THE LIBRARY
ST. MARY'S COLLEGE OF MARYLAND
ST. MARY'S CITY, MARYLAND 20686

Creative Breakthroughs in Politics

CREATIVE

BREAKTHROUGHS

IN POLITICS

Neal Riemer

PRAEGER

Westport, Connecticut
London

Library of Congress Cataloging-in-Publication Data

Riemer, Neal
     Creative breakthroughs in politics / Neal Riemer.
        p.   cm.
     Includes bibliographical references and index.
     ISBN 0–275–95595–8 (alk. paper)
     1. Liberty. 2. Political science. 3. Creative ability.
     4. Problem solving. I. Title.
     JC585.R535   1996
     320.01′1–dc20   96–2201

British Library Cataloguing in Publication Data is available.

Copyright © 1996 by Neal Riemer

All rights reserved. No portion of this book may be
reproduced, by any process or technique, without the
express written consent of the publisher.

Library of Congress Catalog Card Number: 96–2201

ISBN: 0–275–95595–8

First published in 1996

Praeger Publishers, 88 Post Road West, Westport, CT 06881
An imprint of Greenwood Publishing Group, Inc.

Printed in the United States of America

The paper used in this book complies with the
Permanent Paper Standard issued by the National
Information Standards Organization (Z39.48–1984).

10 9 8 7 6 5 4 3 2 1

To my Grandsons

Calmen Eliahu Riemer
Daniel Graan Riemer
Joseph Graan Riemer
Ezra Samuel Riemer

Contents

Preface

In order to confront the challenging problems that bedevil us now and that will still await us in the twenty-first century, we need to engage in the search for and study of creative breakthroughs in politics. The persistent problems are those of war and peace, tyranny and freedom, poverty and prosperity, ecological malaise and balance, social disorder and health. Focusing on creative breakthroughs in politics—past, present, and future—will help us to profit from past successes, understand present tasks, and address future responsibilities.

The end of the Cold War should encourage our endeavor. So should such astonishing events as the collapse of the communist Soviet Union, the reunification of Germany, and the end of apartheid in South Africa. These momentous developments encourage us to believe that we can wrest ourselves free from the intellectual straitjackets fashioned by Cold War mentality and practice, and by a narrow-minded political realism. Such astounding occurrences should also help us to move beyond a social science still too frequently dominated by a behavioral party line unwilling to deal with the crucial ethical and prudential conundrums of political life. Finally, these seemingly miraculous happenings should lead us to reject postmodernism's nihilism and to confidently affirm our belief in efforts to enhance such universal values as peace, freedom, justice, and excellence.

In this book I explore the vital but difficult subject of "Creative Breakthroughs in Politics." I define a creative breakthough in politics as a fruitful resolution of a major problem, a problem the conventional wisdom deems impossible to solve. Genuine creative breakthroughs, I shall argue, are breakthroughs on three interrelated fronts—ethical, empirical, and prudential. I illustrate my argument by examining a number of real or alleged or proposed breakthroughs: some that I consider genuine, some spurious, one incomplete, one necessary but not yet accomplished. Each breakthrough—real or alleged or proposed, genuine or spurious—is prompted by a most difficult practical problem—a problem involving a vision of the good life, understanding of actual (or emergent) political realities, and judgments about wise public policy. Chapter 1 will clarify my understanding of the concept of creative breakthroughs and its place in a larger theory of prophetic politics.

Roger Williams' seventeenth-century argument will be used in Chapter 2 to illustrate a genuine breakthrough to the theory and practice of religious liberty. Religious intolerance, persecution, and bloody religious wars constitute the background for his compelling argument on behalf of religious liberty, separation of church and state, and democratic politics.

James Madison's theory of the "extensive republic" (Chapter 3) constitutes a second genuine breakthrough. The troubled times of the American nation in its early years, especially the effort to reconcile liberty and large size, illuminate the circumstances for Madison's extraordinarily creative efforts in establishing the American federal republic in the late eighteenth and early nineteenth centuries.

The first spurious breakthrough to be examined (Chapter 4) is John C. Calhoun's theory of the concurrent majority. Calhoun's theory, too, was prompted by an agonizing problem: how to protect minority interests in a majority-rule, constitutional system. Calhoun's theory must be understood in terms of the first great trial of American federalism, of the struggle of economic and social interests in nineteenth-century America, of the battle over slavery, and of the ominous specter of secession and civil war threatening to disrupt free and republican government.

I next turn, in Chapter 5, to the thought of Karl Marx and his Promethean effort (in a nineteenth century racked by the Industrial Revolution) to break through to nothing less than universal human emancipation. Marx's struggle against capitalism, against what he held to be its oppression of the proletariat, and against undemocratic political rule is clearly a major struggle of the modern world, and has had—for good or ill—a decisive impact upon modern history. In this chapter I will probe the question of whether or not Marx's theory constitutes a genuine creative breakthrough in politics, or is—as I believe—seriously flawed.

In Chapter 6 attention shifts to a transnational breakthrough in the twentieth century, the West European Community, now known as the European Union. The catastrophes that were World Wars I and II; the historical rivalries of such West European nations as Germany, France, and

Great Britain; the dominance of the Soviet Union in Central and Eastern Europe after World War II; the U.S. stake in free, prosperous, and cooperative nations in Western Europe—these factors constitute the background for this extraordinary transnational breakthrough. Its splendid promise, noteworthy achievements, continuing problems, incomplete fulfillment, and tantalizing future will be my central concerns in Chapter 6.

Looking beyond past and present breakthroughs (actual or potential, genuine or spurious), in Chapter 7 I address an agonizing contemporary problem that cries out for a future breakthrough: how to protect basic human rights against persistent, systemic, and flagrant violations by despotic regimes. My proposed breakthrough—sketched as a provocative thought experiment—calls for the development of an effective Global Human Rights Regime that can, via prudent prevention, effective staged implementation, and just humanitarian intercession, deal with such egregious violations as genocide.

In the Conclusion (Chapter 8), "The Unfinished Prophetic Agenda," I reflect upon the fruitfulness of the concept of creative breakthroughs in politics. A prophetic emphasis on the life-affirming values of peace, freedom, justice, prosperity, and creativity is a common thread running throughout the chapters outlined above. I will reflect, especially, on the difficult task of ascertaining the necessary and sufficient conditions for creative breakthroughs. My hope is that this study will encourage us to address a wide range of significant problems that need our critical attention as we head toward the awe-inspiring millennial year 2001.

Creative Breakthroughs in Politics

CHAPTER 1

Introduction

INTRODUCTION

As we confront the challenging problems that face us in the changed and changing world of the last decade of the twentieth century, we will profit from the search for and study of creative breakthroughs in politics, past, present, and future. These are the age-old problems of peoples learning to live together in greater harmony: in greater harmony with fellow citizens in nation-states; in greater harmony with other nations; in greater harmony, too, with both nature and human institutions. Greater harmony requires a peaceful, free, just, constitutional order. Greater harmony rests upon a prosperous economy that can sustain good jobs, families, homes, schools, and health. War, tyranny, injustice, poverty, and ecological malaise are the historic foes of such constitutional harmony.

Although in this book I undertake to explore only a small sample of creative breakthroughs in politics, I hope that my case studies will demonstrate that—against great odds—significant breakthroughs to a more harmonious constitutional order have occurred in the past, are going on in the present, and are possible in the future. Breakthroughs, then, are not utopian fantasies, but prophetic realities and prophetic possibilities.

Before we sketch our understanding of creative breakthroughs in politics, it will be helpful to review briefly, but critically, features of the changed and changing world of politics since the end of World War II—with particular attention to the outlook that has opened up with the end of the Cold War. This sketch may provide the context for an understanding of one present breakthrough in progress examined in this book (European Union) and for a proposed future breakthrough (global protection against genocidal violations of human rights). It will also provide background for comparing present problems with some of the historical case studies examined in this book (religious liberty, the American federal republic). Finally, this sketch may provide salutary warnings about historical dangers and hopeful encouragement about the opportunities for breakthroughs on problems once deemed incapable of solution.

The world has been changing at an astonishing rate since the end of World War II with momentous—sometimes disturbing, sometimes encouraging, and sometimes quite ironic—consequences for the human race. These changes posed and still pose real challenges and provide real opportunities for leaders of state. And they underscore the importance of the search, which this book undertakes, for creative breakthroughs in politics, breakthroughs in the tradition of prophetic politics.[1] Although in this book I undertake a limited examination of all imaginable breakthroughs—past, present, and future—it will still be most helpful to understand the breakthroughs examined in the context of the larger picture of change since the end of World War II.

World War II saw the defeat, at great cost in lives and treasure, of Nazi Germany and Fascist Italy in Europe, and of militaristic Japan in Asia. These authoritarian regimes were then amazingly replaced over a very short period of time by constitutional democracies, with Japan and Germany soon becoming very powerful actors in the global economy. But why, a thoughtful critic may ask, were these catastrophic wars allowed to occur in the first place? Could anything have been done to prevent the emergence of Fascism in Europe and militarism in Japan? Was the Holocaust inevitable? What might have been done to avoid it and so many of the other horrors brought on by World War II, including the savage bombing of cities and the horrible deaths of innocent women and children? The breakthrough to European Union sketched in Chapter 6 provides one partial answer to some of these troubling questions. And the proposed breakthrough to protection against genocide in Chapter 7 gives one some disturbing clues to an answer on the inevitability of the Holocaust.

A new world organization, the United Nations, came quickly into being to realize the high hopes of humankind for peace and freedom, and moved, unevenly, and often ineffectively, through several postures—anti-Fascist, anticommunist, anticolonial. But—admitting modest successes—why has the United Nations been unable to fulfill its own ambitious hopes? Is an effective global organization an impossibility in a world of nation-states locked into the rigid ideology of national sovereignty? Chapter 7, which focuses on the development of a Global Human Rights Regime, seeks to clarify the possibilities open to key UN actors.

The Soviet Union, which suffered enormous losses in World War II, consolidated its dominance in Eastern Europe with a host of puppet regimes, developed a powerful atomic arsenal, supported anticolonial and revolutionary movements around the globe, and then attempted—after Joseph Stalin's death—to move toward peaceful coexistence and then communist reform, only to collapse suddenly after a failed coup by right-wingers against Mikhail Gorbachev and his policies of glasnost and perestroika designed to usher in an effective communism with a human face. But how do we understand this unexpected collapse of the Soviet Union and the bankruptcy of communism? And how do we assess what is currently taking place in Russia and other former republics of the Soviet Union? Can these developments in Russia really be interpreted as a creative breakthrough in politics? Although none of the following chapters specifically addresses these questions, the demise of the USSR and its communist ideology highlights the significant fact that totalitarian and authoritarian regimes can change in ways favorable to human rights and democratic and constitutional governance—very modestly, I concede, but still significantly, in the case of the new Russia.

China, the world's most populous country, which had suffered grievously under the Japanese onslaught before and during World War II, endured a bitter civil war that resulted in a communist victory, and underwent cataclysmic changes in a Maoist Great Leap Forward and a Cultural Revolution, before settling down to its own pattern of modernization. But what will be the future of the remaining great communist power in the world? Are communism and modernization compatible? Are communism and the protection of human rights compatible? Here, too, the example of the collapse of communism in the Soviet Union holds out hope that other monolithic or fanatical ideologies in other authoritarian regimes may change for the better over time.

The Cold War, featuring the world's two superpowers, the United States and the Soviet Union, both armed with deadly nuclear weapons, followed rapidly after the end of World War II, producing a tremendous military buildup, and savage ideological, political, and military rivalries around the globe. In a number of instances (Korea and Vietnam, for example), the United States found itself embroiled in hot wars with communist states in efforts to stop communist aggression, or prevent a communist takeover. But was the Cold War inevitable? And what were its dangers and costs? Could other ways have been found to deal with the U.S.-USSR rivalry? And with forceful communist efforts to achieve victory in Korea or Vietnam? And with other smaller communist regimes, such as Cuba, around the globe? The ugly reality of the Cold War should stimulate us to explore less costly and more humane alternatives to Cold War tactics—alternative ways of handling the seemingly inevitable rivalries of international politics.

Throughout the world the colonial empires of Britain, France, Holland, and Portugal collapsed under pressure of the anti-colonial impulse, and a host of new nations in Asia, Africa, and the Middle East emerged—new and developing nations struggling against great odds, and most often unsuccessfully, to achieve effective national unity, economic viability, and their own variety of democratic governance. But will the dreams of unity, democracy, and economic development be fulfilled in these new nations? In what time period? At what price? Can these new nations make it into the twenty-first century? Although the case studies analyzed in this book do not feature the painful dilemmas facing many developing nations, the reality of key breakthroughs in history should hearten those who struggle with the problems of so many developing countries.

West European nations banded together, with strong U.S. support, against a further Soviet thrust westward, and sought and significantly achieved internal unity and prosperity in a common market and a new political community. But will this vision of European Union be fulfilled in a deepened and broadened European Community? And can this model of integration and unity serve as a helpful model in other troubled areas of the world beset by national, ethnic, economic, and religious rivalries? Chapter 6 on European Union provides a basis for realistically addressing these provocative queries.

This quick review highlights both dangers and opportunities, as well as the ongoing need to search for creative breakthroughs in politics. In this book we cannot tackle all the possibilities suggested by our examples and questions; but we can underscore the need to seize opportunities. The possibility of seizing opportunities is, of course, enhanced by some of the miraculous developments that have taken place since the end of the Cold War.

The very end of the Cold War is one of those miraculous developments. Assisted by the advent of Mikhail Gorbachev as a reformist Soviet leader and his doctrines of glasnost and perestroika, the Soviet grip on its East European puppets was relaxed. Germany was reunited. Gorbachev's leadership even made possible an invigorated United Nations. Pursuant to U.S. leadership, an invigorated United Nations—with the United States carrying the brunt of the action—was able to turn back Iraq's flagrant aggression against Kuwait.

And then, miracle of miracles, the communist Soviet Union itself collapsed. The old USSR was replaced by a Russia and a Commonwealth of Independent States that now painfully struggle toward a variety of constitutional democracy and a free market economy.

Finally, another astonishing event occurred: South Africa, earlier a rigid bastion of apartheid, sealed its almost incredible move toward a multiracial society with genuinely free elections and the choice of Nelson Mandela—the formerly imprisoned leader of the African National Congress—as president of the new South Africa.

This review cannot, of course, do justice to the complexity of world events since the end of World War II. It serves its purpose, however, if it highlights the momentous changes that have occurred since World War II, and underscores some of the remaining challenges—durable peace, effective protection of human rights, sustainable prosperity—facing those courageous enough to explore the continuing possibilities of creative breakthroughs in politics. In this book I shall argue that creative breakthroughs have occurred in the past, that they are visible in the present, and that we can achieve them in the future. My selected cases should demonstrate that we can, indeed, learn from both our past triumphs and failures, better appreciate present endeavors, and be more intelligently equipped to address our future concerns.

The changing world of politics can be the best of times, or the worst of times. It can be the best of times, *if* opportunities are creatively seized with the help of creative breakthroughs. It can turn out to be the worst of times, *if* theoretical dangers become real, or real dangers become severe. We need to be both realistic about our hopes and prudent about our fears.[2] The critical exploration of creative breakthroughs in politics, undertaken by those who *are* realistic about hopes and prudent about fears, can help us to seize opportunities and avoid dangers and thus achieve the best of times and avoid the worst of times. In this critical endeavor I shall opt for a soundly prophetic approach and seek to distinguish it from a falsely utopian outlook. I shall also endeavor to distinguish the soundly prophetic approach from that of a narrow-minded realism and a complacent liberalism or conservatism.

Let me turn next to a somewhat fuller clarification of that appealing, but perhaps still illusive, concept of "creative breakthroughs in politics."

THE FULLER MEANING OF CREATIVE BREAKTHROUGHS IN POLITICS

By *creative* I mean fruitful, productive of significant results. Religious liberty, for example, leads to peace, respect for other outlooks, and social order; West European Union enhances peace, prosperity, and democracy. The creative is constructive; and it is usually distinctive, novel, unique. Thus, the American federal republic—at its inception in 1787—is something new under the sun; it is a bold effort to build a different kind of political community. West European Union builds an unprecedented community with certain supranational features.

By *breakthrough* I mean a resolution (or discovery or invention) that results in the overcoming of a major problem, difficulty, or obstacle, and that produces a momentous change of outlook, behavior, and judgment. Thus, religious liberty overcomes the problem of religious persecution, and introduces the acceptability of the idea of religious pluralism. The federal republic overcomes the problem of the compatibility of liberty and large size, and introduces the idea of a new kind of republican national union. European Union overcomes the problem of historical national rivalries and devastating warfare, and introduces the idea of integrating economies and establishing other vital linkages among nations.

Politics is a much misunderstood and much maligned word. At its best, politics is a genuinely civilizing process, enabling people to live coopera- tively, safely, and sensibly in a democratic and constitutional community wherein they can seek individual fulfillment within the framework of the common good. At its worst, of course, politics can be authoritarian, uncon- stitutional, malignant, corrupt. Clearly, creative breakthroughs seek to enhance politics at its best. In my treatment of politics I shall realistically address both the best and the worst aspects of politics. I shall view politics as a process whereby public values are expressed and endorsed; whereby political actors cooperate and compete to protect their interests; and whereby public policies are made and implemented.

Genuinely creative breakthroughs in politics are, moreover, significantly fruitful resolutions of major problems on three interconnected fronts: ethi- cal, empirical, and prudential. Creative breakthroughs can occur on one or more of these fronts; but the greatest breakthroughs—those of the first magnitude—successfully deal with problems on all fronts.

The ethical front involves expanded conceptions of the good political life: of democratic and constitutional communities living in peace; of the more generous enjoyment of human rights; of prosperous communities able to sustain good health, housing, and schools; of an ecologically balanced world; of a socially sane and a culturally rich and creative people. A significantly fruitful resolution of a disturbing problem thus inevitably involves ethical considerations—considerations of how people ought to live together better in the political community.

The empirical front involves a deeper, more fundamental, under- standing of cooperation, conflict, and accommodation in the political com- munity; of the intractable knots of politics that seem to defy successful untangling; of the struggle for power in politics and better ways to tran- scend it, use it, harness it, contain it, restrain it; of new perceptions of old realities; of a more penetrating understanding of emergent realities (future operative-ideals, forces, institutions, policies); in brief, a more profound understanding of political health in a complex and ever-changing world.

The prudential front involves the vital, but not fully scientific, matter of wise judgment. At stake here is wise judgment by creative people, about ideas, policies, institutions. Wise judgment is a crucial component of strat- egy and tactics: about how much, or how little, to bite off and chew; about how fast or slow to move; about how to balance competing values, claims, interests; about how to reckon with costs and benefits; about how to balance the promise and peril of enterprises; about how to distinguish between the soundly prophetic and foolishly utopian; about how to take the wise, bold course and avoid both a short-sighted realism or a complacent liberalism or conservatism.

Creative breakthroughs in politics, in brief, result in a better way of handling a serious difficulty or problem. They lead to momentous changes in outlook, behavior, and judgment. They lead to significantly better political values, to a deeper understanding of political phenomena, and to the successful testing in action of imaginative practical possibilities.

As I discuss political breakthroughs in this book, I shall, first, identify the problem that calls for a breakthrough; second, articulate the theory that addresses itself to that problem; third, highlight the breakthrough's ethical, empirical, and prudential contributions; and finally, critically appraise the breakthrough in the light of the history and future of politics. The limited number of breakthroughs I examine—an important sample only—will nonetheless clarify my general argument on the prophetic promise of creative breakthroughs in politics.

SOME INHIBITING FACTORS

By focusing on creative breakthroughs in politics we have a unique opportunity to break out of the intellectual straitjackets fashioned by Cold War mentality and practice, by a narrow-minded realism, by the behavioral party line in social science, and by postmodernism's nihilism. The contemporary task of exploring creative breakthroughs has clearly been made more difficult by these inhibiting factors.

Cold War Mentality and Practice

A major factor inhibiting attention to creative breakthroughs in politics has often been the mentality and practice engendered by the Cold War. The American emphasis on anticommunism, the evil Soviet Empire, a huge military buildup, and support for anticommunist authoritarian regimes often worked against peace, human rights, constitutional democracy, and economic prosperity. For example, the Cold War contributed to anticommunist wars in Vietnam and elsewhere. It contributed to the failure to cope with genocidal actions in Cambodia, Bangladesh, and Uganda. It encouraged, rather than discouraged, repressive (if anticommunist) regimes in Latin America, Africa, Asia, and the Middle East. It made impossible the fuller use of resources in assisting developing countries to achieve constitutional stability and greater economic prosperity. It fed the appetite for arms, which were often used against a regime's own peoples or in catastrophic civil wars.

Moreover, Cold War mentality and practice, in many respects, encouraged a tough-minded—and, unfortunately, often a narrow-minded—realism highly suspicious of prophetic values and creative breakthroughs in politics.

Narrow-Minded, Short-Sighted Political Realism

My quarrel is not fundamentally with a broad-minded, far-seeing political realism, fully appreciative of the limitations of human nature and of politics, of what is involved in the struggle for power that is often politics, especially international politics. Nor do I take issue with the need of leaders of state to protect their truly vital national interests. I am, however, opposed to narrow-minded realists who forget that politics involves cooperation and accommodation as well as conflict. I take issue with short-sighted realists who do not appreciate that long-range national interest should sometimes take precedence over short-range national interest, and that vital national interests may often be best served by fostering vital global concerns.

Unfortunately, a narrow-minded and short-sighted political realism is too often wedded to ideas and policies that make it impossible to address contemporary problems in a more creative way. Such political realists are too wedded, for example, to an unimaginative conventional wisdom, to an ethically indefensible status quo, to a blind protection of national sovereignty, to a foolish safeguarding of a nation's selfish interests, to politics as a brutal struggle for power *only*, to sometimes questionable balance-of-power policies as the *only* alternative to avoid harmful hegemony. My worry is that such a narrow-minded realism is too complacent about admitted evils and so timidly conservative that it will neither seek nor even entertain the very possibility of creative breakthroughs in politics.

My quarrel, then, is not primarily with far-sighted and generous political realists who seek to avoid the illusions of utopians, liberals, idealists, pacifists, and moralists; and who also reject the unacceptable posture of cynics. However, it is important for even such realists to expand their horizons intellectually. Such realists must recognize that safeguarding a nation's vital interests in an increasingly interdependent world may sometimes call for radical transformations in politics, and thus for the exploration of what I have called creative breakthroughs in politics.[3]

The Behavioral Party Line in Social Science

What I call the "behavioral party line"—more accurately, the emphasis on the strictly scientific, empirical approach in the social sciences, including political science—tended to discourage responding to real problems in the real world of politics (and to creative breakthroughs in politics, in particular) for several reasons. Behavioral social scientists tended to ignore or downplay the ethical or normative ingredient in politics: that is, treatment of what ought to be; visions of the good life. They held that what ought to be was not something that social scientists should or could explore. The good life was not a fit subject for science and scientists. It was something that nonscientists should deal with: preachers, ethical philosophers, editorial writers, citizens, elected officials. Scientists should limit themselves to what has been, what is, what will be: to empirical reality. Empirical reality could be observed, measured, explained. The upshot of this approach was to diminish the exploration of the good life (past, present, and future), and thus to destroy the very attempt to envisage imaginative conceptions of a better way of conducting political business. In a very real sense, this approach committed the political scientist to the study and acceptance of the status quo.

Paradoxically, the behavioral approach also limited the very empirical exploration that behavioralists sought to advance. It did so in at least four ways. First, the behavioral approach tended to ignore history and its lessons by focusing primarily on the present. It therefore tended to cut itself off from a vital source of historical knowledge and insight. Second, the behavioral approach, by emphasizing the importance of manageable empirical research (in contrast to the search for larger empirical theories), tended to discourage the articulation and investigation of larger empirical hypotheses. This had the unhappy consequence of discouraging political scientists from investigating vital problems (of war and peace, tyranny and freedom, injustice and justice, etc.), which are almost invariably big and tough problems. Third, and ironically, behavioralists—both because they are leery of prediction and because they tend to focus on dominant present reality— were inclined to ignore or underplay recessive forces (forces not at present powerful, dominant, or visible), which, however, would become dominant, and which would significantly shape future reality. Hence, behavioralists tended to adopt a conservative posture toward the future. Fourth, behavioralists tended to shy away from prudent judgment in the articulation and development of wise public policy. Such judgment, they often affirmed, was the legitimate task of politicians, leaders of state, administrators, and citizens in elections. As scientists, behavioralists did not feel that they were required to move outside the legitimate (scientific) realm of the investigation of what is to pass judgment on what wisely can be.

For all of these reasons, then, the behavioral party line—the scientific commitment to limit social scientists to what can be observed, measured, tested, explained empirically—inhibited responses to a changing world of politics and creative breakthroughs in politics to deal both with that changing world and the tough enduring problems of politics.[4]

Postmodernism's Nihilism

Here I refer to one aspect of a complex, many-sided, intellectual development that has been given the name "postmodernism." Many postmodernists reject a belief in absolutes, such as truth or justice or freedom. They emphasize that all such ideas are culture-bound and time-bound. These ideas have different meanings—not the same eternal, universal meaning— in different civilizations and cultures. The specific meaning of such ideas is largely determined by those who exercise power; and as power-holders change over time so does the meaning of these ideas. One important result of this critique of eternal verities is to legitimize, at least for some, a variety of nihilism—a rejection of key ethical, religious, political "truths." Thus, many postmodernists can affirm that there are no such absolute truths to guide us in politics. The upshot of this outlook, I suggest, is to inhibit the search for creative breakthroughs to peace, freedom, justice, and prosperity. Why, the skeptical postmodernists will ask, search for an absolute, universal verity that does not really exist?[5]

These inhibiting factors tend to limit our ability to deal with real-life problems; and they must certainly discourage the search for creative break- throughs in politics. The sensible response to those troubled by these inhibiting factors, I argue, is fourfold. First, and perhaps easiest, it is important to accept the fact that the Cold War is indeed over, and that it is crucial to move beyond the Cold War mentality and practice that discour- aged creative breakthroughs in politics. Second, a narrow-minded and short-sighted political realism has never been a good approach in an increasingly interdependent world and should clearly be replaced by a more sensible, productive, broad-minded, generous political realism based on a prophetic view of enlightened national interest. Third, while the behavioral approach offers valuable contributions to empirical political science, it cannot be allowed to dominate the field and thereby prevent political scientists from exploring the good life, from profiting from histori- cal lessons, from investigating emergent realities and future empirical possibilities, and from contributing to prudent judgments in politics. Fourth, postmodernism's nihilism must not be allowed to discourage or cripple the effort to pursue ways to curtail savage wars, to protect against egregious violations of human rights, to enhance economic health, or to tackle other problems whose solution requires a confident commitment to a good life.

TOWARD A MORE PROPHETIC POLITICS

I view my analysis of creative breakthroughs in politics in the larger theoretical context of a paradigm of Prophetic Politics.[6] The commitments of Prophetic Politics are: (1) a commitment to the universal applicability of such values as life, peace, freedom, justice, prosperity, and excellence; (2) a commitment to fearless criticism of the existing political, economic, and social order in light of these prophetic values; (3) a commitment to creative constitutional policies and breakthroughs—to sane, practical action—to narrow the gap between prophetic values and existing reality; and (4) a commitment to continuous prophetic scrutiny and futuristic projection—via imaginative scenarios—in order to guard against future evils and to plan for and anticipate problems of even the best imaginable order.

The genuine creative breakthroughs that I examine are all in the tradition of Prophetic Politics and illustrate all four commitments of the paradigm of prophetic politics.

To understand better the perspective of Prophetic Politics, let me compare this outlook with three other model outlooks—those of Machiavellian Politics, Utopian Politics, and Liberal Democratic Politics. My argument is that these models are, at best, inadequate, and, at worst, disastrous; and that the model of Prophetic Politics—a superior democratic and constitutional politics—while true to its own commitments, can successfully incorporate the strengths and avoid the weaknesses of the other models.

Machiavellian Politics: The "Lion and Fox" Politics of the Nation-State

Machiavellian Politics is characterized by a supposedly "realistic" ethical commitment to the protection of the vital interests of the nation-state—its independence, security, power, and prosperity. It is based on a supposedly "scientific" recognition of politics as a struggle for power among contending interests. It is characterized by policy judgments that require leaders of state to be beasts as well as humans, and to be both lions and foxes in the conduct of the affairs of state: that is, to be prepared, as circumstances warrant, to use both force and craft in protecting the vital interests of the state.

This model has much to offer those who seek a wise guiding model.[7] It underscores the need to protect the genuinely vital interests of our own political community; to understand the character of the eternal struggle for power that is politics; and to avoid the confusion of "ought" and "is" in the formulation of public policy. These strengths (which are normally evident in the foreign policy of any sensible nation-state, and can also be seen at work in a nation's domestic policy as well) are, however, offset by the weaknesses of Machiavellian Politics. And these weaknesses raise doubts about the wisdom of its adoption as a model for the future. For example, Machiavellian Politics is often characterized by idolatrous worship of the nation-state—and of the frequently narrow, parochial, shortsighted interests of the nation-state. The practitioners of Machiavellian Politics must often lower their ethical sights in order to make their objectives achievable. This amounts to a loss of civilizing vision in both theory and practice. The Machiavellians, moreover, do not hesitate to use brutal force and to employ the worst excesses of craft to achieve national security and the protection of other vital interests. In recent American history—to select one nation for purposes of illustration—Vietnam and Watergate point out dramatically the weaknesses of Machiavellian Politics and, particularly, a wrong-headed understanding of the meaning of a nation's vital interests.

So it is that Machiavellian Politics, despite some undoubted strengths, is on balance deficient. At best it may protect the vital interests of the nation-state, but often at the expense of other peoples and nations. At worst, Machiavellian Politics threatens to destroy the nation and the globe.

Utopian Politics: The Harmonious Politics of Earthly Salvation

Many critics are tempted to flee from Machiavellian Politics to some version of Utopian Politics. This model of politics is characterized by the dream of earthly salvation, of the harmonious state, of the conflictless society. The Marxist conception of the communist society has been the most influential illustration of this model in the modern world. The harmonious community has a "scientific" foundation. Utopian thinkers hold that Utopian Politics can be brought about by an elite, in touch with the *truth*, and able to "educate" a malleable people. This pattern is illustrated not only by communist party leaders but by the philosopher-kings, Grand Inquisitors, and Fraziers of the world of literature and politics. After utopia has been achieved, the need for significant judgment in politics declines.

The strengths of Utopian Politics are considerable: an inspiring conviction of a better world, a plan for the present; confidence in the truthfulness, fruitfulness, and power of the utopian dream. However, serious weaknesses undermine its strengths. These include (1) a defective vision—which manifests itself in a maddening pride, a tendency to hubris; (2) a serious divorce from reality, illustrated by a loss of a sense of the existent, of power, of the possible; and (3) a loss of prudent judgment, to be seen in the utopian's failure to calculate both costs and benefits, and to perceive the need for a democratic and constitutional order in utopia. In attempting to fulfill utopian ideals, utopians are tempted to violate the very traditions of civility they profess to honor, and, ironically, to succumb to Machiavellian tactics of "lion and fox." Troublemaking poets will be banned from the harmonious republic. Dictatorship will be necessary for the transition to the classless communist society. Miracle, mystery, and authority will be required to overcome unhappiness brought on by the burden of freedom. The gospel of operant conditioning, as practiced by a scientific savior, will usher in the new Garden of Eden. Other utopians, confronted by the difficulty of achieving the reign of earthly harmony, become disillusioned with the real world of conflict and desert politics entirely. And it is even the case that some aspects of the perfectly harmonious society—for example, the decline of judgment in a world without sin—might prove to be undesirable and deadly dull. My allusions have already identified several varieties of Utopian Politics: Platonic, Old (Marxist) Left, Old (Authoritarian) Right, Skinnerian (*Walden Two*). Other varieties abound. They all share a conviction of the need for the triumph of the one true faith against its benighted foes.

A critical assessment of Utopian Politics leads to a gloomy set of conclusions: (1) certain utopian ends may not be desirable; (2) even if Utopian Politics is desirable, it is not achievable; (3) even if desirable and achievable, the cost of its achievement may be too high; (4) the serious utopian is confronted with bleak alternatives: disillusionment, impotence, and costly sacrifice.

Liberal Democratic Politics: The Conservative Politics of Pluralistic Balance

Can we, however, avert jumping from the frying pan of Machiavellian Politics into the fire of Utopian Politics by adopting Liberal Democratic Politics—what we might also call Ordinary Constitutional Politics?[8] Will such a politics enable us to protect the genuinely vital interests of the political community while still holding open the live possibility of sane fulfillment of at least some defensible utopian ideals?

Superficially, the answer seems to be affirmative. Those who believe in Liberal Democratic Politics—as illustrated, for example, by the United States—are dedicated to the "more perfect union." They are committed to balancing liberty and authority. They are convinced that we must see politics as a civilizing process. They have modestly succeeded in establishing in an imperfect world a government that is limited, representative, responsible, and popular—no mean achievement. Such a government does guard, with reasonable success, against arbitrary power. It does seek to balance responsibility to God, nation, people, interests, states, local communities. It does, realistically, perceive the legitimate appeals of conscience, people, party, and the need to balance these in the pursuit of justice. Those who practice Liberal Democratic Politics see the well-established need to umpire the struggle for power according to sound rules that have emerged from our historical constitutional experience—our prescriptive Constitution—and that have been ratified over time by a fundamentally sound electorate. They acknowledge the well-grounded need to balance competing equities in politics. They appreciate the well-grounded need to cultivate and exercise wise judgment on public policy issues in the absence of *the truth* that true believers maintain is the only standard in politics.

Thus the strengths of Liberal Democratic Politics are considerable. This pattern strikes a needed balance between individual freedom and the community's interests. This model operates to overcome the worst features of both Machiavellian and Utopian Politics—and to incorporate their strengths. It recognizes both the strengths and weaknesses of self-interest. It provides an area—an open society—for human fulfillment. It makes constitutional government a living reality. These are unquestionably great historical achievements.

However, a more candid, and more incisive, assessment of Liberal Democratic Politics calls our attention to a number of crucial weaknesses: the limited ethical vision of Liberal Democratic Politics (and its "liberal" and "conservative" supporters); its deficient empirical understanding; and its timid, conservative appraisal of problems and "proximate solutions."

Thus: (1) Liberal Democratic Politics is, too often, complacent (despite campaign rhetoric about fundamental change) about its own ethos and processes. It is too tolerant of fundamental existing evils. It lacks a powerful vision of a more desirable future. It is too often the politics of rich, powerful, white men. (2) Liberal Democratic Politics is not inclined to upset the rich and powerful special interests of the status quo; too frequently it ignores the poorer and weaker forces of society—especially the "least free"—especially poor people, nonwhite people, women. Consequently, the practitioners of Liberal Democratic Politics have a deficient scientific understanding of past, present, and future. Their understanding of what it takes to emancipate the "least free" is especially deficient. (3) Prudentially, over the long haul, those engaged in Liberal Democratic Politics are too conservative, too hesitant, too slow in a world where, at crucial times, truly radical, decisive, and speedy judgments are required. In the United States such Liberal Democratic Politicians (despite the contemporary sound and fury of the fights between "liberals" and "conservatives"—fights that resound with calls for change apropos health care, welfare reform, a balanced federal budget, crime, education, family values, and so on) are to be found in both major political parties and among 99 percent of our politicos.

On balance, then, although Liberal Democratic Politics is a great historical achievement, it is not good enough to address crucial domestic and international problems. A bolder approach is required. That bolder approach—Prophetic Politics—guides my argument on behalf of creative breakthroughs in politics.

Prophetic Politics: The Radical Politics of Life, Growth, and Fulfillment

As I indicated earlier, Prophetic Politics is characterized by four major commitments: (1) to values of a superior universal order; (2) to fearless criticism of existing political orders (in light of the prophetic paradigm); (3) to creative constitutional policies and breakthroughs (to narrow the gap between prophetic paradigm and contemporary reality); and (4) to continuous prophetic scrutiny (in order to monitor historical breakthroughs) and futuristic projection via imaginative scenarios (to plan for future breakthroughs)—in the interest of future political health.

These commitments owe a great deal to biblical prophets and to the Judaic-Christian religious tradition. They also owe a debt to Greek philosophy and the tradition of Natural Law, each of which developed independently of the Judaic-Christian tradition, and yet linked up with that religious tradition in Western thought. They also owe a great debt to those movements of philosophical, social, and political thought we call the Enlightenment as it encapsulates, and brings to fulfillment, aspects of a superior constitution in theory and practice. Finally, they owe a great deal to modern science, and our long tradition of social science, as tools for human understanding, social criticism, and human prognosis.

Let me now outline the key features of Prophetic Politics, especially as they may be compared with or contrasted to the models of Machiavellian, Utopian, and Liberal Democratic Politics.

1. Prophetic Politics is characterized by a superior ethical vision. The vision is universal and applicable to all people. Unlike Machiavellian Politics, Prophetic Politics does not stop with the selfish protection of the vital interests of the nation-state. Unlike Utopian Politics, the outlook of Prophetic Politics is not premised on earthly harmony, salvation, or perfection. Unlike Liberal Democratic Politics, Prophetic Politics is not so enamored of the balance of the existing order in favor of the rich and powerful that it is inhibited in battling, sometimes in radical ways, on behalf of peace, freedom, justice, prosperity, and excellence. Its vital interests are the vital interests of all peoples—not simply of the rich, of the powerful, of whites, of men. But it sees these vital interests being secured best within the framework of a superior democratic and constitutional order. It requires attention both to human needs and human fulfillment *and* to a common good that involves the future as well as the present; and it demands superior patterns of accommodation between individual and group interests and such a common good. This order also looks to sound experimentation to determine the worth of current and proposed social, economic, and political principles, institutions, and practices. The standard for judgment in this superior democratic and constitutional order is civilized life, healthy growth, and creative fulfillment.

2. Prophetic sensitivity opens up exciting ethical and scientific vistas. A sensitivity to the "least free" requires criticism of all political orders—whether liberal-democratic, socialist, capitalist, communist, West or East, North or South, Third or Fourth, white or black or brown—in which the "least free" are struggling for emancipation and fulfillment. Prophetic criticism involves several tasks: clarification and justification of the standards, values, norms, and rules that orient ethical and empirical investigation and permit meaningful appraisal; exploring the necessary and sufficient conditions of human life, peace, freedom, justice, prosperity, ecological health, and excellence; formulating the social science theory that enhances understanding and explanation—particularly our understanding of the

gap between prophetic standard and contemporary reality, and the reasons for this gap, particularly an understanding of the process of sensible constitutional change; and well-articulated alternatives for human action. Such a theory of criticism is characterized by a more realistic, and yet a more generous, understanding of political reality: of what has been, of what is, and of what can be. Political life is to be understood in terms of our purposes and of our rules as well as our actual behavior. Political life is to be understood, too, in terms of political becoming as well as political being. Such criticism thus points toward possibility (and probability) as well as toward impossibility (and improbability). Perfect earthly harmony and salvation is impossible; but a more prophetic world order is not. An earthly hell is quite possible; but so is human effort to avoid the destruction of the human race. Conflict may be ineradicable, but success in overcoming the most disastrous conflicts is possible. The probability of movement toward a superior democratic order in all areas of the world remains to be more fully tested.

3. Those committed to Prophetic Politics are committed to creative constitutional action to narrow the gap between prophetic paradigm and contemporary reality. Long before Marx wrote Thesis ll on Feuerbach,[9] the biblical prophets demanded action to change the world, action based on prophetic values, action rooted in covenantal commandments. In Western thought the Covenant at Sinai has served as a prototype of all sound constitutions. We have inherited the tradition of action that must be creative, sane, superior, and constitutional. Those in the American generation of 1787 (as Chapter 3 will argue) illustrated this brilliantly at the very beginning of our history as a nation. They illustrated that creative breakthroughs in politics are possible. It is possible to move significantly beyond the constitutional status quo. Breakthroughs are ethical, empirical, and prudential: they involve a superior vision of political goals, a fuller understanding of political realities (as they have been, are now, and can become), and wiser judgments as to preferred alternatives. The breakthrough affirms what the conventional wisdom denies. In the American example, as we shall see more fully in Chapter 3, Madison affirmed the sense of reconciling liberty and empire in his proposed "extensive republic." The success of the breakthrough is always measured in light of its ends, its means, and its fruits. Proceeding in this fashion, creative breakthroughs can be attempted with minimum defections to Machiavellian, Utopian, and Ordinary Liberal Democratic Politics.

Creative breakthroughs in politics, in the prophetic tradition, are invariably a response to troublesome problems that seem to defy resolution. Is it really possible to achieve religious liberty in a society committed to the proposition that there is only one true religious faith (Chapter 2)? Can one reconcile liberty and large size (Chapter 3)? Even spurious breakthroughs address troublesome problems: How protect minority interests in a majority rule system (Chapter 4)? How secure universal human emancipation (Chapter 5)? It is also important to recognize that breakthroughs may be in process today (Chapter 6); and that it is important to prepare for future breakthroughs (Chapter 7). And to prepare for future breakthroughs—as well as to recognize the ongoing need to appraise past and present break-throughs—is to appreciate better the fourth commitment of prophetic politics: continuous prophetic scrutiny and futuristic projection.

4. Given the commitment to continuous prophetic scrutiny and futuris-tic projection, we can attempt to do more than simply picture a more messianic age, where swords will be beaten into plowshares and spears into pruning hooks. We can begin to do what in the past we have only rarely done: project the scenarios (positive and negative) of the world we would like to create (or avoid), and—by anticipating problems—work through difficulties we now foresee, and perhaps even uncover some not currently in sight. Chapter 7 illustrates key aspects of this commitment.

In this fashion, then, the pattern of Prophetic Politics can be employed to protect genuine vital interests; to elevate, refine, and harness the struggle for power; while avoiding idolatrous worship of the nation-state and the worst uses of force and craft. In this fashion, too, Prophetic Politics can again provide us with an inspiring image of a future world, a fruitful and powerful image that can enlighten the past, orient the present, and help us understand the future, while avoiding the sin of hubris. Prophetic politics may also assist us to move toward the more nearly perfect union, pursuant to time-tested notions of limited, representative, responsible, popular gov-ernment, in accord with the sensible mandate to balance human equities, while avoiding the limited vision, deficient understanding, and timid assessment of Liberal Democratic Politics.

A vital democratic and constitutional twenty-first century will not be secure unless we are willing to explore, in theory and practice, the prob-ability of the possibility of creative breakthroughs in politics in the tradition of Prophetic Politics. The chapters in this book lend powerful support to the argument that we can go beyond Machiavellian Politics: the "lion and fox" politics of the nation-state. We need to protect the truly vital interests of human beings, and states and local political communities have an important role to play in such protection. But we can no longer convincingly argue that many nations adequately protect those vital interests. Nation-state idolatry remains an obstacle to human life, human rights, human needs in many nations around the globe. Similarly, we can avoid the temptations of Utopian Politics: the harmonious politics of earthly salva-tion. Utopian Politics is wrongly rooted in the premise of an eventual conflictless society. We cannot abolish conflict. We can articulate superior patterns of accommodation among contending interests. And we can also move beyond Liberal Democratic Politics: the conservative politics of plu-ralistic balance. Constitutionalism is an evolving concept. But it is a mistake to assume that the constitutional pattern of Liberal Democratic Politics is the end of the constitutional line. Despite its weaknesses, it is very good; but it is not good enough. We should not be blind to the weaknesses of the "conservative politics of pluralist balance." Liberal Democratic Politics may suit the rich, the powerful, whites, males; but poor people, weak people, many black people, and many women cannot conclude that Liberal Democratic Politics is operating adequately on their behalf.

As we consider the probability of the possibility of creative breakthroughs in the tradition of a more Prophetic Politics, it is particularly important to keep in mind the distinction I have tried to establish between Prophetic and Utopian Politics. It is lamentable that the fear of messianic madness—whether in Left or Right totalitarianism—has led us to equate, and reject, both "utopian" and "prophetic." We have failed to see that the prophetic impulse does not lead to Marx, Lenin, Stalin, and Gulag Archipelago, or to the Grand Inquisitor, Hitler, and Auschwitz. It is also sad that—rejecting Utopian Politics and disgusted with Machiavellian Politics—we have been tempted to conclude that our safest harbor in a world in which false prophets preach "miracle, mystery, and authority," or the end of alienation, is Liberal Democratic Politics. It is sad because that harbor is not the safest harbor. Indeed, if we are to safeguard democratic and constitutional government in the challenging twenty-first century, we are called to voyage, not to rest. Only if we see that we can distinguish between Prophetic and Utopian Politics, can we move away from Machiavellian Politics without embracing Utopian Politics, and without concluding that Liberal Democratic Politics is the way to achieve the right balance in the politics of the twenty-first century. The recovery of the prophetic may be the precondition for a sound and creative, a superior democratic and constitutional, politics in the twenty-first century. The possibility is a live one. Our task is to demonstrate the probability of that possibility.

CONCLUSION

The challenge of change should encourage, not discourage, us as we move toward the twenty-first century. The problems that we face in this world of change should be viewed as opportunities to be seized. Our critical exploration of past and present creative breakthroughs in politics may help us overcome inhibitions that limit us in facing present and future problems and breakthroughs.

Our examination of genuine and spurious breakthroughs—past, present, and future—in the following chapters should also enable us to address the real difficulties facing those committed to a more Prophetic Politics. These difficulties puncture an easy optimism; but they do not, I maintain, destroy prophetic hope. These difficulties can be put in the form of nagging questions, troublesome questions, which confront students of Prophetic

Politics. (1) What conception of the prophetic paradigm can command the support of the diverse forces of the modern world—religious, philosophical, social, economic, political, scientific? (2) How shall fearless criticism go forward in the best ethical and scientific fashion? (3) Can prophetic values, principles, and institutions, if theoretically sound, be successfully translated into superior constitutional practice—without Prophetic Politics itself becoming idolatrous, perfectionist, and complacent? (4) Is continuous prophetic scrutiny and futuristic projection really possible and genuinely fruitful? (5) Is it the paradoxical case that Prophetic Politics is necessary but impossible, or, if possible, highly improbable?

In significant ways the following chapters will address these tough questions and suggest a conclusion on behalf of a more hopeful twenty-first century.

NOTES

1. For my earlier work on prophetic politics, see Neal Riemer, *The Future of the Democratic Revolution: Toward a More Prophetic Politics* (New York: Praeger, 1984). See also Neal Riemer, ed., *Let Justice Roll: Prophetic Challenges in Religion, Politics, and Society* (Lanham, Md.: Rowman and Littlefield, 1996), especially my chapter 12. In my statement about prophetic politics I have drawn generously from these earlier works.

2. See Neal Riemer, ed., *New Thinking and Developments in International Politics: Opportunities and Dangers* (Lanham, Md.: University Press of America, 1991).

3. For a fuller critique of political realism at its best, see Neal Riemer, "Reinhold Niebhur, Political Realism, and Prophetic Politics," Chapter 10, in *Let Justice Roll*. See also John H. Herz, *Political Realism and Political Idealism* (Chicago: University of Chicago Press, 1951) for an analysis that seeks to escape both the pitfalls of idealistic utopianism and cynical realism. In addition, see the perceptive assessments of Michael Joseph Smith, *Realist Thought from Weber to Kissinger* (Baton Rouge: Louisiana State University Press, 1986), and Joel H. Rosenthal, *Righteous Realists: Political Realism, Responsible Power, and American Culture in the Nuclear Age* (Baton Rouge: Louisiana State University Press, 1991). These books represent a sympathetic attempt to move beyond a narrow-minded, shortsighted political realism.

4. For a comparable critique of the behavior persuasion, see David Ricci, *The Tragedy of Political Science: Politics, Scholarship, and Democracy* (New Haven, Conn.: Yale University Press, 1984).

5. For a balanced critique of postmodernism, see Pauline Marie Rosenau, *Post-Modernism and the Social Sciences: Insights, Inroads, and Intrusions* (Princeton, N.J.: Princeton University Press, 1992). For another critique, see Henry Kariel, *The Desperate Politics of Postmodernism* (Amherst: University of Massachusetts Press, 1989).

6. See, again, Riemer, *The Future of the Democratic Revolution;* and also Neal Riemer, Chapter 12, "The Prophetic Mode and Challenge, Creative Breakthroughs, and the Future of Constitutional Democracies," in *Let Justice Roll.*

7. Machiavellian Politics at its republican best shares much in common with political realism at its best. See, again, the references in note 3.

8. My model of prophetic politics, I want to emphasize, builds on the best features of liberal democratic politics. My critique of liberal democratic politics in the American political tradition, I also want to stress, is definitely not a "conservative" or "neoconservative" critique of liberalism. My model of liberal democratic politics reflects the fundamental principles of both "liberals" and "conservatives." Both "liberals" and "conservatives" are committed to freedom, constitutional government, and representative government. They may, of course, differ on the role of national government and on specific policies; but their differences on these matters are minuscule when compared to their agreement on political fundamentals. The model of Prophetic Politics also presupposes agreement on the fundamental principles of freedom, constitutional government, and representative government.

9. Karl Marx, *Theses on Feuerbach* in Robert C. Tucker, ed., The *Marx-Engels Reader*, 2nd ed. (New York: W. W. Norton, 1978).

CHAPTER 2

Roger Williams and Religious Liberty: Harmonizing Truth, Diversity, and Order

INTRODUCTION

In human history it has always been tempting for those who believe they possess the religious truth, expecially if they are the dominant majority in power, to impose that truth upon others: pagans, infidels, the ignorant, the weak. The crusades, jihads, and religious wars of humankind give disheartening testimony to the ugly disasters brought about by those who succumb to that temptation. Religious wars, moreover, have a striking resemblance to national, ideological, and ethnic wars insofar as nationalism, ideology, and ethnicity can also lead zealots who believe that they have a monopoly on truth to extirpate, suppress, or dominate aliens, enemies, foes. Often the ingredients of fanatical religion, intolerant nationalism, crusading ideology, and inflexible ethnicity are combined in a volatile and explosive mixture. The tragic persistence of conflicts combining these ingredients is vividly illustrated all around the contemporary world: for example, in Bosnia, in republics of the former Soviet Union, in India, in the Sudan, in North Africa, in the Middle East, in Tibet. Thoughtful people are led to ask: Can we ever learn from past religious—and kindred—disputes? The case examined in this chapter should help us in our learning process. The problem faced by Roger Williams in seventeenth-century America—and his solution— should be relevant not only to religious disputes in other parts of the globe, but also to national, ideological, and ethnic disputes in the contemporary world.

Is it possible to reconcile the ideal of religious orthodoxy and political order *with* the facts of religious diversity, religious persecution, and political conflict? This was the vexing and deeply troubling problem that faced thoughtful people in the sixteenth and seventeenth centuries. This problem can best be understood if we call to mind two cardinal propositions of the dominant outlook—the conventional wisdom—of the time *and* recall the facts of religious and political life after the Protestant Reformation.

The two cardinal propositions were these: (1) there is only one true religious faith, and (2) it is the duty of the ruler of the state to uphold the true faith.

The facts of religious and political life, however, underscored the realities of disagreement (between Catholics and Protestants, and also between Protestants and Protestants) on who possessed the one true faith. The facts of religious and political life also underscored religious and political warfare. This warfare was rooted—significantly, if not exclusively—in such religious disagreement. This was truly dreadful warfare that in Europe in the sixteenth and seventeenth centuries had turned citizen against citizen, children against parents, brother against brother, families against each other, cities against cities, states against states.

Persecution, of course, was an old story before and after the advent of Christianity. Christians had been persecuted by non-Christian Romans. Catholic Christians had persecuted dissenters within the fold before the Protestant Reformation. The Reformation merely complicated and intensified persecution. Ironically, Christians (when in a minority or out of power) were generally in favor of toleration. In power, however, they generally moved toward persecution of religious heretics. This had been true, for example, of St. Augustine. It was also to prove true of Martin Luther and John Calvin, the great Protestant reformers.

In many respects, as Roland Bainton has pointed out, Protestantism grew "more instransigent as it passed from Lutherism to Calvinism." Conflicts between rival faiths became religious wars,

> first in Switzerland from 1529–1531, then in Germany from 1546–1547, and in France and Holland commencing in the sixties and continuing throughout the sixteenth century. The seventeenth century saw the civil wars in England and the Thirty Years War on the Continent, in both of which religion played no minor role. . . . We see then that the struggle for religious liberty had to be waged at the same time against the intolerance of a Catholicism menaced by a new foe and Protestantism seeking to preserve itself against the Catholic onslaught to the right and sectarian disintegration to the left.[1]

These dreadful religious wars, complicated as they were by political and personal rivalries, resulted in a dreadful carnage, a terrible loss of property, a serious blow to law and order, a significant diminishment of trust, and thus uncertain and unsettling conditions. The Thirty Years War in the seventeenth century, for example, left one out of every three Germans in Central Europe dead. The reality and memory of religious war, of persecution, of attempts to enforce religious conformity was to haunt the minds of sensitive people. As we shall see, this reality and this memory were in the mind of Roger Williams in the seventeenth century. And in the eighteenth century James Madison and Thomas Jefferson were to cry out against the outrage of religious persecution and its consequences.

Wrote Madison in 1784: "Torrents of blood have been spilt in the world in vain attempts of the secular arm to extinguish religious discord, by proscribing all differences of religious opinion."[2]

In his *Notes on Virginia*, Jefferson had asked rhetorically: "Is uniformity possible?" And he had answered: "Millions of innocent men, women and children, since the introduction of Christianity, have been burnt, tortured, fined, imprisoned; yet we have not advanced one inch toward uniformity."[3]

The memory of that persecution lingered on into the twentieth century. In 1947 the U.S. Supreme Court in the *Everson* case summed up the problem eloquently:

> The centuries before and contemporaneous with the colonization of America had been filled with turmoil, civil strife, and persecution, generated in large part by established sects determined to maintain their absolute political and religious supremacy. With the power of government supporting them, at various times and places, Catholics had persecuted Protestants, Protestants had persecuted Catholics, Protestant sects had persecuted other Protestant sects, Catholics of one shade of belief had persecuted Catholics of another shade of belief, and all of these had from time to time persecuted Jews. In efforts to force loyalty to whatever religious group happened to be on top and in league with the government of a particular time and place, men had been fined, cast in jail, cruelly tortured, and killed.[4]

Hugo Grotius, one of the key fathers of international law, writing in 1625 in the midst of the devastating Thirty Years War—a war not unconnected to religious divisiveness—described the anguish of the humane contemporary observer in these memorable words:

> I have had many and grave reasons why I should write a work on that subject [the law of war and peace]. For I saw prevailing throughout the Christian world a license in making war of which even barbarous nations would have been ashamed, recourse being had to arms for slight reasons or for no reason; and when arms were once taken up, all reverence for divine and human law lost, just as if men were henceforth authorized to commit all crimes without restraint.[5]

Grotius witnessed in his life not only the first part of the Thirty Years War, but also the last twenty-five years of the war of the United Provinces (Holland) against Spain, the continuing civil war in France with the assassinations of Henry III and Henry IV, and the sectarian and political troubles in England and Holland, including the execution of Mary Stuart, and the assassination of William of Orange. And we must remember that the Peace of Augsburg and the Peace of Westphalia brought only an incomplete solution, based on the principle of territoriality, a "solution" based on the principle that the ruler of a given state could determine the dominant religion of that state.

Both Catholics and Protestants—we must emphasize—adhered to the two cardinal propositions of the dominant paradigm. Each religious group affirmed with conviction that its religious faith was the true faith. Each also affirmed that it was the duty of the Catholic (or Protestant) ruler to uphold the true Catholic (or Protestant) faith.

And when Protestantism splintered after the Reformation, each Protestant sect affirmed with conviction that its interpretation of the Protestant faith was the true faith and that it was the duty of the Protestant ruler to uphold the true faith.

Clearly, given the existence of substantial numbers of people in disagreement on which, in fact, was the one true faith (i.e., the Catholic or Protestant version, or which Protestant version), and given, too, the will of the ruler of the state to carry out his duty according to the dominant religious and political paradigm, the outcome could only be conflict, persecution, bloodshed, war. And, as we have noted, events in the sixteenth and seventeenth centuries testify eloquently to the ugly, bitter, bloody, and anguished reality of this outcome.

Despite the bloodshed, however, advocates in these bitter religious controversies and wars—made even worse by personal and national ambitions—refused initially to budge from their adherence to the two cardinal propositions of the dominant paradigm. After all, the one true faith must be upheld against schismatics and heretics. People must, of course, live only by the one true faith. And, clearly, unless the ruler of the state upholds the one true faith, disbelief, heresy, and untruth will spread. God's honor will not be upheld. Justice—understood as giving God his due—will not be served. Is it not clear beyond dispute—the advocates of the dominant Christian paradigm argued—that the political community cannot endure unless it is founded on, and guided by, the one true faith? Certainly, they argued, harmony, good faith, justice, order, and prosperity will all be undermined unless the one true faith prevails.

These were arguments of the conventional wisdom—the dominant paradigm—of the sixteenth and seventeenth centuries. And they seemed most persuasive to Christians in Western Europe, and then in America, who were absolutely convinced that belief in and practice of the one true faith were of transcendent importance. Human life on earth, after all, was brief. But life after this earthly existence opened up the glorious vision of immortality to those of the one true faith, and the horrible vision of eternal punishment for disbelievers, heretics, and sinners. Consequently, the cost of bloodshed was a relatively small price to pay to maintain the one true faith and the honor of God.

However, the fact of disagreement on basic religious matters persisted, despite persecution and bloodshed and savage civil war that set Christian against Christian, family against family, town against town, country against country, and that sorely divided people, families, towns, and countries. The one true faith did not triumph. And yet rulers could be found who were convinced of the duty to uphold the true faith by sword and prison. And, moreover, subjects could be found to endorse these efforts.

There were, it is true, other voices than the dominant voices of persecution. There were those—the *politiques*, for example—who advocated a policy of expediency. They held that one should expediently persecute or tolerate, depending on whether or not such a policy did or did not upset law and order, split the community, and threaten the fabric of society. They would persecute and practice a policy of enforced religious conformity only when they could do so without jeopardizing peace, civility, order, strength, prosperity in the state. If, however, persecution led to war, disorder, weakness, economic ruin, then they would desist and practice a policy of toleration of religious dissenters. The *politiques* were thus pragmatists and realists. Their opponents deemed them unprincipled. They deemed their critics fanatics. The *politiques* clearly recognized that a blind and dogmatic policy of persecution, regardless of consequences, would undermine peace, order, law, justice, strength, and prosperity in the state. Such an outcome, they argued, is an evil greater than the toleration of religious dissenters.

Another minority position was that of religious toleration, a position not to be equated with genuine—full and complete—religious liberty. Those who held to this position were often influenced by a humanist philosophy. They held that one should tolerate, and thus permit, the unorthodox faith, even though convinced of its inferiority and even though possessed of the power to hinder its existence. The advocates of toleration, with practical help from the *politiques*, laid the groundwork for the emergence of genuine religious liberty.

In the seventeenth century the policies of persecution and expediency were still operative. However, forces moving in the direction of a policy of toleration were gaining strength. They achieved a triumph in the British Act of Toleration in 1689. This act, however, did not usher in genuine religious liberty. Certain religious groups still suffered liabilities under its terms. Factors encouraging these forces of toleration, and the related forces of genuine religious liberty, did, however, gain momentum in the seventeenth century and then even more momentum in the eighteenth century.

The line between religious toleration and religious liberty is not always easy to see. Let me attempt to clarify these two concepts. Those who believe in religious toleration believe that they possess the one true religious faith, but they are willing to tolerate—allow or endure—the religious faith of those not possessing that true faith. They do so often because they believe that religious conscience cannot be coerced. They may or may not, however, act to remove all disabilities (civic and educational) suffered by those not adhering to the true and dominant religious faith. Toleration is essentially a gift from those of superior faith and political power. The dominant religion would still be the established religion, but its adherents would allow religious dissidents to practice their faith, even though religious dissenters, or those of unorthodox faiths, might still suffer civil disabilities.

Religious liberty, by way of contrast, is based on the following principles. (1) All have a *right* to believe as they see fit. (2) The state is to be prohibited from affirming the one true faith or the superiority of one faith over another. (3) No disabilities—religious, civil, educational—should limit the social, political, or cultural prerogatives of citizens or punish the religiously unorthodox. (4) Religious believers (or non-believers) should not be taxed for the support of religious beliefs or institutions that they do not endorse. Religious liberty is closely related to the principle of separation of church and state. That principle functions to protect religious liberty and, simultaneously, to protect the integrity and impartiality of the state.

Roger Williams, as we shall see, is a key transitional figure between the seventeenth-century doctrine of religious toleration and the modern belief in religious liberty. The modern belief in religious liberty receives a clear and emphatic affirmation with the adoption of the First Amendment to the U.S. Constitution in1791. However, regardless of whether we call Williams an enlightened seventeenth-century advocate of advanced religious toleration (or of real religious freedom) *or* a modern advocate of religious liberty, it is the case that his theory and practice constitute a significant breakthrough.

In the middle of the seventeenth century Roger Williams proposed that it is possible to have the best of two seemingly contradictory worlds. It is possible to pursue the one true faith without insisting upon coerced religious conformity. Moreover, religious diversity, he argued, is not incompatible with the enjoyment of a good, moral, peaceful, constitutional, prosperous political community. Williams thus challenged the conventional wisdom, the dominant paradigm. He did not deny that there is only one true faith, which for him was Christianity. He did hold that humans cannot be absolutely sure what interpretation of the true faith is the correct one. That determination is in God's hands, not the hands of mere human beings. That decision is to be made by God on Judgment Day. Consequently, he rejected the view that it is the duty of the ruler of the state to uphold the one true faith by persecution, and with sword and prison.

But let us next turn to a fuller examination of Williams' interrelated arguments (1) on behalf of religious liberty, and (2) on behalf of separation of church and state.

ROGER WILLIAMS AND THE BREAKTHROUGH TO RELIGIOUS LIBERTY

The religious and political philosophy of Roger Williams is fruitful because it addresses a major problem.[6] How is it possible to reconcile the ideal of religious orthodoxy and political order *with* the facts of religious diversity, religious persecution, and political conflict? This problem has three significant interrelated parts: (1) how to overcome religious and political conflict between Catholics and Protestants; (2) how to arrest disintegration and civil war within the Protestant camp, once Protestantism had triumphed in key countries; and (3) how to work out a proper relationship between spiritual and temporal powers—that is, between church and state. Although the scene of Williams' response is Puritan New England, his argument on behalf of religious liberty—although rooted, as we shall see, in rather orthodox Puritan and Christian ideas—has a relevance not only for Puritan New England and America, but for Europe and indeed for the larger world.

The relevance of his argument, as we shall also see, carries beyond the religious, political, and constitutional controversies in the seventeenth century to national, ideological, and ethnic controversies in the twentieth century—and even beyond into the upcoming twenty-first century. His argument is relevant to the struggle for a constitutional global order that can overcome, or at least more sensibly deal with, national, ideological, and ethnic struggles that continue to erupt around the globe and disrupt political communities with devastating effect.

It is highly significant that Williams' religious and political philosophy is closely related to the development of constitutional theory and practice. We can understand this better if we appreciate that struggles between Catholics and Protestants after the Protestant Reformation produced theories of religious and, then, political resistance in defense of religious and, then, political rights. Such theories—for example, in the famous *Vindication of Liberty Against Tyrants* (1579)—often developed a contract argument in which a ruler was obligated to protect the political and religious rights of his subjects. John Locke's *Second Treatise on Civil Government* (1690) and Jefferson's Declaration of Independence (1776) are both in this significant tradition. But a lot of blood had to be shed before ideas of religious toleration or genuine religious liberty emerged, and became part of the operative constitution of nations.

Let us now restate and explicate each of the three interrelated parts of the problem Williams faced.

First, how was it possible to overcome religious and political conflicts between Catholics and Protestants? As we have noted, sixteenth- and seventeenth-century Europe had been racked by terrible conflicts that pitted Catholic against Protestant. And civil war and persecution did not end, as we have also noted, when Protestants emerged victorious in some countries. Often the tables were simply turned and Protestants persecuted Catholics. In addition, Protestants persecuted Protestants. And as Catholics worried about the splintering of Christianity when the one true Catholic faith was challenged, so Protestants worried about disintegration and splintering and civil war, even when Protestantism was triumphant.

Second, how would it be possible to overcome the splinterization of Protestantism? In seventeenth-century Britain, for example, persecution and civil war overtook Protestants there. The first Puritans—dissenters against the established Protestant Church of England—left England before the Civil War that broke out in the 1640s. But, we must remember, even though they wanted to be free to practice their own faith, they did not advocate religious toleration or religious freedom for all before they left England or after they arrived in the new American world. In New England they had to face the fact that religious dissenters within the Puritan Commonwealth could divide it as Protestants had divided Catholic countries and as Puritans, for example, had divided the Anglican community. Given the existence of nonconformists, how could one end divisions within the Puritan camp? Would religious dissent within the Puritan camp lead to religious disorder and political chaos? The difficulty was compounded because toleration was abominable to orthodox Puritans, because genuine religious freedom was unthinkable to almost all Puritans, and because the number and power of dissenters did not initially encourage a policy of expedient toleration. The problem is illustrated by Catholics confronted by Protestant "heretics," or Anglicans confronted by Puritan "heretics," or Puritans confronted by Puritan "heretics"—or by Quakers, Baptists, and other unorthodox sects. The problem seemed to be an enduring political problem whenever there exists in the political community (1) the belief in a single, true faith (religious or political) *and* the fact of diversity of faith, combined with (2) the conviction that it is the duty of the ruler of the state to uphold the one true faith.

Third, what should be the proper relationship of the spiritual and temporal powers, of what we today call church and state? Williams' conflict with orthodox Puritans in Massachusetts (as the conflict of minority Protestants with majority Catholics, or of minority Puritans with majority Anglicans) must also be seen in light of a problem older than the Catholic-Protestant dispute and Protestant splintering: the problem of the relationship between the spiritual and temporal powers. The conflict here had been foreshadowed in a famous New Testament text (Matthew 22:21): "Render therefore unto Caesar the things which are Caesar's; and unto God the things that are God's." One had an obligation to obey the powers that be. But one also had an obligation to obey God rather than man. What was Caesar's? What was God's? Putting the question in more modern terms: What is the legitimate area of religious liberty? And what is the legitimate area of the state's authority?

Roger Williams' religious and political philosophy will address the troubling issue of religious persecution, war, and disunity and—simultaneously—attempt to distinguish legitimate spheres of religious liberty and state power.

Williams' key arguments can be found in that fascinating debate with John Cotton that erupted in 1644, eight years after Williams fled Massachusetts to escape being deported to England, and ended with Cotton's death in 1652. Williams had gotten into trouble in Massachusetts because he had contended that the Puritans' title to their land was not genuine; that a magistrate must not administer an oath (part of God's worship) to an unregenerate (impure) person; that Puritans must not hear ministers in communion with impure English parishes; and that the power of civil magistrates extends only to the bodies, goods, and outward state of people and not to their relations to God. It is interesting to note, parenthetically, that the English Civil War (the first English revolution) took place in the years 1640–1649. The titles of the key tracts written by Williams and Cotton eloquently reveal the spirit and flavor of the men and the debate. Williams joined the debate in 1644 with *The Bloudy Tenent of Persecution for Cause of Conscience, discussed, in A Conference betweene Truth and Peace.* Cotton responded three years later with *The Bloudy Tenent, Washed, and made white in the bloud of the Lambe.* Williams replied to this salvo with another blast in 1652: *The Bloudy Tenent yet More Bloody: by Mr. Cotton's endeavour to wash it white in the Blood of the Lambe.* John Cotton died in 1652 without replying.[7]

At the risk of making Williams' position more coherent and modern than it was, let me develop his position by setting forth his related arguments on behalf of religious liberty, and on behalf of separation of church and state.

The Argument on Behalf of Religious Liberty

Williams makes a religious and moral argument *and* an historical and expedient argument on behalf of religious liberty. Let me consider each in turn. Williams' religious and moral argument for religious liberty consists of two main points: first, persecution is contrary to the spirit, teaching, and deeds of Jesus Christ; and, second, persecution is hypocritical.

Initially, then, Williams argued that persecution is contrary to the spiritual nature of Christ's gospel and kingdom. Persecution is contrary to the "sweet end of the coming" of the Prince of Peace who came not to destroy bodies and lives but to save bodies and souls. Is it not anomalous, he deftly pointed out, for Christians—in the name of Christ, the Prince of Peace—to persecute, to wield the sword, to spill blood, to divide person against person. God, Williams insisted, does not require that religious uniformity be enacted or enforced in any civil state. Instead, God requires that free-dom of conscience and worship be extended to all people. Moreover, Christ himself indicated that disbelievers must be allowed to live in this world; that their punishment would come in the next. It was contrary to God's message to coerce conscience. People could only come to God freely, not because of fear of earthly persecution, punishment, and coercion. Rape of the soul—Williams' vivid image for religious persecution—was incom-patible with God's message that people be drawn freely to divinity. En-forced uniformity, Williams held, ravishes conscience and violates Christ's message.

Williams used a famous New Testament parable—the parable of the wheat and the weeds (tares) in Matthew 13—to drive home his argument. The weeds (that is, the unregenerate, the impure, the faithless) may grow unmolested among the wheat (the elect) until harvest time—that is, death. Why? Because the wheat may be endangered by plucking (persecuting) the weeds. At harvest time (Judgment Day) the weeds can safely be gathered and burned; that is, at the time of judgment day, punishment can be safely meted out. God's battles in this world, Williams insisted, must be fought with God's weapons—God's word—not with swords and prisons, with persecution and civic disabilities. If Jesus were to return to earth, Williams asked pointedly to clinch his argument here, what Christian religion would he approve: Catholic, Anglican, Presbyterian, Puritan? And would he per-secute those who would not receive him? What, indeed, would be Christ's own answer on the question of who the true believers really are? Catholic or Protestant? And which Protestants? Clearly, if some of each group are being persecuted, then some must be persecuted even if they are the true believers. A policy of persecution, which may result in some true believers being persecuted, cannot be defended. Such a policy is malicious and vicious. It is counterproductive.

Moreover, secondly, persecution is hypocritical. The individual should not be forced to believe against his conscience or support a church against his consent. In an imperfect world how can we, Williams asked rhetorically, say we are godly and, therefore, have the right to persecute the ungodly who adhere conscientiously to their own beliefs?

In his historical and expedient argument Williams argues against relig-ious persecution and for religious liberty. On one hand, he argues that religious persecution undermines civil peace, law, and order, and results in grave injury to true believers. He notes the alternating persecutions of Protestants by Catholics, Catholics by Protestants, and Protestants by Prot-estants; and he contends that true believers—on one side or the other—are being persecuted. This situation all genuine human beings must abhor. In other words, enforced religious conformity destroys the very prerequisites of civilized society, or true civility—law, order, peace, and respect—and injures true believers. He also emphasizes that persecution for cause of conscience has not, in fact, produced the alleged "good" sought by the persecutors. Religious uniformity has not been achieved. "Disbelievers" persist. True believers, moreover, are clearly martyred; and civility is seriously damaged.

On the other hand, Williams argued on the basis of the historical record that religious liberty is in fact compatible with Christ's teaching, with true civility, and with devotion to civilized behavior. This point is developed more fully in Williams' argument on behalf of separation of church and state.

The Argument on Behalf of Separation of Church and State

Williams' argument for separation of church and state, as we shall see, is closely related to and strongly supports his argument for religious liberty. Oddly, from a modern point of view, his argument is rooted in the conviction that only one church-state (biblical Israel) ever possessed the legitimate power to persecute unbelievers. The key question for Williams thus became: What is the proper conception of church and state since Israel and Christ?

The church, Williams argues, is spiritual in nature. It is concerned with souls. The weapons for its rightful defense must also be spiritual. Worldly props, he maintained, would undermine the church. Therefore, a spiritual church can make no use of a secular state for its spiritual purposes. God, Williams eloquently argued, did not appoint the civil sword as a remedy for the sores of God's body and church. The church must be understood as a corporation with an independent existence. Dissent and division within the church need not endanger the peace of the political community.

The state is self-sufficient and has peace as its objective. The state is different in essence from the church. The state existed before corporations or associations and will remain when they are gone. The state is self-sufficient and does not, therefore, need the church in order to preserve peace and order. The political community does not require enforced religious conformity for its continuance. The prince, civil magistrate, or state have limited responsibilities: to preserve peace and order in the political community. Religious uniformity is neither a necessary nor a sufficient condition for such peace and order. Indeed, when the civil magistrate persecutes for cause of conscience, he undermines peace and order. The sword and the prison should not, must not, be used to enforce the alleged one true religious faith. In brief, matters of religious faith were to be left to the individual person and to God. The practice of religious faith should not be a matter of concern to the civil magistrate. Religion should be placed beyond the power of the state.

Here in Williams' argument, let me emphasize, are ideas that contribute to the paradigm of constitutional government: of a government limited in its powers. Later, of course, government will also be effectively and regularly restrained even in the exercise of those powers granted. Certain matters (here religious matters) are to be beyond the power of the state. In the theory and practice of government in Providence Plantation (later Rhode Island), Williams developed other constitutional (and democratic) ideas to supplement these on religious liberty and the integrity of the individual conscience. These ideas and practices anticipated a fuller democratic and constitutional theory.

Williams combined his views on religious liberty and separation of church and state with several other ideas that were being bruited about by such republican and constitutional thinkers as the Levellers and comparable groups. These ideas included the equality of all people, their basic rights, government as an institution entered into by rational people, the consent of the governed via compact, and the right of resistance to tyrannical government. Williams was successful, at least for a short period of time, in incorporating these ideas into the government of Providence Plantation, the first genuinely free charter of government issued to an English colony. His "lively experiment" at Providence Plantation, which incorporated basic ingredients of the American democratic experiment, anticipated the fuller expression of such democratic ideas as popular sovereignty, a written constitution limiting the powers of government, majority rule, referendum and recall, the fuller development of the doctrine of separation of church and state, and the fuller protection of such basic rights as freedom of conscience and worship, of press, of speech, of debate, and of association.

In attending to the practical affairs of governance, Williams encountered the challenge of balancing the claims of liberty (that inclined toward license) and authority (requisite for the common good). One such challenge came from religious extremists, and confronted Williams with the task of establishing some bounds to actions and exemptions demanded on religious grounds. The challenge in this task enables us to see how far Williams would go in developing a theory of bounds—to liberty and to authority.

One such religious extremist was a man named Harris, a Baptist and anarchist living in Providence Plantation. He maintained that all are equal in Christ, held that authority over man is evil, and denied the right of the state to compel obedience by requiring compulsory military service against native Americans (Indians). In reply to the position of such religious pacifists Williams argued that he contended for no such infinite liberty of conscience; that one could indeed punish for breach of civil justice, peace, or sobriety. He might possibly have had in mind not only pacifism but also such other activities as wife-beating or nudity defending on religious grounds. In his argument against Harris, Williams formulated, however crudely, a "clear and present danger" doctrine similar to that we also find in John Milton, Jefferson, and Oliver Wendell Holmes. The passage (1655) is worth full quotation.

> That ever I speak or write a title that tends to such an infinite liberty of conscience is a mistake, and which I have ever disclaimed and abhorred. To prevent such mistakes, I shall at present only propose this case: There goes many a ship to sea, with many hundred souls in one ship, whose weal and woe is common, and is a true picture of a commonwealth or a human combination or society. It hath fallen out sometimes that both Papists and Protestants, Jews and Turks, may be embarked in one ship; upon which supposal I affirm that all the liberty of conscience that ever I pleased for turns upon these two hinges: that none of the Papists, Protestants, Jews, or Turks be forced to come to the ship's prayers or worship, nor compelled from their own particular prayers or worship, if they practice any. I further add that I never denied that, notwithstanding this liberty, the commander of this ship ought to command the ship's course, yea, and also command that justice, peace, and sobriety be kept and practiced, both among the seamen and all the passengers. If any of the seamen refuse to perform their services, or passengers to pay their freight; if any refuse to help, in person or purse, toward the common charges or defense; if any refuse to obey the common laws and orders of the ship concerning their common peace or preservation; if any shall mutiny and rise up against their commanders and officers; if any should preach or write that there ought to be no commanders or officers because all are equal in Christ, therefore no masters nor officers, nor laws nor orders, no corrections nor punishments—I say, I never denied but in such cases, whatever is pretended, the commander or commanders may judge, resist, compel, and punish such transgressors according to their deserts and merits. This, if seriously and honestly minded, may, if it so please the Father of lights, let in some light to such as willingly shut not their eyes.[8]

In brief, the common interest in preserving safety could justify the exercise of civil power against those who jeopardized the ship of state. Williams was at least struggling with the problem of the boundaries of the spiritual and temporal powers, the problem of the reconciliation of liberty and authority, the problem of church and state. Unfortunately, despite the modest help provided in the quotation above, he did not go on to answer some of the difficult questions involved: What is the common interest? What action or inaction jeopardizes the ship of state? Or threatens justice, peace, sobriety? Or interferes with legitimate law and order? We are still struggling with these questions today. It is relatively easy to reject anarchy or totalitarianism, but how do we maintain the vital balance between the legitimate claims of liberty and authority?

Nonetheless, it is the case that the vital religious matters that Williams unquestionably sought to protect against the state would become rights. And rights would be broadened to include freedom of speech, press, and assembly, as well as religious freedom. And (for example, in the Declaration of Independence) the right of the just revolution would be enshrined as a way to protect those rights against tyranny.

Williams emphatically challenged the dominant paradigm of Western Christendom—a paradigm that had seemed so logical and so persuasive. We should note that he did not challenge the proposition that there was a true faith. He did challenge the view that it was the duty of the ruler of the state to enforce the true faith. Williams' new paradigm would protect the rights of conscience, and thus the search of people for the true faith. Simultaneously, his new paradigm eliminated from politics a vital source of discord and division: the duty of the ruler of the state to uphold the one true faith. This duty, he argued, was harmful, indeed potentially fatal, to peace, law, order, justice, civility, prosperity, and strength in the political community. Williams articulated a theory of religious liberty and of consti- tutional protection for the rights of religious conscience. He helped to shape that theory of constitutional government necessary to ensure the successful practice of religious liberty.

The theory and practice of Williams on religious liberty and separation of church and state led to a momentous change in outlook, behavior, and judgment in both religion and politics. Such theory and practice were fruiful: in ending, in time, religious persecution; in securing the effective exercise of religious freedom; in constitutionalizing the exercise of power. His theory and practice—especially as the principle of the free exercise of religion and the prohibition against an establishment of religion became embodied in the First Amendment—contributed mightily to the resolution of a deeply troubling problem that had badly split Western Christendom since the Protestant Reformation, that had led to catastrophic religious warfare in Western Europe, and that had forced a criticial reexamination of the relation of spiritual and temporal powers: church and state.

Before reexamining—and reemphasizing—the ethical, empirical, and prudential breakthroughs involved in Williams' theory, let me endeavor to clarify Williams' Puritan position and to distinguish it from other argu- ments on behalf of religious liberty.

Williams' Puritanism had driven him, on uniquely religious grounds— that is, the search for God's pure church on earth—to recognize that such a church has not existed and could not exist since ancient Israel. Conse- quently, efforts to achieve it were fruitless, presumptuous, and dangerous. Ironically, the search for purity on earth had led him from a holier-than-thou search for purity (and a rejection of the impure) to the necessity of accepting all religious seekers. It had led him to the conviction that one must use only spiritual weapons—God's good word—in contest with the misguided. It had also led him to accept this "dunghill" of a world, a world wherein purity could not be achieved. And, finally, it had led him to limit the functions and objectives of the state in the maintenance of peace and order.

At Judgment Day only, and in another world only, could true and false believers be safely separated and appropriately rewarded or punished.

These ideas are by no means entirely in agreement with modern arguments on behalf of religious freedom. To test the modernity of Williams' argument readers might ask themselves whether they would base their own belief in freedom of conscience on Williams' entire argument.

Williams' thinking represents only a partial, albeit a highly significant, advance on the emerging notion of religious toleration. Religious toleration, we have suggested, is not the same as religious liberty. Toleration assumes a superior worship. Toleration is a gift of a superior believer to those who are inferior. Sometimes, toleration rests not upon the ethical principle of true respect, but upon expedient grounds. Williams did not depart completely from the notion of toleration, since he assumed a superior worship in Christ and based his argument, at least in part, on expedient grounds. Yet Williams did urge upon the dominant church and the dominant powers in the state the principle of liberty of conscience as a fundamental matter of religious principle, even if he used historical and expedient arguments to buttress the cogency of this religious principle.

Despite the lack of political realism in his early puritanical attitudes, Williams—in seeing the disastrous consequences of persecution—was more realistic than the orthodox Puritans who expelled him. He magnificently underscored the dangers of persecution: civil strife and destruction, the martyrdom of "true believers," the hypocrisy of forced belief, righteous people playing God. Here Williams developed arguments to which most liberal democrats would say "amen," even if they sometimes fail to accept the application of these arguments to unpopular dissidents.

But let us now turn to a comparison of Williams' arguments to those of others. This may help us to understand the arguments that Williams did not use or did not fully exploit. For example, he did not exploit fully one of the central arguments of Milton's *Areopagitica*: that in a fair battle we need have no doubts that truth will triumph over falsehood.[9] Perhaps he did not exploit this argument because he was less concerned with what Oliver Wendell Holmes, Jr. later called the competition of the marketplace of ideas, and was more concerned with a person's inward seeking of the truth before God's holy altar. In this connection, however, we should note that Williams (unlike Milton and Oliver Cromwell, whom he knew as friends) was willing to extend freedom of conscience to Catholics, despite the fact that he thought Catholics wrong in their religious beliefs.

Moreover, Williams—although he used historical and expedient arguments—did not base his case primarily on utilitarian notions of the greatest good for the greatest number. Nor did he use John Stuart Mill's utilitarian arguments on behalf of liberty.[10] Mill had argued that we cannot suppress truth because we cannot postulate our own infallibility; because what is almost the whole truth may be perfected by the little truth that may exist in major error; and because truth remains most rational and vigorous and effective when it has to compete actively (with error) for people's minds. Although Williams appreciated human fallibility and the need to search for the truth, he did not use these arguments because he was not a utilitarian but a devout Christian convinced that Christ's word constituted the true belief. In addition, he held that competition in this world (despite the fact that we must accept it) was less important than true judgment in the next world.

Finally, Williams did not use the natural rights argument of Jefferson and Madison: that freedom of religion is an inalienable right that people enjoy in a state of nature and that society and government are instituted to protect. This natural rights argument, not Williams' uniquely religious argument, is the one that has probably exerted the greatest influence in America. This is true, I believe, even though Williams' conviction that it is un-Christian to coerce belief did indeed underlie Madison's natural rights argument on behalf of religious liberty. However, Williams did not argue, as Madison did, that religious diversity is a positive good—as a precondition of freedom; that both political and religious freedom are nourished by and flourish under religious and political competition and diversity.

CREATIVE BREAKTHROUGHS AS BREAKTHROUGHS ALONG SEVERAL FRONTS

The most creative breakthroughs are breakthroughs along several fronts—ethical, empirical, and prudential—and are well illustrated by Williams' political and religious philosophy. *Ethically*, Williams articulated an admirable philosophy of politics, of how we ought to live together in the political community. He articulated a philosophy of people of different religious faiths living freely, happily, harmoniously, civilly, orderly, peacefully, prosperously together in the same political community. For Williams, in practice, this community was to be a democratic political community. Religious freedom, the separation of church and state, a democratic and constitutional polity—these were for Williams preferred crucial values. They became in the eighteenth century the basis of expanded notions of basic rights and republican rule, and served also to ensure a more generous democratic and constitutional regime.

Empirically, Williams articulated a new hypothesis, which would become a cornerstone for his "lively experiment" in what is later to be called Rhode Island, and which would subsequently be more fully tested in the United States. That hypothesis stipulated that in Christendom people of different religious faiths, enjoying religious liberty, can in fact live together without the evil effects that many feared—incivility, immorality, disrespect for law and order, war, economic ruin; that in fact religious persecution is the great enemy of society, harmony, prosperity, and peace.

Prudentially, Williams made the judgment that it was wise to ensure religious liberty and to separate church and state. He did so by calling attention to the ill effects, hypocrisy, and illogic of persecution; by acting to limit the abusive power of the state in religious matters; and by establishing legitimate domains of operation for church and state. Those who follow him can then more easily endorse theories of just resistance and, if necessary, of just revolution to ensure the return to constitutional government in the event the state violates basic rights. They can more easily establish the principle of separation of church and state, and thus protect both the purity of the church—and of religious conscience— and the legitimacy of the state in its proper sphere of operation.

In reflecting on this particular creative breakthrough, we emphasize again that, initially, the ethical recommendation on behalf of religious liberty seems outrageous; that the empirical proposition that religious liberty and political peace are compatible seems false; and that the prudent judgment that religious liberty and separation of church and state are wise seems absurd. However, when the decision on behalf of religious liberty is tested, it works. In time, religious liberty becomes enshrined in the First Amendment as a cardinal and admired value. Religious liberty serves *in fact* to advance social harmony. Both religious liberty and separation of church and state function to protect against the abuse of religious and political power.

Reflection on this creative breakthrough strongly suggests the need in politics (and in political science) to be open to and willing to test new possibilities for living together better in the political community. These new possibilities are suggested by new and prophetic ethical views. They are prophetic because they are dedicated to peace, freedom, and justice. They are reinforced by a willingness to try new and prophetic patterns of conflict resolution. And these new and prophetic possibilities are suggested by people searching for wise decisions to live political problems.

Such prophetic men and women are not discovering a scientific mystery long shrouded in our past and present—in nature—although they may be inspired by ancient prophetic aspirations for peace, freedom, and justice. They are in a significant sense creating the future. They are divining political becoming. They are discerning future possibilities that illuminate the contemporary meaning of such prophetic values as covenant, law, peace, freedom, justice, prosperity. They are significantly influenced by untried and unfulfilled ethical possibilities; by a glimpse of new empirical possibilities, keen insights about human realities; and by an intimation of a fresh and inspiring wisdom.

Looking beyond the breakthrough to religious liberty, it is possible to see the relevance of this breakthrough to other struggles—to other conflicts of faith, political as well as religious, national as well as ethnic—in our own century. Here I think of the East-West ideological and political struggles of the post–World War II Cold War, now perhaps happily behind us with the end of the Cold War, but only after great losses—losses that might have been avoided or mitigated if the principles underlying Williams' argument had been accepted by East-West adversaries. Here, too, I think of all struggles by all those seeking real freedom within authoritarian regimes, and real peace in ethically diverse societies. Alas, in too many of these struggles, Williams' principles have been also been rejected.

In the Cold War period (1945–1989), if we interpret communism and liberal democracy as faiths, we immediately see some parallels that make the religious battles of the sixteenth to the eighteenth centuries strikingly relevant in the years 1945–1989. Was communism (or liberal democracy) considered to be the one true faith? And was it the duty of the communist (or liberal democratic) state to uphold the one true faith throughout the world? Did this mean, therefore, that conflict is inevitable between communist and liberal democratic states?

It is true, some will argue, that the parallel between Williams' argument and the East-West struggle may not be cogent. After all, the communists are atheists and don't believe in God or Judgment Day. We live now and must work out our breakthroughs in a secular world. Disturbing questions emerge here. If we reject the view of a God who forbids "soul rape" (or "political rape") and who will judge the communist (or liberal democratic) believers only at Judgment Day, must we come up with a convincing secular substitute? Or must we reject such a secular substitute as mere rubbish? Do we then recognize that we are modern day *politiques*—advocates of "peaceful coexistence" on purely expedient grounds? Or can we in the modern world develop a convincing constitutional theory that will be persuasive to theists, agnostics, and atheists? Is conflict inevitable (when one side or the other concludes that it can risk aggressive action and forceful conversion) unless both sides concede that neither side can be absolutely certain about the true faith, *and* unless both sides agree to back away from enforcing their political or ideological or religious dogmatism? Must we at least move away from persecution of political or ideological conscience?

With regard to freedom and constitutionalism within authoritarian regimes, and real peace in ethically diverse societies: Will we be able to place religious, political, economic, social, and scientific beliefs beyond the power of the state to enforce against a person's conscience? Will we be able to get authoritarian states to limit their power and to cease their abuse of power? Will we be able in such authoritarian states to move toward constitutionalism and constitutional change? Can political communities, composed of ethnically diverse populations, live together harmoniously?

Or will arguments on behalf of freedom, liberal or social democracy, and constitutionalism prove unavailing until our reaction to international war or civil war or ethnic war carried on by intolerant states and peoples produces a new, a prophetic constitutional receptivity?

These questions adumbrate the character of a major creative break-through in the future, a breakthrough to genuine peaceful and constitutional accommodation within authoritarian or repressive states or among the armed nations of the modern world. They highlight the work that remains ahead as we seek to maximize the benefits and insights of Williams' breakthrough to religious liberty.

CONCLUSION

Williams sought to reconcile the ideal of religious orthodoxy (the belief in one true faith) and political order *with* the facts of religious diversity, religious persecution, and political conflict. He did so not by abandoning the belief in one true faith or the need for political order but by contending that religious diversity was not incompatible with the one true faith or political order, that—indeed—religious persecution was contrary both to the one true faith and engendered political conflict, not order. Religious liberty, he maintained, was the way to overcome conflicts between Catholic and Protestant, Protestant and Protestant, or between members of other religious denominations. One need not fear disintegration within the Protestant camp. There should exist what we today call a separation of church and state—with the temporal power not dictating matters of conscience, and the spiritual power not seeking to use temporal power for its sectarian purposes; with individuals free to pursue their religious beliefs free of state interference.

Williams' religious and political philosophy constituted a major break-through, but it was not an absolutely perfect solution in the sense that it solved all future difficulties. Given fallible human beings in a nonangelic world, life seems to defy absolutely perfect solutions. However, Williams' position went a long way in delineating the legitimate bounds of church and state in a democratic America soon to be committed more fully to the novel principle of separation of church and state and the emerging principle of religious liberty, both of which were to achieve brilliant expression in the First Amendment to the U.S. Constitution. It is too much to expect that Williams' argument could completely resolve all the inevitable tensions between liberty and authority generated in a free, human society, particularly when either church or state push too far. Ongoing tensions always remain to be worked out by sensible people employing sensible constitutional principles and rules. These principles and rules, although we can certainly improve upon them over time and in response to new situations, nevertheless owe a great debt to Williams' religious genius. It is in the spirit of that genius that we need to tackle our continuing conundrums.[11]

We are still struggling with the question of the meaning of "pushing too far." Does the church push too far when a religious majority imposes its position on a religious (or irreligious) minority? When religious leaders, and their lay followers, impose their religious views on their fellow core-ligionists (particularly those in public life) and on the general public who may be informed by a different conscience on difficult issues that overlap the concerns of church and state: say, for example, on the issues of abortion, or capital punishment, or nuclear weapons, or Bible reading, or prayer in the public schools, or evolution, or poverty. To identify these issues is to indicate the complexity of the problem.

With regard to the state pushing too far, our problem (for example, in the United States today) is not the problem of a state-established church, wherein the state compels a single worship or persecutes unbelievers or those of a different religious faith. Nor is ours the problem of a state run indirectly by the "godly." Ours is the more difficult problem of ascertaining what action the state may take without infringing upon the free exercise of religion and without establishing a church. The state has the difficult job of deciding what the church or religious individuals may legitimately do in influencing public policy; and of deciding in controversial cases what religiously inspired persons may do without committing a substantive evil that the state may legitimately prevent.

Considerable controversy surrounds a number of questions of great interest to both church and state. Where does one draw the line between the religion's legitimate constitutional as well as moral and religious con-cerns *and* unacceptable meddling and involvement in the affairs of state? Where does one draw the line between the state's legitimate constitutional and political responsibilities *and* unacceptable meddling and involvement in matters of concience? (1) Is abortion the criminal taking of human life (murder) or a constitutional right of a pregnant woman to exercise control over her own body? (2) Is capital punishment a punishment forbidden to the state on religious and moral grounds or a legitimate punishment in a constitutional and just society? (3) Is nuclear war an unacceptable option on religious and moral grounds or a legitimate and necessary means of deterring a potential and dangerous aggressor? (4) Do religious bodies have immunity from violating the law when they grant sanctuary to illegal aliens fleeing political persecution in their home countries? (5) Is Bible reading or prayer in the public schools a violation of the Fourteenth Amendment (and thus the First Amendment) or the legitimate exercise of freedom of religion? (6) Is indirect federal aid to parochial schools a breach of the wall of separation of church and state or legitimate protection to, or support of, all school children? (7) May religious groups, on religious grounds, constitu-tionally ban public school texts because they allegedly interfere with the free exercise of religion of such religious groups? (8) What pressures may the hierarchy of religious organizations bring upon coreligionists, who are in political office or who are candidates for political office, on issues of public policy that are also religious concerns?

It is, of course, asking too much to expect Williams to provide us with answers to these ticklish and troublesome questions. I raise them only to indicate that difficult problems persist even in a democratic and constitutional society committed to religious liberty. These problems revolve around the issues of religious freedom and religious power, of individual freedom and state power, of separation of church and state. These problems are complicated by the fact that controversy rages about what constitutes permissible but unwise action on the part of both church and state.

Nevertheless, despite the difficulties suggested above, Williams' reasoning and conclusions may still provide considerable guidance for us in the contemporary America and in the contemporary world. He still helps us to see that we often have to be as leery of the virtuous as of the sinful, particularly when the virtuous are so sure that they possess the truth in controversial matters and insist upon imposing their understanding of the "truth" upon all who disagree with them. Religious diversity, he emphatically emphasized, is not incompatible with either religious truth or political order; and democratic governance by people of diverse religious views does not produce anarchy. Williams still helps us to see that religious liberty, interpreted as the freedom of a person's mind and soul to receive the truth, remains the most basic of our freedoms.

It is striking, I believe, that James Madison—whose breakthrough to the theory and practice of the federal republic we consider next—strongly emphasized in his political philosophy the crucial importance of religious diversity, religious and political freedom, and republican rule.

NOTES

1. Roland H. Bainton, *Studies of the Reformation* (Boston: Beacon Press, 1966), p. 213.

2. Quoted in Leo Pfeffer, *Church, State and Freedom* (Boston: Beacon Press, 1953), p. 27.

3. *Ibid.*, p. 95.

4. *Everson vs. Board of Education*, 330 U.S. 1 (1947).

5. See Hugo Grotius, *The Law of War and Peace* (1625), quoted in Francis W. Coker, *Readings in Political Philosophy* (New York: Macmillan, 1938), p. 409.

6. In my account I draw generously upon my earlier analysis of Williams in Neal Riemer, *The Democratic Experiment* (Princeton, N.J.: Van Nostrand, 1967), pp. 78–89. I have also profited from the excellent essay by Irwin H. Polishook in his *Roger Williams, John Cotton and Religious Freedom: A Controversy in New and Old England* (Englewood Cliffs, N.J.: Prentice-Hall, 1967). Polishook's book also contains helpful extracts from the writings of Roger Williams, John Cotton, and other contemporaries.

7. These essays can be found in Perry Miller, editor, *Roger Williams: His Contribution to the American Tradition* (Indianapolis: Bobbs-Merrill, 1953).

8. This passage will be found in Miller, *Roger Williams*, pp. 225–226; in Perry Miller and Thomas H. Johnson, eds., *The Puritans: A Sourcebook of Their Writings*, 2

vols. (New York: Harper and Row, 1963 [originally published in 1938]), Vol. 1, p. 225; and in Bainton, *Studies of the Reformation*, p. 226.

9. See John Milton, *Areopagitica* (1644). (New York: Payson & Clarke, 1927); and also in *Complete Poems and Major Prose* (New York: Odyssey Press, 1957).

10. See John Stuart Mill (1859), *On Liberty* (Indianapolis: Hackett, 1978).

11. For perspective on the continuing conundrums, see Luis E. Lugo, ed., *Religion, Public Life, and the American Polity* (Knoxville: University of Tennessee Press, 1994). Part I explores "Contending Models of Church-State Relations," Part II examines "The Founders and the Church-State Question," Part III deals with "Religion and the Law," Part IV assesses "Religion and American Political Culture." My chapter (pp. 37–50) on "Madison: A Founder's Vision of Religious Liberty and Public Life" throws light on Madison's debt—direct or indirect—to Williams' argument.

CHAPTER 3

James Madison and the Extensive Republic: Reconciling Liberty and Large Size

INTRODUCTION

The theme of this chapter is the most significant, the most momentous breakthrough that occurred in the spring, summer, and fall of 1787, that was developed with fertile results in the 1790s, and that was ignored with tragic consequences in the decades prior to the American Civil War. In order to appreciate Madison's breakthrough—which achieved initial political expression in 1787, and classic literary expression in Madison's numbers in *The Federalist*—we must first understand Madison's problem (indeed, the problem of Americans in 1787) in the context of the literature and experience of several millennia.[1]

The problem that faced thoughtful Americans in 1787 was this: Is just republican government in a large state possible? This was the central question that challenged the political genius of James Madison, America's first great political scientist. What political theory would provide guidance for republican statesmen struggling with the task of reconciling liberty and authority in the new American world? How could one maintain free, strong, and popular government in the huge expanse of the American domain?

This problem illustrated the two horns of the dilemma that faced the more thoughtful constitutional fathers: a despotic empire as a necessity of government in a large state; or faction, injustice, and weakness as the inevitable outcome in a confederate republic with major power residing in the thirteen states? What Americans wanted—just and strong republican government in a large state—thus seemed to contradict the historical and theoretical realities.

It was a problem for Madison (as it was for all republicans in America) because he was (as they were) committed to republican government (government by the people, through majority rule; government, moreover, dedicated to the protection of basic rights) in a new American nation that required requisite power and authority for survival. Was it possible, however, to reconcile such liberty (and self-government) and such authority (in a union of the states) in a large country? This was a problem because the conventional wisdom about democracy and large states—according to the evidence of history, according to the testimony of political philosophers—decreed the impossibility of reconciling liberty and authority in a large state.

According to the conventional wisdom of history and political theory, republican government (based on popular self-government and liberty) was possible *only* in a small political community—for example, a city-state such as Athens or Venice or Geneva. But, alas, the new United States was a large state. Moreover, according to the conventional wisdom, the political science of the day, a large state could *only* be governed under the authority of a monarch or a despot and within the framework of a nonrepublican empire, one incompatible with self-government and liberty, at least the degree of self-government and liberty that Americans had presumably fought their revolution to secure. Anything less than such republican self-government and such republican liberty was a state of affairs that good American republicans could never accept.

How, then, deal with this problem? How respond to this dilemma? Could American republicans have the best of two, seemingly contradictory, worlds? Could they have self-government and liberty in a republic *and* also enjoy legitimate power, authority, order, security in the large country that was America?

Others had refused to face up to the problem because they believed it to be insoluble. Patrick Henry and other anti-Federalists, for example, argued that republican government is possible only in a small political community. They therefore opposed the new Constitution of 1787 and the stronger government it created. They did not lift their sights beyond the loose political confederation of the Articles of Confederation. They rejected the possibility of a greatly strengthened central government.

Alexander Hamilton and John Adams and other advocates of "high toned" government maintained—before the adoption of the new Constitution—that only an Empire, or a strong central government on the British model, could hold together a political community as large as the new American nation. Confederations, they insisted, were notoriously weak and unstable and detrimental to the interests of justice. If Henry and his friends argued that great strength in a central government jeopardized republican self-government and liberty, Hamilton and Adams and their friends held, initially, that faction prevailed in the small political community and jeopardized both the public good and the Union.

So the battle raged about authority or tyranny at the center (with a new national government) and about liberty and anarchy at the circumference (among the several states). Neither Henry nor Hamilton challenged the accepted political science of their day or perceived that the traditional statement of the problem of how to reconcile liberty and authority (in the large expanse of the new United States of America) had to be reexamined. Only Madison challenged the conventional wisdom and was bold enough to look at the problem in a new light and to ask if a new concept—what Madison called the extensive republic, what we today call the federal republic—suggested a way out.

The traditional answer to the problem of reconciling liberty and authority in a large state had been overwhelmingly "no." Both history and theory joined in rendering this answer. Here Aristotle joined hands not only with rabble-rousers like Patrick Henry who opposed the new Constitution but also with solid citizens like John Adams and the Alexander Hamilton of the Convention who felt initially that the proposed new Constitution would not be strong enough to work.

And, interestingly enough, both sides—those like Henry who opposed a stronger central government, and those like Adams and Hamilton who favored a much stronger central government—had the overwhelming evidence of history to support their (initial) lack of faith in the new Constitution.

Central government too strong would produce tyranny and injustice—so argued those who favored a decentralized government that would enable a liberty-loving and republican people in the states to keep power in their own hands. Central government too weak would produce anarchy and injustice—so contended those who favored a powerful, more centralized government to maintain union and liberty. Both sides could appeal to history to support their respective arguments.

The historical, theoretical answer to the question of the possibility of just republican government in a large state had, prior to 1787, been emphatically negative. Both Aristotle and Thucydides had noted the despotic character of the great empires of the East. Aristotle and Machiavelli had also noted that democracy is fit only for a country of small size and that in such a country democracy is subject to the notorious democratic disease of faction—a disease whose symptoms were selfishness, self-aggrandizement, injustice, and brute power.

Those who favored a strong central government were familiar with the troubles of Greek democracy, and of the civil war among Greek city-states that had done such harm to Greek civilization. Shay's Rebellion was so alarming to conservatives because it seemed to many like a chapter out of the Peloponnesian War. Faction, lawlessness, bloodshed, civil war—this was the spectre that haunted many of the minds of the fifty-five hard-headed men gathered in solemn conclave in Philadelphia in the hot, decisive summer of 1787. Many of them were educated in the classical tradition. They had read Thucydides, Aristotle, and Polybius. They remembered the bloody scenes of Greek civil strife. They knew about the weaknesses of Greek democracy, democracy understood in Aristotelean terms as government by the many (ignorant and poor) in their own selfish interest. They knew with Aristotle that "without virtue" man "is a most unholy and savage being . . . worse than all others in the indulgence of lust and gluttony."[2] Without a standard of the common good to guide a political community, the polity is doomed to misfortune. Greek democracy, the confederation of Greek city-states—these were not happy models for the Americans of 1787.

In light of political literature and actual history, confidence in the long-term maintenance of republican government seemed a delusion. The hard fact seemed to be that republican government was possible only in a small state, as in Athens or Venice; but, unfortunately, it was precisely in such a state that faction, the omnipresent disease of popular rule, was most prevalent. Neither Aristotle, nor Cicero, nor Machiavelli, nor James Harrington, nor John Locke—thinkers and writers who influenced the republican tradition—had anything to say that contradicted this "hard fact." Small republics, said the influential Baron Charles-Louis Montesquieu—reflecting the accepted position of political literature—were more easily destroyed by foreign force. "It is natural for a republic to have only a small territory; otherwise it cannot subsist."[3]

Such conventional wisdom unquestionably reinforced the initial convictions of statesmen like Hamilton and Adams that only a "high-toned" government could prevail in America, a country of large size. Such a government would be a "mixed government"; and this meant a monarch-like executive with strong power to hold the nation together, and an aristocracy to protect the rich and the well-born. Such an executive and aristocracy would then be able to balance the popular element—the many poor—and thus keep faction in check. In moving in the direction of a high-toned government Hamilton and those who shared his perspective were struggling in their own way to reconcile republicanism and empire in view of the conventional wisdom that affirmed that republicanism and empire were incompatible. They were not unaware of Montesquieu's argument that large empires can be governed only by a despotic prince; that large republics could not be held together on republican principles. But they worried less about power at the center than about anarchy at the circumference.

Patrick Henry and those who became known as the anti-Federalists (really the opponents of a stronger central government) were considerably worried about a high-toned central government. They would not forget Montesquieu's contention that a large empire could be governed only by a despotic prince, that a large republic (and clearly the new American nation was a large republic) could not be held together on republican principles. If Hamilton, for example, initially had little faith in democracy, Henry had little faith in the proposed new Constitution. To Henry and many of the other anti-Federalists, the proposed new government of 1787 was but a thin disguise for monarchy or aristocracy. They wanted no such high-toned government. They wanted to keep power close to the people. Henry declared typically "that one government cannot reign over so extensive a country as this is, without absolute despotism."[4] Montesquieu's dictum here was very much alive in his mind. He thus agreed emphatically that republican government was possible only for a relatively small territory and a relatively small homogeneous population.

Strikingly, both Hamilton and Henry grounded their arguments in essentially the same history and political literature. Oddly, the conventional wisdom that cast serious doubts on the possibility of just republican government in a large state led Alexander Hamilton to one conclusion and Patrick Henry to another. As we have seen, Hamilton—fearing the actuality of faction in the states and a weak union more than the possibility of a despotic empire—sought refuge in a high-toned government that would subordinate the states to a strong nation. Fundamentally, John Adams, in England in 1787, favored a comparable solution.

Such a scheme, as we have also seen, was abhorrent to Patrick Henry and the anti-Federalists who were also the captives of the conventional wisdom. They would take their chances with a loose and weak confederation, with power close to the people in the states.

Madison's great contribution was to demonstrate that both sides were wrong. He was to show that an extensive republic was indeed possible. Madison's theory and practice is a paradigm case of a creative breakthrough in politics, a breakthrough that has been so assimilated into our political thinking or so obscured by uncritical patriotic history that it has become embarrassing for honest students to appreciate its genuine greatness.

However, to appreciate Madison's breakthrough more fully, we must return to the political literature again and note some "luminous truths" that Madison detected in such thinkers as Montesquieu and David Hume.[5] We must note how he was able to combine the bare hints that he found in these men with the insights of other republican thinkers and develop a theory that could cope with the problem facing the infant American republic—the problem of reconciling strength at the center with freedom in both the center and circumference.

Of the political thinkers better known to us today, only a few—Althusius, John Milton, Montesquieu, J.-J. Rousseau, Hume, A.R.J. Turgot, M.J.A.N. Condorcet—had touched directly or indirectly upon the problem of federalism. However, with the important exceptions of Montesquieu and Hume, these men (like the great classical masters of political thought) provided little help in coping with the republican dilemma in the new world: the reconciliation of republican government and large size.

If Milton, for example, did recognize in his two essays on a "Free Commonwealth" the worth and role of "county councils" in dividing power between central and local governments, he provided no clues for the reconciliation of liberty and empire or for the republican control of faction. Similarly, no clues were to be found in Condorcet's *Lettres d'un Bourgeois de New Haven*, which also advocated a division of power between national and provincial assemblies; or in Turgot's comparable plan in his *Memoire au Roi sur les Muncipalites*. All three envisaged plans that would have made the central government a powerless slave or an unhappy captive of the local assemblies. Rousseau in the *Social Contract* had announced his intention to treat of confederations in a later work, but—exercising the prerogative of genius—he never did. As for Althusius, his *Politica Methodice Digesta* (Politics Methodically Digested) was rediscovered in the nineteenth century.

Montesquieu and Hume, however, it seems reasonably clear, had both (in Madison's words applied only to the enlightened Frenchman) "lifted the veil from the venerable errors which enslaved opinion, and pointed the way to those luminous truths of which" they "had but a glimpse themselves."[6]

But what was this glimpse?

Montesquieu, as I have already noted, had echoed classical thought on the question of republicanism and large size. Yet he had also hinted that mankind could contrive a "constitution that has all the internal advantages of a republican, together with the external force of a monarchial government." Montesquieu held that such a "confederate republic" could withstand both external force and internal corruption.[7] This was only a hint. Unhappily, Montesquieu's picture of a confederate republic was too close to the government under the Articles of Confederation; and Madison knew from bitter intimate experience that this government could withstand neither external force nor internal corruption. Furthermore, nothing in Montesquieu threw new light on the operational principles of a new kind of confederate republic or informed anyone how such a republic could effectively unite central strength and local liberty, how it could preserve popular government without succumbing to factional danger.

Hume's "Idea of a Perfect Commonwealth" provided some of the missing clues, and undoubtedly encouraged Madison to press on to a more satisfactory solution. Hume, a strange combination of skeptic and tory, had branded as a "falsehood" the "common opinion" "that no large state, such as France or Great Britain, could ever be modeled into a commonwealth but that such a form of government can only take place in a city or small territory." Not so said the skeptical Scot! "Though it is more difficult to form a republican government in an extensive country than in a city, there is more facility, when once it is formed, of preserving it steady and uniform, without tumult and faction." This would be the case, Hume maintained, because fragmentized election districts (that is, thousands of election districts) and indirect elections would serve to give the people a chance to elect their rulers at the same time as this process operated to refine popular passions. Moreover, the multiplicity and competition of competing interests in a large state would operate to neutralize the dread forces of faction.[8]

MADISON'S THEORY OF THE EXTENSIVE REPUBLIC

Madison undoubtedly perceived the significance of those "luminous truths" in Montesquieu and Hume because of his own devotion to religious liberty. Here we cannot help but be struck by the centrality of religious liberty in Madison's thought—a devotion, as we have seen in Chapter 2, that he shared with Roger Williams. Madison's devotion to religious liberty enabled him to see that the same principle—of the salutary consequences of the multiplicity of sects—that operated to ensure religious liberty might also operate (now as the multiplicity of political, economic, and social interests) to ensure civil freedom. Human wit could perceive that pluralistic diversity might advance freedom without interfering with civil decorum and harmony.

In 1785 Madison had written to Jefferson: only a coalition between religious sects "could . . . endanger our religious rights." Two years later Madison again expressed his worry about a religious sect forming a majority and using its power to oppress other sects. And he noted that civil as well as religious rights could be endangered by an oppressive majority. The multiplicity of religious sects guarded against such oppression.

In the Virginia Ratifying Convention of 1788 Madison drove home his point with unmistakable clarity:

> If there were a majority of one sect, a bill of rights would be poor protection for liberty. Happily for the states, they enjoy the utmost freedom of religion. This freedom arises from that multiplicity of sects, which pervades America, and which is the best and only security for religious liberty in any society. For where there is such a variety of sects, there cannot be a majority of any one sect to oppress and persecute the rest.[9]

It would be an easy step from this proposition to one of Madison's cardinal ideas about the multiplicity and diversity of political, economic, and social interests as a safeguard for political freedom.

Thus Madison's religious convictions—which reflect the late-eighteenth-century emancipation from religious orthodoxy and authoritarianism characteristic of both Catholics and Protestants in earlier centuries—carried over into the political arena. Again, the concern for religious freedom would strike another great blow for democratic and constitutional government. And so it was that Madison could easily sympathize with Hume's argument that the wit and will of men could devise a new commonwealth "in some distant part of the world," a commonwealth that would reduce "theory to practice" and, in so doing, improve on "the common botched and inaccurate governments" of the moment.[10]

Thus Madison would take a stand against those in America who maintained that "republican government was possible only for a relatively small territory and a relatively small and homogeneous population," against those who argued that the real locus of power must remain with the states in a loose confederation.[11] And, similarly, Madison would argue against those who insisted that history proved that a country of great size and diverse interests could be governed only by a mixed government or a limited monarchy—that is, by a strong central government that would deprive the individual states of any significant powers.

Madison's theory of the extensive republic—the theory of the new federal republic—constituted a creative breakthrough because he proposed that Americans could work out a new political synthesis. The new Constitution of 1787 was that synthesis. The new republican Constitution greatly strengthened the central government by equipping it with powers to hold the Union together, and to protect the common interests of the people in the new nation. Yet liberty, justice, and self-government would be ensured for the people in their state and local governments. This new federal republican model thus gave to the new central government legitimate authority in matters of concern to all members of the Union, and yet continued control by the states over their local affairs. The new federal republic enhanced the strength of the Union as it simultaneously operated to control the effects of faction, primarily but not exclusively at the state or local level. The new Constitution created a central authority—the new federal government—that rested more legitimately on popular consent and the Union's component states, and yet possessed greater strength than any confederation in history. The features of the American federal republic are today well known. But in 1787 they constituted a breakthrough in governmental theory and practice: a federal government with significant powers operating directly on the people; a unique division and sharing of powers between the central government and the states; constitutional limitations on federal and state governments; a strong chief executive in the president; and so on.

Before we review the cardinal features of Madison's theory of this new extensive republic more fully, it makes sense to identify explicitly the four interrelated difficulties that disturbed Madison in the crucial year, 1787, and that complicated his life-long efforts to make republican government in a large state possible: disunion, large size, faction, and the anti-republican danger. (1) The potent forces of disunion were strongly entrenched in the thirteen jealously "sovereign" states. (2) The large geographic size of the United States seemed to make free and effective republican government extraordinarily difficult if not impossible. It did so, ironically (as we have noted above), by encouraging both those who favored almost complete autonomy for each state and those who favored great centralization of power in the Union's government. Thus those who endorsed decentralization were inclined to play down strength for the Union in order to ensure liberty in each state. And those who approved of consolidation were disposed to regard liberty for people and states less highly than authority for the nation. (3) Selfish factional interests—groups opposed to the nation's common interest—operated within each of the states and obstructed the central government of the Union. (4) Finally, people and movements unsympathetic to genuine republicanism were potentially dangerous.

Understanding these difficulties enables us to understand the strands of Madison's response. Madison was a *nationalist* who saw in a greatly strengthened, more nearly perfect federal Union the instrument to cope with the danger of disunion. Madison was a *federalist* defending the new principle of federalism as the republican answer to the problem of large size. Madison was an *empirical political scientist* who articulated an explanation of how faction, the disease of liberty-loving republics, might be brought under control in an extensive, representative republic. And Madison was a *republican* passionately concerned with the antirepublican danger who worked his way toward a theory of democratic politics, a theory based on the significance of civil liberties, bold republican opposition, and a loyal republican opposition party. In each of these capacities Madison was attempting to demonstrate that the conventional wisdom was wrong, that republican government in a large state was not only desirable but feasible.

Let us now examine Madison's key, interrelated arguments.

Coping with Disunion via a Greatly Strengthened Federal Union

Madison's diagnosis of disunion suggested the need for a new concept of strengthened federal Union with a federal government capable of operating directly on the individuals who compose the states of the Union. The treaty principle of the Articles of Confederation was inadequate. The Union could not be an alliance of sovereign states, each of which possessed the power to dissolve the Union when a breach of the treaty establishing the alliance had in the judgment of any state occurred. Each state could not on key matters of concern to the Union be a law unto itself. Each of the states in the Union could not be allowed to encroach on the government of the Union, or on the rights of its own citizens. The government of the Union must have the crucial powers to raise revenue, to regulate interstate commerce, to handle the western lands, and to deal with other matters of common concern.

Strengthening the Union would guard against the danger of republican anarchy and also against a reactionary attempt to overcome such anarchy via tyranny. Madison emphasized the tie between a strong and effective

Union and republicanism: the failure of republican union might lead to the repudiation of republicanism. Madison saw the greater threat in 1787 to be factionalism in the states, not the tyranny of the proposed central government. So it was that the Union must be given necessary strength, authority, energy, stability, confidence, and respect. So it was that the Union must be protected against selfish state interests that threatened the "aggregate interests of the community" in either domestic or foreign affairs. So it was that the power of the states, and hence the power of faction within the states, must be limited by the new Constitution of the Union.

The powers of the new Union would be safely exercised because they were based on the sovereign power of the people, because they were limited, and because they would function within the structure of the new federal government. Madison actually sought greater powers for the government of the Union than those finally approved in 1787. But he was persuaded that the new Constitution—with its taxing/spending/interstate commerce powers—was a vast improvement over the Articles of Confederation. The "due supremacy" of the nation would be safeguarded. An independent president would help here; so would an independent judiciary. The president would be a truly national officer. The Supreme Court would ensure the due supremacy of the Union.

Madison did not achieve in 1787 as strong a central government as he desired. Yet he recognized that it was immensely superior to the government under the Articles of Confederation. The new central government would be strong enough to preserve the Union. And it would be a genuinely republican government. Let us next look more closely at the operation of the federal republic, and especially at its ability to deal with the problem of large size.

Coping with the Problem of Large Size via a New Kind of Federal Government

The new federal republic, Madison insisted, divided power between the Union and its component states in a way that would be satisfactory to both. The new federalism would, then, not only be a response to the problem of disunion, but also to the problem of large size. The Constitution of the new Union would be strong enough to cope with the danger of disunion; yet it would leave ample powers—and freedom—to the states. The new federalism would affirm (1) a unique division of powers between nation and states, (2) the direct operation of federal law on the individuals of the nation, (3) the amplitude but yet limited character of national power, (4) the robust pragmatic temper that must guide judgment of the proper operation of the federal system, (5) the experimental character of the new federal laboratory, (6) the Supreme Court's crucial role in maintaining the proper division of powers in the federal union, and (7) the role of consensus in ensuring the new federalism's success.

1. Madison saw the new Constitution as a "middle-ground" solution between a unitary government and a confederated one. It was "neither a national nor a federal Constitution, but a composition of both." The people, as "composing the states," ratified the Constitution; hence in its "foundation" the new Constitution was "federal." In the source of its power, the Constitution was "partly federal and partly national." The new central government's legislators were chosen either by the people of the states (representatives), or—then—by the state legislatures (senators). Representatives were alloted roughly in proportion to each state's population. Each state was entitled to two senators. The president was chosen by electors from the states, electoral voters being weighted both as to population and statehood. In the operation of its powers, the Constitution was "national" because its powers affected "indvidual citizens composing the nation, in their individual capacities." However, the Constitution was federal with regard to the extent of its powers because the jurisdiction of the central government "extends to certain enumerated objects only, and leaves to the several States a residuary and inviolable sovereignty over all other objects." Finally, amendments to the Constitution were neither wholly "federal" nor wholly "national," for they could not be made by a "majority of the people of the Union," and did not require a "concurrence of each State of the Union," but instead required action by both the central government and the states.[12]

2. The significance of a new central government able to operate directly on the individuals composing the states of the new federal union has been noted previously. I emphasize it here again because this operational feature of the new federalism enabled the central government to reach the individual citizen of the Union directly and immediately without the intervention of state governments. National law, affecting the individuals of the entire nation, would be obeyed throughout the land. Federal tariffs and other sources of revenue would give the central government an independent source of national income. Money could thus be raised without having to rely on state taxes and treasuries.

3. The new federal Constitution endowed the government of the Union with ample, elastic, but yet limited and enumerated powers. In *Federalist* No. 14 Madison stated:

> The general government is not to be charged with the whole power of making and administering laws. Its jurisdiction is limited to certain enumerated objects, which concern all the members of the republic, but which are not to be attained by the separate provisions of any. The subordinate governments, which can extend their care to all those other objects which can be separately provided for, will retain their due authority and activity.

But generous power must be given the new government of the entire nation and its key clauses must be generously interpreted. "No axiom is more clearly established in law, or in reason," Madison contended in *Federalist* No. 44, "than that wherever the end is required, the means are authorized: wherever a general power to do a thing is given, every particular power necessary for doing so is included." A constitution must be "accommodated . . . not only to the existing state of things, but to all the possible changes that futurity may produce. . . ." (Madison's later shift to a stricter interpretation we will consider subsequently.)

4. Madison's approach to the new federalism was pragmatic. The powers of the central government and of the state governments would, in the last analysis, depend upon their success in doing a good job for their respective constituents. In the healthy competition to serve the people of the Union, Madison pointed out, the states had many natural advantages. State governments were closer to the people. State leaders knew the people better. State officials had more rewards to offer and more services to render. All that they had to do was a good job in the eyes of their constituents. If, however,

> the people should in the future become more partial to the federal government than to the State governments, [it will be because of] such manifest and irresistible proofs of a better [federal] administration, as will overcome all their antecedent propensities. And in that case, the people ought not surely to be precluded from giving most of their confidence where they may discover it to be most due.[13]

5. Madison also saw the new federal Union—with its multiple governments—as an experimental laboratory wherein successes could be copied, and failures limited and avoided. As Madison put the point later in his life, the federal system encouraged "local experiments," [which,] if failing, are but a partial and temporary evil; if successful, may become a common and lasting improvement." Happily, given the federal character of the Union, dangerous practices in a given state could inflict only limited harm. Abuses in a given state could, moreover, be corrected by the influence of other states or of the central government. Large size, therefore, need not lead to anarchy or injustice. On the contrary, a federal republic—which "excites emulation without enmity"—permitted a free and diverse people to experiment responsibly in responding to their problems.[14]

6. Madison also appreciated the role of the U.S. Supreme Court as a way to keep the states in their proper places, and to arbitrate clashes between the nation and the states. "Some such tribunal is clearly essential" Madison wrote in *Federalist* No. 39, "to prevent an appeal to the sword and a dissolution of the Union. Later in his life Madison expanded on this argument. He held that there was a need to give to the "Judicial authority of the U.S. [the power] to provide for a peaceful and authoritative termina-

tion [of] "controversies concerning the boundary of Jurisdiction" between nation and states. The federal courts alone could not, of course, hold the large American nation together; but, in conjunction with other features of the new federal Constitution, they had a vital role to play in maintaining the Union. The courts represented a feasible alternative to anarchy in deciding jurisdictional disputes. The courts offered a sensible way to avoid disastrous diversity on fundamental matters of national policy. They provided a practical solution to inconvenient, expensive, constitutional amendment. They suggested a reasonable technique for avoiding a return to the "treaty" concept of federation, which had been the bane of the Articles of Confederation.[15]

7. However, if the federal courts could help to umpire the federal system, they would be successful in helping to keep the American "empire" together, Madison emphasized, only if there existed an underlying consensus in the new nation on key matters. This agreement on fundamentals would operate to hold the Union together. Without shared emotions, mutual trust, and common principles, the Union would disintegrate. American nationality and republican rights constituted two crucial fundamentals. In *Federalist* No. 14 Madison stressed the "many chords of affection" that "knit together" the American people, and called attention to the blood that Americans had "shed in defense of their sacred rights." In *Federalist* No. 43 Madison called attention to the "considerations of a common interest" that would link the states together. In the extensive republic it was true that multiple and diverse interests might divide the nation; but, on the other hand, common interests—kindred political, economic, social, and religious interests—would also serve to keep the new large republic together. Abraham Lincoln, in the midst of the American Civil War (the catastrophe that Madison had so much feared) was to return to Madison's insight on this point. We will return again to Madison's efforts to cope with disunion when we examine his effort to cope with the antirepublican danger.

Coping with the Problem of Faction via an Extensive Representative, Federal Republic

Madison argued that the American nation could cope with the problem of faction by profiting from the advantages of an extensive, representative, federal republic functioning under a constitution armed with requisite powers of governance, denying certain powers to the states, resting upon a fundamentally capable electorate, and utilizing the principle of separation of powers. To appreciate more fully Madison's operational theory, it is important to summarize Madison's understanding of the problem of faction.[16]

"The instability, injustice, and confusion introduced [by faction] into the public councils," Madison wrote, "have, in truth, been the mortal diseases under which popular governments have everywhere perished." Madison defined a faction as a "number of citizens, whether amounting to a majority or minority of the whole, who are united and actuated by some common impulse of passion, or of interest, adverse to the rights of other citizens, or to the permanent and aggregate interests of the community." It was unwise to destroy liberty and impractical to give "to every citizen the same opinions, the same passions, and the same interests." Free people, "diverse" people, fallible, heterogeneous, heterodox, opinionated, quarrelsome people were the raw material of faction, "the most common and durable source of factions" being traceable to "the various and unequal distribution of property." Thus, the ever likely danger of abuse of power, or of injustice—possible in all governments—was rooted in the very nature of people, and especially how they earned a living. Such people were no angels or philosopher-kings.

Moreover, elected officials and the electorate did not necessarily stand as guardians of the public weal. Of the motives that guided political candidates—ambition, personal interest, and the public good—"the two first" were unhappily "proved by experience to be the most prevalent." And, unfortunately, succeeding elections did not throw unscrupulous politicians out.

Madison did not flinch from a soberly realistic analysis of the people's contribution to faction. "A still more fatal if not more frequent cause of injustice lies among the people themselves" who, not being sufficiently restrained by enlightened self-interest, respect for character, or religion, were prone to form factional majorities. The result was that "measures are too often decided, not according to the rules of justice and the rights of the minor party, but by the superior force of an interested and overbearing majority." Such would almost always be the case when a powerful faction acted as a judge (in the legislature) in disputes to which said faction was a party.

How, then, Madison asked, was it possible to "secure the public good and private rights against the danger of faction, and at the same time to preserve the spirit and the form of popular government"? Madison's own answer to this crucial query constitutes, I believe, the greatest contribution yet made to republican theory in the modern world. Madison clearly recognized that a proper answer was "the greatest desideratum by which this form of government can be rescued from the opprobrium under which it has so long labored, and be recommended to the esteem and adoption of mankind."

Madison wrote as a thoroughly republican thinker. He had, in the opening paragraph of *Federalist* No. 10, declared that the "friend of popular governments never finds himself so much alarmed for their character and fate, as when he contemplates their propensity to this dangerous vice of faction. He will not fail, therefore, to set a due value on any plan which, without violating the principles to which he is attached, provides a proper

cure for it." And in the closing paragraph of No. 10 he had again emphasized his republican commitment:

> In the extent and proper structure of the Union, therefore, we behold a
> *republican* remedy for the diseases most incident to republican govern-
> ment. And according to the degree of pleasure and pride we feel in being
> republicans, ought to be our zeal in cherishing the spirit and supporting
> the character of Federalists (emphasis added).

But what was that "republican remedy" and how would it work? Madison recognized that a "Utopia exhibiting a perfect homogeneousness of
interests, opinion, and feelings [has] nowhere yet [been] found in civilized
communities." Moreover, "the *causes* of faction"—the key self-destructive
force within republican governments—"cannot be removed." So Madison
concluded that "relief is only to be sought in the means of controlling its
effects." But how?

As a convinced republican—who rejected minority rule based on force,
blood, money, or slaves—Madison argued that minority faction could
normally be controlled by the republican principle of majority rule. (This
view assumed a working republican constitutional order, an assumption
Madison was to explore more fully in the 1790s in his opposition to key
Hamiltonian legislation and, then, the Alien and Sedition Acts.) But what
of the more real and the more pressing danger—majority faction? This
Madison argued could be controlled only by one of two means: by preventing the "existence of the same passion or interest in a majority at the same
time" or by rendering such a majority "unable to concert and carry into
effect schemes of oppression."

What kind of government system would be most conducive to such
control? Here we come to Madison's operational theory already outlined
above: an extensive, representative, federal republic, functioning under a
Constitution armed with requisite powers of governance, denying certain
powers to the states, resting upon a fundamentally capable electorate, and
utilizing the principle of separation of powers.

First, an *extensive republic*—a republic embracing a large geographic area
and therefore a large number of diverse interests—would "lessen the
insecurity of private rights." This would be true, Madison maintained,
because the multiplicity, diversity, and conflict of factional interests, plus
their larger sphere of operations, would diminish the possibility of factional
agreement and unified faction action.[17]

Second, the technique of *representative government* in an extensive republic would control the effects of faction. Madison was by no means blind to
the possibility that "Men of factious tempers, of local prejudices, or of
sinister designs, may, by intrigue, by corruption, or by other means, first
obtain the suffrages, and then betray the interests of the people." But he
believed that an extensive republic is more likely to produce the "election

of proper guardians of the public weal" than a "small" republic. Madison thought this true for at least two "obvious" reasons: (1) The extensive republic, having a larger population, would normally have more fit people capable of representing it; and this larger number of potential representatives would ensure a "greater probability of fit choice." (2) The greater number of citizens in the "extensive republic" would (in comparison with the process in a small republic) make it "more difficult for unworthy candidates to practice with success the vicious arts by which elections are too often carried." Such representative government would provide that purified and ennobled "process of elections" that would "refine and enlarge the public view."[18]

Third, a *federal form of government* would guard against factional evil. Madison argued that this advantage, as we have already noted, is implicit in the very concept of an extensive republic of large size, many interests, and innumerable group conflicts. This advantage, moreover, is reinforced by a federal system wherein division of power—between the nation and its component states—minimizes the prize of factional victory, wherein compartmentalization of power renders the Union less vulnerable to factional contagion, and wherein the states of the union would act as watchdogs "to detect or to defeat a conspiracy" by the central government "against the liberty of their common constituents."[19]

Fourth, the Constitution of the new Union must provide for *requisite powers of governance*. These expanded and invigorated powers—necessary to establish the due supremacy of the central government—would help to counter factional mischief in the states (since certain powers—for example, the regulation of interstate and foreign commerce—could no longer be exercised by state governments). Moreover, in the stronger central government of the new extensive republic, it would be difficult for faction to form a majority and carry out its mischief.

Fifth, a factor related to requisite powers of governance was *constitutional prohibition*, particularly certain restrictions on the power of the states. Most important was the injunction of Article 1, Section 10: "No state shall . . . emit bills of credit; make anything but gold and silver a legal tender in payment of debts; pass any . . . law impairing the obligation of contracts." Madison strongly contended that justice, private rights, and the preservation of the very character of republican government required these constitutional bulwarks against faction in the states.

A sixth feature of Madison's operational political theory—as it functioned to control the effects of faction—was his conviction that a *fundamentally capable electorate* was the prime safeguard of republican institutions. Here we come to the neglected "other side" of Madison's understanding of human nature. As we noted earlier, Madison was no blind and uncritical admirer of the sovereign capacity of the people. He clearly recognized that people were often passionate, fallible, shortsighted, unjust, ambitious, fickle, quarrelsome, opinionated, heterodox, depraved, capricious, wicked, foolish, avaricious, and vain. Nevertheless, Madison also appreciated that as "there is a degree of depravity in mankind which requires a certain degree of circumspection and distrust, so there are other qualities in human nature which justify a certain portion of esteem and confidence." Indeed: "Republican government presupposes the existence of these qualities in a higher degree than any other form." What were these qualities? They included "sufficient virtue among men for self-government," and sufficient intelligence. These were of vital importance. One must operate on the "great republican principle" that "the people will have virtue and intelligence to select men of virtue and wisdom." Similarly, basic—if qualified—confidence must be placed in the representatives of the people, who would be "bound to fidelity and sympathy with the great mass of the people" by the "chords [of] "duty, gratitude, ambition itself."[20] Madison thus affirmed— anticipating Reinhold Niebuhr—that whereas a person's inclination to vice makes republicanism necessary, a person's capacity for virtue makes republicanism possible.

Finally, Madison affirmed a truism of republican thought—the concept of *separation of powers* (particularly as this concept embraced a wise and stable Senate). Here was another safeguard against factional abuse of power, abuse stemming either from the "various and interfering" factional interests in the nation or from government itself should it set "up an interest adverse to that of the whole society." The branches of government must, he held, be sufficiently connected to permit mutual "constitutional control" and mutual self-protection.[21] Madison—here, perhaps, a bit naively— hoped that the concept of separation of powers might ensure a "Neutral Sovereign," which would operate in the public interest, and would control the governed without itself becoming tyrannical.

Coping with the Antirepublican Danger via a Theory of Democratic Politics

The difficulty of balancing liberty and authority in a large state was a life-long problem for Madison and in his political theory. The year 1787 represented only one constitutional struggle. Two other constitutional struggles have often been ignored because of the focus on the momentous breakthrough, in 1787. But to appreciate the fullness of Madison's break-through these additional struggles must be addressed. A second major constitutional struggle erupted in the 1790s in connection with Hamilton's efforts at nation-building and reached a troublesome climax in the passage of the Alien and Sedition Acts. A third constitutional struggle broke out in the late 1820s with the enunciation of Calhoun's theory of the concurrent majority and the doctrine of nullification, and reached its tragic climax on the battlefields of the Civil War several decades after Madison's death in 1836.

These two latter struggles are significant because they forced Madison to develop a theory of democratic politics, which features Madison's views on bold republican leadership, civil liberties, and a republican political opposition. Such a theory is crucial to the democratic experiment in reconciling liberty and authority in a large state. These additional constitutional struggles also illustrate clearly the incompleteness of even the most creative breakthroughs in politics and the difficulties encountered in attempting to improve on a breakthrough. To focus on Madison's battles in the 1790s and then in the 1820s and 1830s is to call attention to weaknesses as well as strengths in Madison's theory; but it is also to highlight a theory of democratic politics that, despite its shortcomings, reflects Madison's efforts to reconcile liberty and large size.

In the 1790s Madison had to respond to what he deemed faction in control of the national government. In the 1820s and 1830s he had to respond to factional mischief in the states of a kind more ominous than that of the 1780s. What I have called his theory of democratic politics was his attempt at a response, which built on his earlier efforts but, as necessary, added new elements.

Always Madison sought *to analyze the danger* to republican government in a large state. With the adoption of the Constitution in 1787, the pressing dangers of disunion and faction, inherent largely in state action, seem to have been faced and at least momentarily overcome. But in the 1790s, Madison—who had played a key legislative role in helping the new government get under way—perceived new dangers in key aspects of the Federalist program. Earlier Madison had sought to forestall an anticipated reaction against republican government by establishing a more nearly perfect union. Now in the 1790s he had to contend with the worst possible threat: the actual effectuation of a factional program by what he deemed an antirepublican party.

This party arose, Madison contended, with "the regular and effectual establishment of the federal government in 1788." It consisted, he believed, of

> those who . . . are more partial to the opulent than to the other classes of society; and having debauched themselves into a persuasion that mankind are incapable of governing themselves, it follows with them . . . that government can be carried on only by the pageantry of rank, the influence of money and emoluments, and the terror of military force.

Indeed, the antirepublican party believed that to the "stupid, suspicious, licentious" people one should pronounce "but two words—*Submission and Confidence.*"[22]

Throughout Madison's argument against such measures and actions as the funding of the debt, the bank bill, Washington's neutrality proclamation as defended by Hamilton, Adams' supposed "monarchical principles" and "heretical politics," and the Alien and Sedition Acts, there runs the common threat of the danger to republicanism. Madison feared the corruption of the public interest to the advantage of special interests, the conversion of a limited govenrnment into an unlimited one, the obliteration of basic civil liberties, the consolidation of the states into one sovereignty, the undue extension of presidential power, and—eventually—the transformation of "the present republican system of the United States into an absolute, or, at best a mixed monarchy."[23]

Madison was convinced that to allow an expansive interpretation of federal power by antirepublican forces to go unchallenged was to court suicide. His earlier parade of horribles, mobilized against such measures as the first bank bill, might have been discounted as partisan exaggeration; but the antirepublican danger manifest in the Alien and Sedition Acts was clear for all to see. The Sedition Act, in particular, was a dramatic illustration of "a power which, more than any other, ought to produce universal alarm because it is levelled against the rights of freely examining public characters and measures, and of free communication among the people thereon, which has ever been justly deemed the only effectual guardian of every other right."[24]

If a touch of partisan exaggeration did characterize Madison's analysis of the Federalist Party as antirepublican, there can be no doubt that his efforts helped greatly to maintain the pure republican faith. And, we must remember, Madison helped to maintain this faith in light of the candid antipathy to some of the fruits of republican principles that appeared in America with the conservative reaction against the French Revolution.

Later in his life, after he had retired from the presidency, and when the "republican ascendency" seemed assured, Madison again went forth to battle against the antirepublican forces: this time against the antirepublican principles inherent in the ideology of nullification and secession. In this connection he cannot be accused of partisan exaggeration. However, his characteristic tendency to "write large" antirepublican principles, designs, and actions is unmistakable. Those who held majority government to be the most oppressive of all governments, Madison maintained, were anti-republican. Such a "doctrine strikes at the roots of Republicanism, and if pursued into its consequences, must terminate in absolute monarchy, with a standing military force." Those who—like Calhoun and his supporters—held such a doctrine in order to attack the tariff "must either join the avowed disciples of aristocracy, oligarchy or monarchy, or look for" a utopian society.[25]

Madison brilliantly criticized the dangers lurking in Calhoun's theory of the concurrent majority, the theory that gave to an aggrieved minority (say a group of states or even a single state) the right to prevent passage or execution of objectionable policy. He was so vehemently opposed to Calhoun's doctrine because, prophetically, he saw and feared its consequences. He saw more clearly than Calhoun and those who would defend nullification and secession that Calhoun's ideas would, for all effective purposes, reestablish the treaty principle of Union that had prevailed under the Articles of Confederation. This principle held that the Union was an alliance of sovereign states or sovereign sectional interests, each possessing a veto power on the law and administration of the nation. Madison deftly pointed out that Calhoun's attack on majority rule in the nation was really an attack on all government.

Calhoun's argument, logically employed, could be turned against majorities in state governments as well as against a majority in the national government. Its ultimate implication was anarchy. Since there was no unanimity of interests within a state, and since each state would have to rely on majority rule in its own government, the minority would not find within a state, or ultimately outside the Union, the greater safety it sought. Abuse of power, stemming from the conflict of interests, would occur within a single state as well as within the Union. Hence, if majority government could be legitimately attacked in the Union, it could also be attacked as it operated within each of the several states. The alternative to majority government in an extensive republic was either nonrepublican government or anarchy.

The dangerous consequences of the twin heresies of nullification and secession were portrayed in one particularly prophetic passage. Here Madison foresaw

> a rupture of the Union; a Southern confederacy; mutual enmity with the Northern; the most dreadful animosities and border wars, springing from the case of slaves; rival alliances abroad; standing armies at home, to be supported by internal taxes; and federal Governments, with powers of a more consolidating and monarchical tendency than the greatest jealousy has charged on the existing system.[26]

Keen analysis of the antirepublican danger is closely connected to a second key feature of Madison's theory of democratic politics: *political debate and popular or party protest*. Sometimes the political debate would precede the popular protest; sometimes the popular debate would support or follow the political argument. Here we need only note that popular protest was an old revolutionary strategy; whereas the organization of an opposition political party, with intent to take over the government by peaceful and constitutional means, was, in part, novel and of great significance for the evolution of democratic government—especially democratic government in an extensive republic.

Early in his political career, in the *Memorial and Remonstrance Against Religious Assessments* (1785), Madison had utilized successfully the technique of strong popular protest to rally first a popular and then a legislative majority against actions threatening republican liberties in Virginia. His strategy was "to take alarm at the first experiment on our liberties"; to blast the first deviation from the republican faith.

Comparable protests were used against objectionable policies of the Federalist Party, and especially against the Alien and Sedition Acts. This time political power was marshalled against the national government. And this time a national opposition political party—drawing upon people throughout the Union—was organized and mobilized. Political argument was carried on in the halls of Congress as well as in state legislatures and in the press. The political debate—still controversial today—involved both the wisdom and the constitutionality of Federalist Party measures. It is only in light of the actual effectuation of objectionable policies of the Federalist program by an alleged antirepublican party that Madison's somewhat restricted interpretation of two key clauses of the Constitution—the necessary-and-proper clause and the general-welfare clause—can be squared with his early nationalism.

Madison accepted as indispensable the necessary-and-proper clause, but opposed any construction of it that would give Congress an "unlimited discretion." Implied powers must naturally, obviously, appropriately, directly, evidently, and immediately pertain to the Constitution's delegated powers. The tie between the delegated power and the implied power must be obvious if the government was to remain one of enumerated, limited powers. Implied powers that were merely convenient or conducive to the exercise of delegated powers were not necessary and proper. The necessary-and-proper clause should not be used to legitimatize a "distinct," "independent," "substantive," "great and important" power—in contrast to "an accessory or subaltern" power.[27]

In connection with the general-welfare clause, Madison held that there was no blanket power to spend for measures related to the general welfare clause, but only a power to spend for that general welfare as explained and limited by the specifically enumerated powers of the Constitution. To Madison it made little difference whether the general-welfare clause authorized every measure directly or whether it would merely authorize every measure for which money could be expended. Both interpretations would transfer a limited government into an unlimited government.

Madison's more limited interpretation of these key constitutional clauses did not prevail in American history. What did prevail was respect for the Constitution as a secular covenant of the American people. Madison's argument against the Alien and Sedition Acts—particularly the Sedition Act—is more compelling than his interpretation of the necessary-and-proper and general-welfare clauses. In protesting against these acts his attack ran virtually the gamut of constitutional argument. The acts, he said, represented an exercise of power not delegated; contravened explicit prohibitions of the federal Bill of Rights; violated the principle of separation of powers; would "inflict a deathwound on the sovereignty of the States"; subverted the "general principles of free government"; were not authorized by a Constitution that, it was wrongly argued, embodies common law by implication; could not be sanctioned by the Preamble to the Constitution; were not a legitimate exercise of "preventive justice"; were not justified by any governmentally inherent power of self-preservation; stifled liberty under the guise of controlling the licentiousness of the press; could not be used to justify domestic tyranny under the pretext of combating foreign danger.[28]

Despite some exaggerations—in the heat of partisan battles—about his political opponents, and despite a perhaps too narrow interpretation of national power, Madison's use of and emphasis on constitutional argument and his work in organizing a loyal and responsible opposition political party helped greatly to establish the idea of peaceful change to overcome factional control of the national government.

Let us pursue this devotion to orthodox constitutional means a bit more fully. Madison hoped that argument—based on the merits and constitutionality of a given measure—might kill antirepublican measures before passage. If such argument failed, however, Madison was prepared to fight against such measures after passage. He held that enlightened public opinion would respond to anti-republican measures by using legitimate techniques of electoral opposition. Petition by state legislatures to Congress for repeal of obnoxious and unconstitutional measures, requests by state legislatures to the state's own congressmen to propose constitutional amendments, petition by sufficient state legislatures asking Congress to call a convention to propose amendments to the Constitution—these were some of the techniques that might be used to rid the nation of unconstitutional, antirepublican measures. Impeachment could be used against a president violating his trust. And as public opinion could result in a legislative change of mind, it could also bring about a judicial change of mind. Madison defended the freedom of states, and of people in the states, to take the initiative in seeking change via appeal, elections, and amendment. Since some of Madison's opponents denied that a state might protest against the constitutionality of federal legislation or appeal a constitutional question beyond the federal judiciary, Madison's position becomes not a commonplace defense of the obvious but a vindication of republican principles under challenge.

Madison contended, however, that these (now orthodox) means did not exhaust the possibilities open to the sovereign people of the states—as parties to and creators of the Constitution—who could, therefore, explain, amend, and remake the Constitution. He maintained that *ultraconstitutional interposition* remained as a penultimate resort in "those great and extraordinary cases in which all the forms of the Constitution may prove ineffectual against infractions dangerous to the essential rights of the parties to it." The exact nature of this ultraconstitutional remedy—this extreme remedy to be employed only in very rare cases—still remains somewhat mysterious, ambiguous, and unorthodox. Unfortunately, Madison never fully and clearly spelled out its exact nature. He did, however, indicate that such a remedy must secure a peaceful and effective decision. It cannot be employed when the oppressed are a minority and the oppressors a majority. In other words, there is no ultimate, constitutional power on the part of a minority to explain, amend, or remake a constitution. Apparently, only a majority (presumably a majority of people in a majority of states) possess this ultimate, constitutional power as the parties to and creators of the Constitution. So long as the minority stays within the Union and under the Union's Constitution, not even its desperate, oppressed position enables it constitutionally to invoke Madison's doctrine of ultraconstitutional interposition.[29]

Madison's position on interposition got him into considerable trouble in the 1820s and 1830s. Then, and especially in the midst of the nullification controversy, Madison insisted that the interposition called for by the Virginia Resolutions would not justify South Carolina's nullification of federal legislation. He denied South Carolina's claim that such single-state nullification was valid until overridden by three-fourths of the other states in the Union. Rather, he insisted, interposition called for the collective, aggregate, concurrent action of the sovereign people of the states.

If Madison's position on interposition was not as clear as it might be, it is the case that his penultimate remedy for tyranny at the center was peaceful, constitutional, and republican.

Madison was a strong believer in constitutional government and in constitutional resistance to antirepublican measures. But he never abandoned that republican orientation that justified *revolution* by the majority *as the ultimate remedy* against intolerable oppression. In taking this stand he was endorsing an orthodox philosophy immortalized in the Declaration of Independence. However, Madison clearly recognized that this ultimate remedy of revolution was a natural right and not a constitutional right. It was a natural right because "intolerable oppression" of the people by government, and "abuses or usurpations" by government, released the sovereign people in the states from their obligations under the Constitution. They were thus, in good Lockean fashion, back in a state of nature because of the government's violation of the people's trust embodied in the constitutional agreement. Clearly, as far as those who were intolerably oppressed were concerned, government was dissolved, and the parties were in a state of nature, and might therefore use their "natural right of self-preservation" to revolt against governmental tyranny. The obligation of the revolting majority was always to weigh carefully the consequences of both resistance and oppression; and, once revolution was decided upon, to reestablish constitutional republican rule and rights. What, however, about an oppressed minority? Madison answered:

[should] power usurped be sustained in its oppressive exercise on a minority by a majority, the final course to be pursued by the minority must be a subject of calculation, in which the degree of oppression, the means of resistance, the consequences of its failure, and the consequences of its success must be the elements?[30]

If put into a series of aphoristic imperatives, Madison's theory of democratic politics might be phrased as follows: Safeguard the basic civil liberties, for without freedom of speech, press, and assembly there can be no free elections, no criticism of public officials, and no republican policy. Be prepared to exert bold leadership in anticipation of the antirepublican danger. Know your friends and foes; take alarm at the selfish friends and scheming foes, and be prepared to organize a genuinely republican party to advance truly republican principles. Resist the beginning of trouble and tyranny by protesting loudly and intensely. See the untoward consequences in the wrong principles and thus avoid the consequences by denying the principles. Be careful to distinguish among a usurpation, an abuse, and an unwise use of power. Use orthodox constitutional interpretation and constitutional weapons first, but do not abandon peaceful, majoritarian recourse to the people—the highest source of constituent power—if such resource beyond the existing legal order is necessary. Always keep in reserve the natural right of militant revolt in the event that tyranny is continued by a powerful minority against the majority, or by the majority against a minority.

Madison's theory of democratic politics thus emerges as an important element of his overall theoretical and practical effort to ensure just republican government in a large state.

THE ETHICAL, EMPIRICAL, AND PRUDENTIAL BREAKTHROUGHS IN MADISON'S THEORY

Ethically, Madison's theory—particularly as fully developed—embodied a breakthrough to a broadened conception of how Americans ought to live: enjoying broadened conceptions of liberty, self-government, pluralist democracy, the good political life in a strengthened and more nearly perfect Union. He extolled the vision of religious and political liberty—especially religious liberty, and freedom of speech, press, and association. He endorsed the vision of just popular rule, operating through republican representation, and resistant to factional dominance. He accepted the value of the multiplicity and diversity of interests, of an informed and vigilant public opinion, and of competing political parties, including a loyal opposition party. He fought for a republican Union and nation, operating under a powerful, but still limited, Constitution.

Empirically, Madison's theory of the extensive, federal republic constituted another breakthrough. This theory involved a new empirical hypothesis designed to explain how Americans could enjoy the best (and escape the worst) of two worlds: how they could enjoy liberty without fear of anarchy and the adverse effects of faction; how they could enjoy authority without fear of tyranny and the adverse effects of an overpowerful central government. The large size of, plus the diversity and multiplicity of interests in, the new federal republic would defeat or inhibit the operation of factions and thus ensure greater success for the public good. The federal division of power would keep government at the local level close to the people, and yet give to the central government authority in matters of common national concern. Representation would operate to filter the evil effects of faction.

Constitutional limitations on power and separation of powers were additional "auxilliary precautions" that would help to ensure the successful reconciliation of liberty and authority in the new republic. Moreover, a loyal republican and constitutional opposition party would guard against tyranny at the center. The constitutional operation of majority rule, a sound public opinion, a free press, a healthy two-party system, the federal judiciary, wise statesmanship that could distinguish between a usurpation, an abuse, and an unwise use of constitutional power—these features would protect against the evils of monarchy, plutocracy, or tyranny in the central government and against antirepublicanism and anarchy in the component states of the Union. In brief, just republican government in a federal republic was feasible.

Prudentially, Madison's theory and political judgments illustrate a number of practical breakthroughs in politics. In 1787 he saw the need to strengthen the powers of the central government. He insisted wisely on the possibility, and feasibility, of a new federal republic that could reconcile liberty and authority. He wisely rejected the counsel of those who denied the possibility of republican government in such an extensive domain as America. He was willing in 1787 to settle for a central government not as strong as he had originally wanted because he perceived correctly that the new Constitution was a major step in the right direction. Guided by his political theory, he articulated key features of the new federal republic in Philadelphia in 1787, explained the new Constitution brilliantly and effectively in *The Federalist* and in the important Virginia Ratifying Convention, worked to establish the new Constitution on a firm foundation with a Bill of Rights and with other supporting legislation in the first Congress, exercised leadership on behalf of a republican constitutional opposition party in the 1790s, and defended the Union against nullfication and secession at the end of his long life.

Madison's theory constituted an illuminating guide to generally successful action throughout his lifetime effort to demonstrate that Americans could reconcile liberty and authority in a large state. His role in braintrusting and securing the adoption of the Constitution, and then the Bill of

Rights, is perhaps his outstanding prudential success. Still to be fully recognized is his contribution to a theory of democratic politics, centered on a loyal opposition party. Despite Madison's inability, in retirement, in the last several decades of his life to stop the movement that would lead to the Civil War, his argument against Calhoun and the Southern fire-eaters pointed toward the wise statesmanship that might have prevented that disaster.

CONCLUSION

Madison's creative breakthrough occurred at the dawn of constitutional democracy in the modern world. The American republic was the first great federal experiment in a large country. Madison's contribution to this democratic and constitutional experiment was enormous. Despite critical questions that we may have about aspects of Madison's argument, we have to affirm clearly that Madison's creative breakthrough demonstrated—in both theory and practice—that just and effective republican government in a large state was not only possible but feasible.

Madison argued persuasively that an extensive, federal, representative republic—endowed with requisite, yet limited, powers—could reconcile liberty and authority. The central premise of this new experiment was that an extensive republic (that is, a republic embracing a large area and a variety of interests) could effectively safeguard the rights of citizens and yet effectively advance the common public interest. The heart of Madison's penetrating argument was that an extensive republic would safeguard these rights and this interest because the very multiplicity, diversity, and conflict of factional interests, plus their large sphere of operations, diminished the possibility of factional agreement and unified factional action. Madison thus proposed ingeniously to make a virtue out of necessity: large size and heterogeneous interests would support, not destroy, the proper functioning of the republic.

The extensive republic, moreover, would be a new kind of federal constitutional republic. Federalism contributed to the same end of reconciling liberty and authority by ensuring both strength at the center and freedom at the periphery of the republic—requisite power in central government to hold the new nation together and attend to common needs, and requisite freedom in the states of the Union to attend to more local concerns. Federalism, too, operated to control faction because it made it more difficult for factions to corrupt and disrupt the government of the strengthened Union. A federal form of government, moreover, minimized the prize of national factional victory and diminished the risk of factional contagion spreading from state to state.

Representation in an extensive and constitutional republic would also operate as a filter to ensure the choice of better representatives. And such representatives would be more inclined to keep the public interest in mind in their deliberations.

A fundamentally virtuous and intelligent—if not a completely angelic—people operating within the constitutional framework of an extensive, federal, representative, limited government—and utilizing such other "auxiliary precautions" as separation of powers and a federal judiciary—could function to maintain the proper balance of liberty and authority.

It is to Madison's credit that he did not stop his efforts to consolidate the breakthrough of 1787 with the Bill of Rights in 1789, but grappled with the problem of faction in actual control of the central government in the 1790s, and in the process articulated a fuller theory of democratic and constitutional politics. Here he extended the breakthrough of 1787. Here he articulated a theory of a loyal constitutional opposition party—utilizing freedom of speech, press, and association—functioning to keep the party in control of the national government responsive to the republican will and to republican principles. Truly republican forces in the extensive republic would thus be able to cope with the danger of tyranny at the center (in 1798) as well as with anarchy at the circumference (1787). Madison helped to give definite form to the constitutional role of the opposition party in a republican society. He helped to establish firmly in the American political firmament the idea of peaceful change: change in accord with basic republican principles; change based on public opinion functioning through constitutional machinery; peaceful republican change, which was impossible if the right to freedom of speech, press, and communication were denied; peaceful change based upon a party system including a loyal opposition.

Unfortunately, Madison's political philosophy and his prudent statesmanship—especially his diagnosis of Calhoun's mischievous theory and of the perils of nullification—were not able to exercise a dominant influence in the last decade of his life. The evil of a civil war, which he so prophetically feared in the United States, was not avoided. That tragic war had to be fought before factional mischief was again laid to rest, and the indestructible union of indestructible states again affirmed.

The failure of Americans to adhere to Madison's political philosophy and his prudent statesmanship in the period before the Civil War underscores the fact that no creative breakthrough can be counted upon to usher in utopia. No creative breakthrough is perfect. Creative statesmanship, even in the best of constitutional systems, is an ongoing imperative. New problems emerge under changing conditions and require diligent attention and, often, additional creative breakthroughs. Moreover, it is important to assess the thought and practice of even the most creative political minds with a critical eye.

There are certainly some weaknesses in Madison's political philosophy of the extensive republic. A disturbing weakness is Madison's failure to appreciate more fully how his federal republic might inhibit strong positive action on behalf of the common good. Madison's political philosophy may explain how faction may be controlled in the states and why it would be difficult for faction to unite and dominate the central government. But, some might argue, in the absence of a "Neutral Sovereign" pursuing the common good (Madison's early unrealized hope), Madison's logic also explains why good government by the right people may also be obstructed. Did Madison underestimate the ability of factions to obstruct good government?

Ironically, Madison—the strong nationalist of 1787—himself contributed somewhat to the governmental philosophy of a weaker central government by his limited interpretation of the necessary-and-proper and general-welfare clauses of the U.S. Constitution in his partisan struggles with Hamilton and the Federalists in the 1790s. Knowing how to strike the balance between a central governmental authority seeking the common good and the preservation of liberty (in both the Center and the circumference) is no easy matter.

Other weaknesses are also apparent: the difficulty, for example, of defining the faction whose unjust actions are to be controlled; the dubious assumption that somehow the public interest will emerge from the clash of contending interests; the sometimes questionable refinement of the popular will that takes place through representation and indirect elections; Madison's failure to clarify the meaning of "interposition."

Other problems plague us today and require us to ask troublesome questions about the historic Madisonian model, and how we might amend it to fit new and changing conditions. Can it really be adapted successfully to the changing conditions of modern twentieth-century—or twenty-first-century—America? To the decreased size of America brought on by science and technology? To the great facility that factions have to obstruct if they cannot completely dominate? Is Madison's theory too negative in character to do justice to the "least free" in society—to the poor, African-Americans, Native Americans, Hispanic Americans, women? These questions call upon us not to reject Madison's model, but to ask about adjustments in it or about other creative responses to new problems posed by a changing political world.

When all is said and done, however, we must conclude that Madison's political philosophy has worked reasonably well when followed. Certainly, the possibility of just republican government—via federalism—in a large state has been demonstrated. The pessimistic prophecies of classical thought have not been fulfilled. Moreover, federalism has demonstrated reasonably well its openness to republican experiments: if successful, they can be emulated; if failures, they can be contained. In addition, Madison's theory of democratic politics—featuring as it does the importance of civil liberties, a loyal opposition party, keen criticism of the party in power, the primacy of peaceful constitutional change—has demonstrated its worth in ensuring just republican government in a large state.

What, finally, of the future of the paradigm of the federal republic? The paradigm of federalism holds out hope for use as a model at the transnational, and perhaps even at the global, level. Similarly, it holds out hope for organization and decision-making at very local levels through new patterns of participatory democracy. Here we have intimations of what the future will hold.

In a time when many are afflicted by intellectual gloom and doom, or existentialist fear and trembling, it is indeed heartening to call to mind a great creative breakthrough in politics, one that suggests that we are not the inevitable victims of accident and force. Such breakthroughs as Madison's in the last decade or so of the eighteenth century can inspire us to move up to new levels of political creativity as we face our current problems in the last decade or so of the twentieth century.

NOTES

1. In this chapter I have drawn generously from my earlier work on the political theory of James Madison. See Neal Riemer, *James Madison: Creating the American Constitution* (Washington, D.C.: Congressional Quarterly, 1986). This book is a revised edition of my *James Madison* (New York: Washington Square Press, 1968).

2. Aristotle, *Politics*, Bk. 1, Ch. 2.

3. Charles-Louis Montesquieu, *The Spirit of the Laws* (1748), trans. Thomas Nugent (Cincinnati, Oh.: Robert Clark, 1892), quoted in Riemer, *James Madison* (1986), p. 31.

4. Quoted in ibid., p. 33.

5. Along with other Madisonian scholars, I am greatly indebted to the brilliant historical detective work of Douglas Adair. See especially his famous article, "That Politics May be Reduced to a Science: David Hume, James Madison, and the Tenth Federalist," *The Huntington Quarterly*, Vol. 20, No. 4 (August, 1957), 343–360. Adair's important essays may be found in Douglas Adair, *Fame and the Founding Fathers*, ed. H. Trevor Colbourn (New York: W. W. Norton, 1974).

6. Quoted in Riemer, *James Madison* (1986), p. 31; for the original source see Madison's essay on "Spirit of Governments" *National Gazette* (1792), in Gaillard Hunt, ed., *The Writings of James Madison*, 9 vols. (New York: G. P. Putnam's Sons, 1900–1910), Vol. 6, p. 93. Hereinafter citation to this edition will follow form of 6 *Writings* 93 (1792).

7. See Montesquieu, *The Spirit of the Laws*, Vol. I, pp. 139, 142, 145–146.

8. See Adair, "That Politics May Be Reduced to a Science," pp. 349, 351, 351–353; and Riemer, *James Madison* (1986), pp. 31–32.

9. The quoted remarks in this paragraph may be found in Riemer, *James Madison* (1986), p. 105.

10. Quoted in Adair, "That Politics May Be Reduced to a Science," p. 349; and in Riemer, *James Madison* (1986), p. 32.

11. See Cecilia M. Kenyon's brilliant "Men of Little Faith: The Anti-Federalists on the Nature of Representative Government," *William and Mary Quarterly*, Third Series, Vol. 12 (January 1956), pp. 6, 38. Also see Riemer, *James Madison* (1986), p. 33.

12. See *The Federalist* No. 39 (1787–1788) (New York: Modern Library, 1937). Hereinafter reference to *The Federalist* will be to this edition. Also see Riemer, *James Madison* (1986), pp. 79–80.

13. See *The Federalist* No. 46, p. 306.

14. 9 *Writings* 385–386 note (1830); and Riemer, *James Madison* (1986), p. 85.

15. Ibid.

16. See *The Federalist* No. 10 for source of quotes that follow.

17. See, for example, 2 *Writings* 368 (1787) ("Vices . . ."); *Debates*, p. 65. *The Federalist* No. 10, pp. 61-62; and Riemer, *James Madison* (1986), p. 11.

18. See *The Federalist* No. 10, pp. 56–60; and Riemer, *James Madison* (1986), p. 114.

19. *The Federalist* No. 10, p. 363. See also Nos. 14 and 51; and Riemer, *James Madison* (1986), pp. 116–117.

20. *The Federalist* No. 51, p. 337, and No. 57, pp. 373–374; and Riemer, *James Madison* (1986), pp. 120–121.

21. See *The Federalist* No. 10, p. 56; 2 *Writings* 368 (1787) ("Vices . . ."); *The Federalist* No. 48, p. 321; and Riemer, *James Madison* (1986), p. 121.

22. 6 *Writings* 113–116 (1792) ("A Candid State of Parties," essay in *The National Gazette*); 6 *Writings* 120 and 122 (1792) ("Who Are the Best Keepers of the People's Liberties?"—essay in *The National Gazette*).

23. 6 *Writings* 327 (1798) (Virginia Resolutions of 1798); and Riemer, *James Madison* (1986), p. 140.

24. 6 *Writings* 328–329 (1798) (Virginia Resolutions of 1798); and Riemer, *James Madison* (1986), pp. 140–141.

25. 9 *Writings* 520, 526 (1833) ("Memorandum on Majority Governments"); and Riemer, *James Madison* (1986), p. 141.

26. *Madison's Works: Letters and Other Writings of James Madison*, 4 vols. (New York: R. Worthington, 1884), Vol. 4, p. 273 (1833) (To Andrew Stevenson); and Riemer, *James Madison* (1986), p. 54.

27. 6 *Writings* 29–34 (1791) (Speech against Bank Bill); and 6 *Writings* 383–385 (1799–1800) (Report on the Virginia Resolutions); and Riemer, *James Madison* (1986), p. 91.

28. 6 *Writings* 326–331 (1798) (Madison's Virginia Resolutions of 1798); 6 *Writings* 332–340 (1798) ("Address of the General Assembly to the People of the Commonwealth of Virginia"); 6 *Writings* 341–406 (1799–1800) (Report on the Virginia Resolutions).

29. 9 *Writings* 575, 583, 592, 597–599, 606–607 (1835) ("Notes on Nullification").

30. 9 *Writings* 573–574, 575, 588–591, 604, 597 (1835) ("Notes on Nullification").

CHAPTER 4

John C. Calhoun and the Protection of Minority Interests: The Theory of the Concurrent Majority—A Spurious Breakthrough

INTRODUCTION

We can, I believe, profit from an examination of both genuine break-throughs and false breakthroughs. We can learn from unsuccessful as well as successful breakthroughs. With this in mind let me now turn to a false candidate for a creative breakthrough in political science: John C. Calhoun's theory of the concurrent majority.

Calhoun has often been highly praised as a great American political theorist. I hope to demonstrate in this chapter why this claim cannot be substantiated. Certainly, he is not a great political theorist in the tradition of prophetic politics. I also hope that my analysis will make clear why his reputation as a great conservative political theorist cannot be sustained. In order, however, that Calhoun may have a judicious hearing, I will endeavor in this chapter to present Calhoun's argument as fully and as fairly as possible.

Superficially, the problem that Calhoun posed is a major one: How can we protect the vital interests of the minority in a majority-rule system? However, phrased differently—and more accurately—Calhoun's question (his real question in nineteenth-century America) is considerably less appealing: How can we protect the vital economic, political, and social interests of the slave-holding, agricultural South in a Union more and more dominated by a majority in the North (and West) favorable to free labor in factory and on farm, to industrial, commerical capitalism, and to the republican principle of majority rule?

Calhoun, it should be clear, wanted to have the best of two worlds: on one hand, perpetuation of the institution of slavery, of the South's social and economic institutions, of the South's political power; and, on the other hand, enjoyment of the blessings of liberty, constitutionalism, and federal union. But let me attempt now to pose the problem as Calhoun himself saw it.

Fundamentally, then, Calhoun's troubling question was this: How achieve an understanding of popular, constitutional, federal government that would protect the vital interests of the minority of southern states in a Union increasingly controlled by an oppressive northern and western majority?

Calhoun was not happy with the conventional wisdom that affirmed that legitimate minority rights and interests would be protected under the Constitution of the United States. He was, of course, particularly concerned with the legitimate rights and interests of southern states. He explicitly rejected the argument that the federal government—operating under the principle of rule by the numerical majority, and employing the usual safeguards of the American constitutional system—could be prevented from abusing its power and thus violating the rights of the minority of southern states. Thus he rejected as inadequate such safeguards for the rights of the minority as the right of suffrage, a written constitution, strict constitutional construction, limited government, separation of powers, the U.S. Supreme Court, federalism (as interpreted by the northern majority), the competition of political parties, a free press, public opinion, and such miscellaneous protections as a "higher power," "superstition, ceremonies, education, religion," "appeals to reason, truth, justice."[1] These safeguards, although valuable, would not—Calhoun insisted—adequately safeguard vital minority interests.

Calhoun stated that without his own remedy—his theory of the concurrent majority—all "other provisions . . . would be of little avail." He explicitly identified such "other provisions" "as the right of suffrage, written constitutions, the division of the powers of government into three separate and independent departments, the formation of the people into individual and independent States, and the freedom of the press and of speech."[2] Calhoun conceded that these "all have their value," but would prove unavailing in the absence of a theory of the concurrent majority.[3]

Calhoun recognized that the right of suffrage was a "first and indispensable step toward *forming* a constitutional government." But he insisted that the right of suffrage "of itself" was not "sufficient" to protect minorities from abusive majorities. For voters might still abuse their power. Suffrage led to party contests and majority victory in elections, and majority control of government, and the danger of majority abuse of power.[4]

Similarly, a written constitution, alone, could not "counteract the tendency of the numerical majority to oppression and abuse of power."

> A written constitution [including the principle of separation of powers] certainly has many and considerable advantages; but it is a great mistake to suppose, that the mere insertion of provisions to restrict and limit the powers of the government, without investing those for whose protection they are inserted with the means of enforcing their observance, will be sufficient to prevent the major and dominant party from abusing its powers.[5]

Calhoun was explicit in his rejection of separation of powers as a protective device:

> Nor would the division of government into separate, and . . . independent departments, prevent this result [i.e., oppression]. Such a division may do much to facilitate its operations, and to secure to its administration greater caution and deliberation; but as each and all the departments,—and, of course, the entire government,—would be under the control of the numerical majority, it is too clear to require explanation, that a mere distribution of its powers among its agents or representatives, could do little or nothing to counter its tendency to oppression and abuse of power.[6]

Calhoun was also not convinced that the threatened minority could rely upon "strict construction" of the Constitution. He noted that the majority would adopt a policy of "liberal construction." And the "liberal construction" of the major party would win out over the "strict construction of the minor party."[7] For Calhoun "liberal construction" meant that limited government would not prevail in view of a majority determined to have its way in unconstitutionally expanding the powers of the Union government.

Similarly, one could not rely upon the U.S. Supreme Court, or the majority's interpretation of federalism. Calhoun's adverse critique of the majority's understanding of the federal system and the federal Constitution, including the power of the U.S. Supreme Court, is a major theme of his *Discourse on the Constitution and Government of the United States*. Calhoun wanted to reserve to the states of the Union the power to interpret the reserved powers. These views also dominate many of Calhoun's speeches in the U.S. Senate. Calhoun insisted that the states must have the power to protect "the reserved rights of the States" and that "to suppose that the Senate, or any department of this government, was intended to be the guardian of the reserved rights, was a great and fundamental mistake."[8]

Nor could one rely on the competition of political parties, a free press and public opinion, or other possibilities to prevent majority abuse of governmental power.[9] Calhoun explicitly recognized but rejected as a proper safeguard for minority rights and interests the competition of political parties for office and governmental power. Such competition could not protect against an "absolute" and abusive majority power. Thus:

> It is true that, in such governments ["of the numerical majority"], the minority and subject party, for the time, have the right to oppose and resist the major and dominant party, for the time, through the ballot-box; and may turn them out, and take their place, if they can obtain a majority of votes. But, it is not less true, that this would be a mere change in the relations of the major and dominant party, with the same absolute majority and tendency to abuse power; and the major and dominant party would become the minor and subject party, with the same right to resist through the ballot-box; and, if successful, again to change relations, with like effect. But such a state of things must necessarily be temporary. The conflict between the two parties must be transferred, sooner or later, from an appeal to the ballot-box to an appeal to force.[10]

Calhoun saw the operation of a party system based on rule by the "numerical majority" as leading to "confusion, corruption, disorder, and anarchy" and then to "an appeal to force;—to be followed by a revolution in the form of government."[11]

Calhoun's doubts about party competition were deepened by his recognition that the South was becoming a permanent minority: that, in brief, southern states would be unable to use the party and electoral process to become a majority in control of the federal government. In 1847 Calhoun had declared.

> We are already in a minority in the House of Representatives and the Electoral College; so that, with the loss of the Senate, we shall be in a minority in every department of the Federal Government, and ever must continue so if the non-slave-holding States should carry into effect their scheme of appropriating to their exclusive use all the territories of the United States.[12]

And on March 4, 1850, four weeks before his death, Calhoun had stated that the "northern section" has a "predominance in every part of the Government."[13] The North, he argued,

> has acquired a decided ascendency over every department of this Government, and through it a control over all the powers of the system. A single section, governed by the will of the numerical majority, has now, in fact, the control of the Government and the entire powers of the system. What was once a constitutional Federal Republic is now converted, in reality, into one as absolute as that of the Autocrat of Russia and as despotic in its tendency as any absolute government that ever existed.[14]

Calhoun also did not place any confidence in the ability of a free press or public opinion to safeguard the minority at the hands of an oppressive majority. He wrote:

> It may be thought . . . that the defects inherent in the government of the numerical majority may be remedied by a free press, as the organ of public opinion . . . so as to supersede the necessity of the concurrent majority to counteract its [the numerical majority's] tendency to oppression and abuse of power. It is not my aim to detract from the importance of the press, nor to underestimate the great power and influence which it has given to public opinion. . . . But, however important its present influence may be, or may hereafter become,—or, however great and beneficial the changes to which it may ultimately lead, it can never counteract the tendency of the numerical majority to the abuse of power,—nor supersede the necessity of the concurrent [majority], as an essential element in the formation of constitutional governments.[15]

Calhoun argued that a free press could not provide protection for oppressed minorities for "two reasons." First, a free press "cannot change that principle of our nature which makes constitutions necessary to prevent government from abusing its powers,—and government necessary to protect and perfect society." Second, the press' political influence affected not public opinion understood as "the united opinion of the whole community" but only "the opinion or voice of the strongest interest, or combination of interests." Hence, the free press and public opinion, so understood, could not "counteract the tendency to oppression and abuse of power."[16]

Finally, Calhoun maintained that education, religion, "appeals to reason, truth, and justice"—however valuable—would not safeguard the minority against majority oppression.

The conventional wisdom, then, in Calhoun's eyes could not protect the minority of Southern States from oppressive northern majorities in the Union. That oppression Calhoun saw in such economic policies as the 1828 "Tariff of Abominations," in Henry Clay's American System, in a host of measures designed to exclude slavery from the territories; in the agitation against slavery; and in the ultimate design of abolitionists to abolish slavery itself.[17]

Calhoun's central economic complaint was twofold: that the unconstitutional protective tariff hurt the South; and that revenue disbursements favored the North.[18] The tariff was designed not to raise revenue but to protect largely Northern industries. Calhoun's central territorial complaint was that the Union government, by a series of acts had "excluded the South from the common territory belonging to all the states" of the Union.[19] This process had started with the Northwest Ordinance of 1787, enacted even before the new federal government was under way, and had continued through the Missouri Compromise, and had included the act that "excluded the South from the whole of the Oregon Territory."[20]

Calhoun was alarmed at what he took to be the dangerous consolidating nature of the Union government in the hands of an oppressive northern numerical majority, and the consequent destruction of what he held to be true constitutional and federal government. This meant the sacrifice of southern interests.[21]

Particularly alarming was the agitation over slavery. Calhoun felt that such agitation would end in disunion. "Unless something decisive is done," he worried, "what is to stop this agitation" from achieving its "great and final object," "the abolition of slavery?" And then he asked ominously: "Is it, then, not certain that if something decisive is not now done to arrest it, the South will be forced to choose between abolition and secession?"[22]

Here, then, we see Calhoun's analysis of the problem that faced the Union. He was convinced that the conventional constitutional vision of the United States afforded no solution to this deeply disturbing problem. It was necessary, he was convinced, to adopt a new remedy for the illness that beset the Union. His appropriate remedy, he strongly believed, was the theory of the concurrent majority.

CALHOUN'S THEORY OF THE CONCURRENT MAJORITY

Calhoun's remedy involved a new political paradigm, a new majoritarian model, a new concept of constitutional government. Theoretically, Calhoun's remedy would protect the vital interests of any minority from oppression by any majority in the Union. Indeed, theoretically, Calhoun's remedy would (if the majority, indeed, needed such protection) safeguard the majority's vital interests at the hands of a destructive minority. Theoretically and practically, however, the primary purpose of Calhoun's remedy was to protect a southern minority against a northern majority.

Calhoun's formulation of the theory of the concurrent majority is not always perfectly clear. Let me, however, initially state it in a more clear-cut fashion than he did in order to get at the heart of his argument. I will then reproduce, in Calhoun's own language, his statement of his theory so that readers can judge for themselves.

Simply put, Calhoun argued in his *A Disquisition on Government* that the South must obtain "either a concurrent voice in making and executing the laws, or a veto on their execution."[23] Translated, this meant that no policy on a vital matter could prevail in the government of the United States unless all states were in unanimous agreement. Concurrence required unanimity. Clearly, this would solve Calhoun's problem of how to protect the vital interests of the southern minority. The numerical majority would thus not be able to pass or execute any policy without the concurrence of the South, or—indeed—of any state in the South.

How was this to be accomplished? First, let us look to the matter of a veto on the execution of Union policy.

South Carolina, as a southern state, had already illustrated how a state could veto or nullify what it considered to be unconstitutional federal legislation. Here we should note that Calhoun was prepared to resort to a constitutional amendment to ascertain if a state veto would be overriden by such an amendment to the federal Constitution, or sustained. However, even if overridden, Calhoun held, a state could ultimately decide if it wanted to remain in the Union or secede.

What about a "concurrent voice in making and executing the laws?" Here, Calhoun suggested as one possibility a "dual presidency": a southern president and a northern president.[24] Such a dual presidency, he argued, could be obtained through an amendment to the federal Constitution. Such an arrangement would ensure that a southern president could exercise his voice in shaping and executing legislation. The southern president could veto legislation contrary to the vital interests of the South. He could also, presumably, prevent execution of legislation contrary to the vital interests of the South. Calhoun is not explicit on what would happen if Congress voted to override a southern president's veto. Presumably, legislation passed over a southern president's veto could be nullified by a state, until such nullification were overriden by a constitutional amendment reaffirming such federal power.

In this fashion, then, the vital interests of the minority of Southern states would be protected in the Union.

Calhoun's theory contrasted sharply with the theory of government by the numerical majority. Persistently, Calhoun emphasized that crucial contrast. He wrote in the *Discourse* that "the government of the United States is a democratic federal Republic." It is "democratic in contradistinction to aristocratic, and monarchical." It is "federal, in contradistinction to national, on the one hand,—and to a confederacy, on the other." It is "a Republic—a government of the concurrent majority, in contradistinction to an absolute democracy—or a government of the numerical majority."[25]

Now let me present Calhoun's own still somewhat ambiguous formulation of his theory of the concurrent majority. It is quite a mouthful, but bears careful reading:

> There is but one certain mode in which this result [guarding against "oppression and abuse of power" and against aggrandizement by the government of the Union] can be secured; and that is, by the adoption of some restriction or limitation, which shall so effectually prevent any one interest, or combination of interests, from obtaining the exclusive control of the government, as to render hopeless all attempts directed to that end. There is, again, but one mode in which this can be effected; and that is, by taking the sense of each interest or portion of the community, which may be unequally and injuriously affected by the action of the government,

separately, through its own majority, or in some other way by which its voice may be fairly expressed; and to require the consent of each interest, either to put or to keep the government in action. This, too, can be accomplished only in one way,—and that is, by such an organism of the government,—and, if necessary for the purpose, of the community also,— as will, by dividing and distributing the powers of government, give to each division or interest, through its appropriate organ, either a concurrent voice in making and executing the laws, or a veto on their execution. It is only by such an organism, that the assent of each can be made necessary to put the government in motion; or the power made effectual to arrest its action, when put in motion;—and it is only by the one or the other that the different interests, orders, classes, or portions, into which the community may be divided, can be protected, and all conflict and struggle between them prevented,—by rendering it impossible to put or to keep it in action, without the concurrent consent of all.[26]

Again and again, Calhoun returned to his emphasis on the need for a concurrent majority. Thus:

The necessary consequence of taking the sense of the community by the concurrent majority is . . . to give to each interest or portion of the community a negative on the others. It is this mutual negative among its various conflicting interests, which invests each with the power of protecting itself;—and places the rights and safety of each, where only they can be securely placed, under its own guardianship. Without this there can be no systematic, peaceful, or effective resistance to the natural tendency of each to come into conflict with the others; and without this there can be no constitution. It is this negative power,—the power of preventing or arrest- ing the action of the government,—be it called by what term it may,—veto, interposition, nullification, check, or balance of power,—which, in fact, forms the constitution. They are all but different names for the negative power. In all its forms, and under all its names, it results from the concur- rent majority. Without this there can be no negative; and, without a negative, no constitution. The assertion is true in reference to all constitu- tional governments, be their forms what they may. It is, indeed, the negative power which makes the constitution,—and the positive which makes the government. The one is the power of acting;—and the other the power of preventing or arresting action. The two, combined, make consti- tutional governments.[27]

Calhoun had hinted about a dual presidency in the *Disquisition*.[28] In his *Discourse on the Constitution and Government of the United States*, he made his proposal more explicit:

How the constitution could best be modified, so as to effect the object [to protect the "weaker section" of the country against a majority in the government of the Union], can only be authoritatively determined by the amending power. It may be done in various ways. Among others, it might be effected through a reorganization of the executive department; so that its powers, instead of being vested, as they now are, in a single officer, should be vested in two;—to be so elected, as that the two should be constituted the special organs and representatives of the respective sections, in the executive department of the government; and requiring each to approve all the acts of Congress before they shall become law.[29]

Calhoun maintained that the two executives—"elected by different constituencies"—"would have to act, concurringly, in approving the acts of Congress,—and, separately, in the sphere of their respective [presumably foreign and domestic] departments."[30]

As I have indicated, Calhoun's formulation of the doctrine of the concurrent majority is not perfectly clear. What is clear, however, was his search for a device that would protect the southern minority from the northern majority—that would protect southern states and their vital interests from what Calhoun considered to be oppressive action by the numerical northern majority in control of the Union government.

Sometimes he emphasizes the supreme importance of a "negative" (or veto) by a state. Sometimes he emphasizes either a concurrent voice for states in the government of the Union or a "negative" (or veto) by states on the acts of the Union government. Sometimes he emphasizes both the concurrent voice and a veto.

Thus on the "negative" alone: "Nothing short of a negative, absolute or in effect, on the part of a government of a State, can possibly protect it against the encroachments of the government of the United States, whenever their powers come in conflict."[31]

Thus on either the "concurrent voice" or the "negative":

> But the several States, as weaker parties, can protect the portion not delegated [reserved powers or reserved rights], only in one of two ways; either by having a concurrent voice in the action of the government of the United States; or a negative on its acts, when they disagree as to the extent of their respective powers. One or the other is indispensable to the preservation of the reserved rights,—and to prevent the consolidation of all power in the government of the United States, as the stronger.[32]

Thus on both the "concurrent voice" and the "negative" (or "veto"):

> By no other device, could the separate governments of the several States, as the weaker of the two, prevent the government of the United States, as the stronger, from encroaching on that portion of the reserved powers allotted to them, and finally absorbing the whole; except, indeed, by so organizing the former, as to give to each of the States a concurrent voice in making and administering the laws; and, of course, a veto on its action.[33]

My judgment is that Calhoun preferred both the concurrent voice and the veto. But what must not be lost in trying to ascertain clearly Calhoun's meaning of his doctrine of the concurrent majority is that this doctrine—whether concurrent voice or veto—requires unanimity among the states and in the Union government on vital matters.

Any state, then, could obstruct the achievement of unanimity if it held an act of the federal government to be unauthorized by the U.S. Constitution. Such obstruction, Calhoun did concede, could be overcome, presumably, when a constitutional amendment to the federal Constitution was adopted that sustained the exercise of federal power to which a state objected. But even then, as noted earlier, states—and here, of course, we are talking about southern states—reserved the right to secede from the Union if they were deeply unhappy about what they deemed federal action contrary to their vital interests.

Let me next set forth Calhoun's views on the amending power, which seems to provide constitutional relief from the principle of unanimity, but no relief from absolute majority rule.

Calhoun maintained that "it is the duty of the federal government" to utilize the amending power "should any dangerous derangement or disorder result from the mutual negative of the two co-ordinate governments, or from the interposition of a State, in its sovereign character, to arrest one of its acts,—in case all other remedies should fail to adjust the difficulty."[34]

Moreover, Calhoun held that "it is the duty of the federal government to invoke the action of the amending power, by proposing a declaratory amendment affirming the power it claims, according to the forms prescribed in the constitution; and, if it fail, to abandon the power."[35]

Thus, failure to achieve a constitutional amendment would mean that the federal government's assertion of power would be denied, and thus the state's denial of federal power would be sustained.

However, if the amendment to the Constitution carried, the state would be overruled; and the power of the federal government on the matter at issue would be sustained.[36]

So, apparently for Calhoun, a constitutional amendment affirming federal power that properly belongs to the federal government would be upheld in the state that had previously declared such federal power null and void.

However, if the constitutional amendment was not proper (because not consistent with the character and ends of the federal union), the state would not be obligated to obey. Rather it could choose whether to obey or to secede from the Union. Thus:

> But if it [the federal power claimed] transcends the limits of the amending power,—be inconsistent with the character of the constitution and the ends for which it was established,—or with the nature of the system,—the result

is different. In such case, the State is not bound to acquiesce. It may choose whether it will, or whether it will not secede from the Union.[37]

Here Calhoun clearly affirms the right of a state to secede from the Union:

> That a State, as a party to the constitutional compact, has the right to secede—acting in the same capacity in which it ratified the constitution,—cannot, with any show of reason, be denied by any one who regards the constitution as a compact,—if a power should be inserted by the amending power, which would radically change the character of the constitution, or the nature of the system; or if the former should fail to fulfill the ends for which it was established.[38]

Calhoun was well aware of the adverse arguments—loss of strength and effectiveness, conflicts, anarchy, disunion—that would be directed against his theory of the concurrent majority. He counterattacked by contending (1) that there were historical and contemporary precedents to support his view of the practicality and strength of his theory of the concurrent majority; (2) that his theory would produce not debility, collisions, anarchy, and disunion in the Union but genuine strength and healthy compromise.

Thus, Calhoun pointed to the requirement of unanimity in juries to refute those who held that unanimous agreement could not be achieved on vital matters. Trial by jury required twelve individuals to "unanimously concur." "And yet, as impracticable as this mode of trial would seem to a superficial observer, it is found, in practice, not only to succeed, but to be the wisest and the best that human ingenuity has ever devised." Necessity, the "necessity for unanimity," Calhoun argued, produced concurrence, produced the "disposition to harmonize." The same necessity, Calhoun maintained, would predispose "the various interests of the community to agree in a well organized government, founded on the concurrent majority."[39]

Calhoun also found, or thought he found, in the Roman Republic, in Poland, in Great Britain, and in the Confederacy of the Six [Indian] Nations examples of governments by the concurrent majority.[40] Apropos of Rome and Great Britain, Calhoun argued as follows:

> But, however different their origin and character, it will be found that the object in each was the same,—to blend and harmonize the conflicting interests of the community; and the means the same,—taking the sense of each class or portion through its appropriate organ, and considering the concurrent sense of all as the sense of the whole community.[41]

And again: "The constitutions of both rest on the same principle—an organism by which the voice of each order or class is taken through its appropriate organ; and which requires the concurring voice of all to constitute that of the whole community."[42]

And again:

> In the government of Great Britain, the three orders are blended in the
> legislative department; so that [the] separate and concurring act of each is
> necessary to make laws; while, on the contrary, in the Roman, one order
> had the power of making laws, and another of annulling them, or arresting
> their execution.[43]

The need to concur, based on the importance of safeguarding all vital
interests—Calhoun was persuaded—would produce a peaceful, effective,
and harmonious compromise. Government of the concurrent majority
would not only exclude the "possibility of oppression" "by giving to each
interest . . . the means of protecting itself, by its negative, against all measures calculated to advance the peculiar interests of others at its expense."
Such government would prevent potentially oppressive majorities from
"attempting to adopt any measure calculated to promote the prosperity of
one, or more [interests], by sacrificing that of others" and thus would force
different interests "to unite in such measures only as would promote the
prosperity of all, as the only means to prevent the suspension of the action
of the government,—and, thereby, to avoid anarchy, the greatest of all
evils." Thus: "it is by means of such authorized and effectual resistance, that
oppression is prevented and the necessity of resorting to force superseded,
in governments of the concurrent majority;—and, hence, compromise,
instead of force, becomes their conservative principle."[44]

So it was that Calhoun extolled the virtues of his theory of the concurrent
majority and attempted to refute the arguments of those who maintained
that such a theory was impractical and ineffective and disastrous.

Calhoun held that such a constitutional theory was a genuinely conservative theory. It would conserve genuinely popular, republican, constitutional, federal government. It would conserve the proper combination of
legitimate power and liberty. It would thus fulfill the ends of genuinely
constitutional government.

WHY CALHOUN'S THEORY OF THE CONCURRENT MAJORITY
IS NOT A BREAKTHROUGH ON ANY FRONT

Superficially, Calhoun's theory seems attractive. Here, it would seem, is
an effective way to protect legitimate minority rights and interests against
oppressive majorities. Here is a desirable way to advance true constitutional, federal, government: to combine liberty and power; to advance
peace, the common good, mutual prosperity.

More deeply understood, however, Calhoun's theory reveals serious
ethical, empirical, and prudential weaknesses. Instead of revealing a creative breakthrough in politics, Calhoun's theory turns out to be a failure on
all fronts. His theory turns out to be an argument that contributed signifi-

cantly to secession and the Civil War. Strikingly, many of the most hard-hitting adverse criticisms of Calhoun's theory were made by James Madison.

Not an Ethical Breakthrough

Despite Calhoun's high-sounding talk about constitutional liberty, and his rhetorical devotion to federal Union, it should be clear that Calhoun was seeking a federal Union that would perpetuate the status quo in the South, and particularly the institution of slavery. Clearly, Calhoun's theory is defective because it is dedicated not to the protection of all minority rights and interests—and especially such individual rights as freedom of religion, speech, press, assembly—but to the protection (in a federal union) of slavery, and the slaveholder's economic and social way of life. Although Calhoun talked of a good future for the American federal Union if his views were adopted—of a peaceful, stable, prosperous, liberty-loving, constitutional future—it is clear that Calhoun did not anticipate a genuine Union democracy that included emancipation for America's enslaved black population.

Calhoun sought to sustain a slaveholding present or, worse, resurrect an obsolescent and indefensible past, that of a slaveholding Greek-style democracy. In this sense—making a pitch for a slaveholding Greek-style democracy—Calhoun was not simply conservative; here Calhoun was deeply reactionary. Moreover, Calhoun proposed a reactionary alliance between a united slaveholding South and a "sensible" northern party free of abolitionist sentiment and of partisan politics. Such an alliance he argued, at one point, might be an alliance of the slaveholding South and a capitalistic North against abolitionists, labor agitators, and egalitarian ideologues.[45]

I use the world "reactionary" advisedly. Madison, Jefferson, and many of the founding fathers of 1776 and 1787—although slaveholders themselves—at least deplored the institution of slavery and looked forward to its demise over time. Calhoun turned his back on these more enlightened Americans and resurrected less enlightened arguments: in defense of slavery, adversely critical of the proposition that all people are created ethically equal.

Similarly, capitalism in Calhoun's time, however rough and sometimes oppressive, was premised on free labor, a free market, and was opposed to perpetuation of the economic status quo. Calhoun's efforts, if successful, would have perpetuated an economic system in the South hostile to free labor, a free market, and private enterprise—in the interest primarily of a slaveholding elite.

It is certainly ethically laudable to guard against oppression and to seek to maximize agreement on vital matters. But one must ask critical questions about the oppression claimed and not close one's eyes on oppression ignored—namely, slavery in the South! To ask the North and West to close their eyes to slavery in the South and slavery in new territories and states is asking too much ethically.

Calhoun's understanding of constitutionalism, majority rule, the amending process is also ethically suspect. Here many disturbing questions arise. Does consitutionalism require unanimity or silence on the issue of slavery? Or on other economic issues that the South claimed as vital issues? Did Calhoun wildly exaggerate the dangers of majority rule? Majority oppression? Did he wildly exaggerate the benefits of the doctrine of the concurrent majority? Is such exaggeration ethically healthy? One must also raise questions about the desirability of constitutional amendment as the cardinal device to overcome conflicts between the federal government and state governments.

These questions and comments highlight serious doubts about the ethical ends to be advanced by Calhoun's theory and about the ethical sense of the means to be employed to reach such dubious ends.

Not an Empirical Breakthrough

We can, of course, appreciate aspects of Calhoun's political realism: for example, some of his views about human nature, the naturalness of society, the necessity of government, human self-interest, conflicts of interests in society and government, the danger of the abuse of power, and the need for constitutional government. Yet we may still conclude that these do not lead to an empirical breakthrough in politics in the form of the doctrine of the concurrent majority. We can also appreciate the fact that he was not oblivious of the value of a free suffrage, of numerical majority rule, of a written constitution, separation of powers, judicial review, the competition of parties, and a free press. Yet we may still fault him for failing to see how these factors could indeed operate to guard against majority abuse of legitimate minority rights and interests, even if not the southern interest in slavery or the southern opposition to a protective tariff. And, similarly, we can fault him for thinking that only his remedy—of the concurrent majority—would work to protect the southern minority against the northern majority.

We can also raise other serious questions—on empirical grounds—about his argument on behalf of the doctrine of the concurrent majority. For example, we have reason to doubt that the jury analogy that Calhoun employed to defend his theory of the concurrent majority—as it required unanimity—is applicable to the larger operation of government: the electoral process by which legislators and chief executives are chosen; the legislative process by which laws are enacted; the administrative process by which public policy is executed. Similarly, we have reason to doubt the cogency of Calhoun's examples of Poland and the Indian Confederacy as they support the reality or the feasibility of the need for unanimity in governmental action. Moreover, it is by no means clear that either the British or Roman precedents that Calhoun cited in support of his theory of the concurrent majority strongly support his argument for a concurrent majority in a federal United States. Republican Rome and republican America are not really analogous. And Great Britain and the United States do not have identical political systems. Moreover, rule by the numerical majority was more prevalent in Great Britain than Calhoun supposed; and British history illustrates not the triumph of something resembling Calhoun's concurrent majority but the triumph of numerical majority rule.

In addition, Calhoun badly read a number of powerful forces that were shaping the United States of his day. He missed the power of democracy in America that Alexis de Tocqueville saw as equality in America, a free and equal democratic society that could not long coexist with the institution of slavery. He missed the power of American capitalism, a capitalism fundamentally unsympathetic to slave labor and agricultural interests. He missed the democratic and egalitarian impulse and the geography of the westward movement. Western Americans would not easily perpetuate slavery. And the Northwest and West were really not suitable for slavery. He missed, too, the power of American nationalism, a nationalism that was making Calhoun's compact theory of Union, of states rights, of severely limited federal powers increasingly obsolescent. His proposed breakthrough—the concurrent majority—could hardly be sustained when it attempted to fly in the face of these powerful empirical factors shaping American society in the nineteenth century.

Finally, one must raise serious questions about the South's real hurt at the hands of the numerical majority in the federal government. For example, the South did suffer economically as a result of the protective tariff. For example, the ban on slavery in the territories and new states did inhibit Southern slaveholders who might have desired to move to those territories and new states with their slaves. But did these injuries justify nullification and the threat of secession? Did they justify a repudiation of more traditional devices to protect legitimate minority rights and interests in favor of a very questionable theory of the concurrent majority? The answer to these questions must be negative.

Not a Prudential Breakthrough

My comments in the preceding two sections highlight Calhoun's deplorable lack of prudential judgment. They also underscore the ethical and empirical contributions to wise judgment. Calhoun's basic failure of judgment was that he sought, futilely, to protect such anachronistic interests as slavery by means of a veto incompatible with democratic rule. He simply did not understand the character of the new federal republic created in 1787. Differently put, he was fighting, vainly and foolishly, for a view of the federal Constitution as a compact, with the states free to nullify federal legislation and secede from the Union if their interpretation of reserved powers was not accepted by the nation. He could not grasp or accept the view of the Union as an "indestructible union of indestructible states."[46] Ethically, politically, economically, socially, he was trying to push the clock back, or to maintain an impossible status quo. He never appreciated that the principle of the concurrent majority that he sought to use to protect slavery against majority decisions in the Union might also be used by whites and blacks to oppose slavery itself. For if human freedom is a vital interest, then majorities in southern states should not be able to perpetuate slavery. Indeed, even one black slave should be able to veto the action of that majority that keeps him or her a slave.

Calhoun's values, as we noted above, were at odds both with the libertarian and egalitarian trends of democratic America and with the individualistic and capitalistic trends of the industrial East and the agrarian West. His reading of America's operative ideals, its economic interests, its political patterns was simply wrong-headed empirically. Hence, his prudential recommendations—grounded in both indefensible values and mistaken economic, social, and political reality—were bound to fail. The theory of the concurrent majority was simply not a prudential possibility for America.

The conclusion that Calhoun's theory is impractical, unfeasible, difficult to achieve, and foolish is underscored if we consider, more fully, his ideas on nullification, the amending process, secession, and dual presidency. Here his failures of prudential judgment become even more obvious.

To give to each state the power to nullify federal legislation (even when the state claims that its reserved rights are being violated) is to make a mockery of national unity and to introduce elements of chaos into the American system. Would nullification mean that one southern state, or several southern states, or all southern states could nullify a law in that state or states while the federal law would be operative in the other states? Does nullification mean that such a situation would prevail until a constitutional amendment either sustained the action of the federal government or sustained the position of the nullifying state or states? Would the American nation survive if states, unhappy with a constitutional amendment sustaining the federal government, could opt to secede from the Union? And what would be the consequences of secession—if not what in fact happened: the Civil War?

And what of the sense of Calhoun's idea of a dual presidency—one from the North, one from the South—to effectuate Calhoun's doctrine of the concurrent majority? First, it is extremely doubtful that the nation would pass such a foolish constitutional amendment to secure a dual presidency. But even assuming that such a dual presidency could be established, there would still be the question of a majority in Congress overriding a veto by the southern president. What then? Would state nullification then come into effect, and would the scenario for a constitutional amendment and eventual secession, in the paragraph above, then play out? To state these scenarios is to underscore their imprudence or impracticality, their downright foolishness if not outright dangerousness.

Calhoun argued that the idea of the concurrent majority illustrated a sensible compromise. Who can give much credence to that argument? One is impressed not only by Calhoun's imprudence (in a statesman who prided himself on being prudent); but also by Calhoun's unwillingness to see that other constitutional and political devices could and would protect legitimate minority rights and interests. Despite imperfections, a free suffrage, a competitive party system, rule by the numerical majority, separation of powers, judicial review, a free press, public opinion, the ultimate good sense of the American electorate—these have generally acted to protect legititimate minority rights and interests.[47]

There is one final point that needs to be reemphasized about the logic of the theory of the concurrent majority. If one pushes the logic of the theory to its conclusion, every minority claiming that a vital right had been violated by the oppressive majority would have the right to veto the action of the oppressive majority. Thus if a state (as a minority in the Union) could veto the action of the majority in the federal government, a county (as a minority in a state) could claim the right to veto the majority action of the state. And, then, a city or town (as a minority in the county) could claim the right to veto the majority action of the county. And the ward (as a minority in the city or town) could claim the right to veto the action of the majority in the city or town. And, thus, ultimately, a minority of one individual (one black slave) could claim to veto the action of the majority in the ward! This way is indeed the way to anarchy, understood as no coercion by the majority on the minority. This may be a *reductio ad absurdum*, which Calhoun either ignored (because states like South Carolina were sovereign and could therefore interpret the rights reserved to groups or individuals within the state) or finessed (by arguing that the doctrine of the concurrent majority actually was in practice in a state such as South Carolina).

Strikingly, Madison in the last years of his life provided us with one of the keenest and most potent criticisms of Calhoun's doctrine. He clearly saw that Calhoun's theory, if played out, would indeed lead to the destruction of republican government.

Calhoun's failure was foreseen by Madison, who first clearly criticized and exposed the theoretical and practical weaknesses of Calhoun's theory. Madison was convinced that the theoretical weakness of Calhoun's argument made its practical failure a certainty. Madison maintained that Calhoun's theory led either to anarchy or to tyranny. Both, for Madison, were incompatible with republican and constitutional government. Diversity of interests made unanimity impossible; and Calhoun was really seeking unanimity on at least key vital issues. To depart from the principle of the numerical majority, to endorse nullification, as Calhoun suggested, was to move toward anarchy and this would mean the death of republicanism, which was based on the majority principle. Moreover, given the rejection of anarchy, and given the inability to act when a majority sought to act, those seeking the need for action would sooner opt for tyranny rather than accept anarchy. Hence, the twin evils of anarchy and tyranny—traditional enemies of republican government—were theoretically rooted in Calhoun's theory and vitiated his argument.

Madison foresaw, prophetically, what would happen if the Union refused to buy Calhoun's theory of the concurrent majority, and the South insisted on following Calhoun and his followers down the road of nullification and secession, ultimate weapons that Calhoun and his followers in fact endorsed to protect the vital interests of the South against majority rule in the Union. Madison saw the breakup of the Union in nullification, and civil war in secession. These, indeed, were the imprudent—unwise—consequences of Calhoun's efforts to ensure the operation of the theory of the concurrent majority: the anarchy of nullification and secession, and the dangers of tyrannical actions (in both the Confederacy and the Union) required to maintain unity in the light of nullification and secession.

Madison's critique of Calhoun merits fuller attention. Madison saw nullification and secession as twin heresies—dangerous evils. These evils, Madison prophetically declared, involve a "rupture of the Union; a Southern confederacy; mutual enmity with the Northern; the most dreadful animosities and border wars, springing from the cause of slaves."[48]

Dissolution, Madison argued, would be "fatal to the hopes of liberty and humanity." Madison was vehemently opposed to the doctrines of nullification and secession because he saw more clearly than Calhoun and other defenders of the southern cause that these doctrines were incompatible with a more nearly perfect union. The power of a state to nullify a federal law, the power of a state to secede from the federal union—these would admit the validity and legitimacy of a principle of union which Madison had so strongly condemned in his earlier criticism of the weaknesses of the Articles of Confederation. This was the "treaty" principle, which held that the Union was, in the last analysis, an alliance of sovereign states, each of which possessed the power to dissolve the Union when a breach of the treaty establishing the alliance had occurred. The theory of nullification and secession would, in effect, cancel the attempt to secure a more perfect union. The nation would return to a condition not unlike that under which it had lived under the Articles of Confederation. Each state would again possess at least a temporary veto power over federal legislation. Unanimity would again be required for the orderly functioning of national law, even if an overwhelming majority of states could theoretically obligate a single state to withdraw its nullification of a national law. The more nearly perfect republican, federal union could not long survive if these doctrines were to prevail. This is why Madison so bitterly condemned them as spurious, heretical, and dangerous.[49]

Madison contended, perceptively, that it was "madness in the South to look for greater safety in disunion. It would be worse than jumping out of the Frying-pan into the fire; it would be jumping into the fire for fear of the Frying-pan." Nullification and secession were not the principles that would provide protection against either anarchy or tyranny. On the contrary, these principles militated against both individual liberty and state authority. They were not, in brief, the prudent alternative to a new republican, federal sytem.[50]

The absurd and dangerous consequences of Calhoun's logical, but imprudent, doctrine seem never to have been perceived by the rash advocates of nullification and secession. Few were alive in the 1830s who remembered the state of disunion in the 1780s. Madison in 1833 did perceive these consequences because he had been burned once before by the principle of unanimity under the Articles of Confederation. A lack of basic uniformity and the absence of fundamental concert had been vices of the Union under the Articles. They remained vices inherent in the doctrine of nullification and secession.

There cannot be

> [Madison insisted] different laws in different states on subjects within the compact without subverting its fundamental principles, and rendering it as abortive in practice as it would be incongruous in theory. . . . In a word, the nullifying claims if reduced to practice, instead of being the conservative principle of the Constitution, would necessarily, and it be said obviously, be a deadly poison.[51]

Madison also noted what would happen if the principle of unanimity were to be followed in each state. If one could not operate on the principle of the unanimity of states in 1787, one could not rely on the same principle in the 1820s and 1830s. And unanimity *within* states was equally impossible. If it were accepted *within* each state, such a state would be as paralyzed in its action as would the United States of America. The result would be anarchy *within* each state. If unanimity were not accepted, each state would have to operate within its sovereign area on the same principle of majority rule which Calhoun and his followers opposed for the government of the Union. The result would be inadequate protection—following Calhoun's own logic—for the minorities within such a state.[52]

Madison did not mince words in his sharply adverse critique of Calhoun. He recognized that the principle of unanimity—whether in the government of the Articles of Confederation or in Calhoun's doctrine of the concurrent majority—could only lead to anarchy and impotence. The doctrine of the concurrent majority—linked as it was to nullification and secession—would give each state or major section of the nation the power to veto national action. Nullification gave to a state the power to set aside national laws; secession, the power to withdraw from the national union. And Madison made no effort to conceal his condemnation of these heretical doctrines. He wrote: "Nullification has the effect of putting powder under the Constitution and Union, and a match in the hand of every party to blow them up at pleasure."[53]

If majority government in the Union was improper, it was also improper as it operated in each state. The alternative to majority government was either nonrepublican government or anarchy. In brief, Madison contended that the doctrine of the concurrent majority—which was an attack on the majority principle as it operated in the government of the Union—did not really solve the problem of protecting minorities against the conflict of interests or against majority decision at lower levels or against majority abuse of power. And, in addition, this doctrine was destructive of union.[54]

Madison hammered relentlessly at Calhoun's republican credentials. Those who hold majority government to be the most oppressive of all governments Madison believed to be antirepublican. Such a doctrine, he wrote, "strikes at the roots of Republicanism, and if pursued into its consequences, must terminate in absolute monarchy, with a standing military force." Those who hold such a doctrine in order to attack the tariff "must either join the avowed disciples of aristocracy, oligarchy, or monarchy, or look for" a utopian society.[55]

Madison perceived that Calhoun's politics, grounded as it was in a rejection of rule by the numerical majority, was really the politics of anarchy or the politics of tyranny. Calhoun wanted to protect slavery and the South's other economic and social interests within the Union, but he was unwilling to extend the power to nullify and secede to geographical, political, or economic interests within a given state. In rejecting majority rule Calhoun was rejecting democratic politics; and he must therefore opt either for nonrepublican government or for anarchy. Nullification and secession were clearly republican heresies and they would destroy not only republican government but the Union as well.[56]

Calhoun's doctrine of the concurrent majority does not work; it is simply not sensible. Indeed, it is dangerous for the ongoing operation of constitutional government based on the principle of the numerical majority. It would be destructive of federal union.

To make the argument above—that Calhoun's theory of the concurrent majority is not an ethical, or an empirical, or a prudential breakthrough—is also to deny that Calhoun can legitimately be called a conservative in the best sense of that word. At best, he is a seriously flawed conservative. At worst, he is deeply reactionary. Clearly, he emerges as a very troubled defender of a seriously flawed ethical, empirical, and prudential theory.

CONCLUSION

Calhoun's theory was not a creative breakthrough. It was defective in theory. It could not work and did not work in practice. It was crucially responsible for the greatest catastrophe the American nation has ever faced—the American Civil War. Despite the arguments of those who see in other devices (e.g., electoral politics, the power of committee chairpersons based on seniority, the filibuster) the accomplishment of the objectives of Calhoun's theory of the concurrent majority, the fact remains that no section, state, or vital interest in the United States has a secure permanent veto on making policy and its execution. In brief, we have not followed Calhoun's very questionable interpretation of true constitutional government.

To argue against the weaknesses of Calhoun's theory of the concurrent majority is not to say that prohibitions against certain majority action should not be institutionalized. But we must, for example, distinguish between protecting slavery *and* protecting religious liberty or freedom of speech and press. And we must, for example, distinguish between institutionalizing a veto on all matters of alleged vital interest *and* defending certain crucial freedoms against genuinely tyrannical majorities in a clearly undemocratic and unconstitutional system.

The problem of how to protect minority or individual rights in a majority system is still a problem that challenges our ingenuity. And, as we shall see in Chapter 7, the problem of protecting human rights against egregious violations in authoritarian systems worldwide remains an excruciatingly troublesome matter. Clearly, we have not worked out a completely foolproof system to ensure protection for individual rights even in a democratic and constitutional system. And we are very, very far from protecting human rights in authoritarian systems.

As we explore possibilities here, we must be clear on the worth of the vital rights and interests to be protected and on the effectiveness of the mechanisms we choose to achieve the desired protection. The real problem that should engage us should be this one: How can we secure the more adequate protection of the legitimate rights and interests of the weak against the abusive strong (majority or minority) in the interest of justice? Here there is need for continuing breakthroughs—to enable people to overcome poverty, to assist vulnerable workers, to protect maltreated ethnic groups, to aid disadvantaged women, to help struggling developing nations.

The breakup and troubles of federalism in many countries in the post–Cold War era (e.g., the former Soviet Union, the former Yugoslavia) highlight the continuing problem of the search for a governmental organization—and the necessary and sufficient means to advance constitutional democracy—that can genuinely reconcile liberty and authority.

In our next chapter—on Karl Marx and communism—we turn to a most ambitious effort to achieve nothing less than universal human emancipation.

NOTES

1. See, especially, John C. Calhoun, *A Disquisition on Government* (1851), in *Calhoun: Basic Documents*, John C. Anderson, editor (State College, Pa.: Bald Eagle Press, 1952).

2. *A Discourse on the Constitution and Government of the United States* in John C. Calhoun, *The Works of John C. Calhoun*. Vol. 1 (Columbia: General Assembly of the State of South Carolina, 1852), p. 310.

3. Ibid.

4. See *A Disquisition on Government*, pp. 36–39.

5. Ibid, pp. 48–49.

6. Ibid., p. 50.

7. Ibid., p. 49.

8. On the Supreme Court, for example, see Calhoun's speech "On The Revenue Collection (Force) Bill, February 15–16, 1833," in *Calhoun: Basic Documents*, pp. 138–139.

9. See *A Disquisition on Government*, pp. 48–49.

10. Ibid., p. 54.

11. Ibid., p. 55.

12. "Remarks At The Meeting Of Citizens Of Charleston, March 9, 1847," in *Calhoun: Basic Documents*, p. 254.

13. "On Henry Clay's Compromise Resolutions On The Bill To Admit California, March 4, 1850," in ibid., p. 301.

14. Ibid., p. 306.

15. Ibid., p. 75.

16. Ibid., pp. 76–77.

17. See "On Henry Clay's Compromise Resolutions,"especially pp. 302–310; and *A Discourse*, especially pp. 364–374.

18. "On Henry Clay's Compromise Resolutions," pp. 302–304. See also *A Discourse*, pp. 264–367.

19. "On Henry Clay's Compromise," p. 302.

20. Ibid., p. 303.

21. Ibid., pp. 305–306.

22. Ibid., p. 310.

23. *A Disquisition on Government*, pp. 44–45.

24. *A Discourse*, pp. 392–395.

25. Ibid., p. 187.

26. *A Disquisition on Government*, pp. 44–45.

27. Ibid., p. 51.

28. See ibid., p. 50, where Calhoun states that it might be necessary to "make the several departments the organs of the distinct interests or portions of the community; and to clothe each with a negative on the others." This Calhoun wrote would "change the government of the numerical into the concurrent majority."

29. *A Discourse*, p. 392. Calhoun went further in his proposal for a "dual executive." He wrote: "One might be charged with the administration of matters connected with the foreign relations of the country;—and the other, of such as were connected with its domestic institutions; the selection to be decided by lot."

30. Ibid., pp. 394–395.

31. Ibid., p. 241.

32. Ibid., pp. 266–267.

33. Ibid., p. 266. It should also be remarked that there is some ambiguity about the veto. The veto could be a state veto as in nullification. The veto could also be the veto of the southern Dual President over acts of Congress.

34. Ibid., p. 296. By the "mutual negative" Calhoun apparently meant the ability of a state to veto an act of the Union government that encroached upon the reserved power of the states; and the ability of the federal or Union government to prevent any state action that encroached upon the federal government's clearly delegated powers. (Why the state's negative is different from interposition is not made clear. Conceivably, Calhoun understood that a southern president [as part of his proposed dual presidency] could exercise a veto on Congressional legislation.)

35. Ibid., pp. 299–300.

36. Ibid., p. 300.

37. Ibid.

38. Ibid., p. 301.

39. *A Disquisition on Government*, pp. 70 and 71.

40. Ibid., pp. 74–75 and 87–96.

41. Ibid., p. 87.

42. Ibid., p. 85.

43. Ibid., pp. 95–96.

44. Ibid., pp. 52–53.

45. See Richard Hofstadter's essay on "Calhoun: The Marx of the Master Class," in his *The American Political Tradition and the Men Who Made It* (New York: Knopf, 1948).

46. See *Texas* v. *White*, 7 Wallace 700 1869).

47. On majority rule, see Neal Riemer, "The Case for Bare Majority Rule, *Ethics*, Vol. 62 (October 1951); and Neal Riemer, *The Revival of Democratic Theory* (New York: Appleton-Century-Crofts, 1962), especially pp. 117–131.

48. See Neal Riemer, *James Madison: Creating the American Constitution* (Washington, D.C.: Congressional Quarterly Press, 1986), p. 54. Madison wrote on February 10, 1833—twenty-eight years before the Civil War.

49. Again, see ibid., pp. 54–55. For Madison's critique of the Articles of Confederation, see his "Vices of the Political System of the United States," in Gaillard Hunt, ed., *The Writings of James Madison*, Vol. 9 (1787) (New York: G. P. Putnam's Sons, 1900–1910), pp. 361–369.

50. Ibid., p. 55.

51. Ibid.

52. Ibid., pp. 55–56.

53. Ibid., p. 64.

54. Ibid., p. 64.

55. Hunt, *The Writings of James Madison*, pp. 520, 526.

56. Ibid., pp. 141-142.

CHAPTER 5

Karl Marx and Universal Human Emancipation: A Flawed Prophetic Breakthrough

INTRODUCTION

John C. Calhoun sought to preserve slavery and the status quo in the American South. Karl Marx sought a revolutionary breakthrough beyond the global status quo to nothing less than universal human emancipation. In the previous chapter on Calhoun, particularly in our critique of Calhoun's flawed constitutional theory of the concurrent majority, we highlighted Calhoun's misguided efforts to protect minority rights. In this chapter, as we explore Marx's communist theory, we will examine and appraise his efforts to advance the freedom of the overwhelming majority. As our critique of Calhoun's alleged breakthrough (falsely conservative at best, deeply reactionary at worst) contrasts with the creative breakthroughs of Williams and Madison, so our critique of Marx's alleged communist breakthrough will illuminate significant differences between the soundly prophetic and the foolishly utopian traditions.

After presenting Marx's troubling problem and ambitious solution I shall argue that, although Marx's analysis is powerful and often illuminating, there are serious flaws in his understanding of both problem and solution. These flaws, I shall contend, characterize his ethical values, his empirical understanding, and his recommended prudential course of action; and they prevent one from characterizing his proposed breakthrough as a genuinely creative breakthrough in the prophetic tradition.

First, however, in this section, let me attempt to pose Marx's problem. Briefly put, it is this: How can we achieve universal human emancipation? Marx is especially concerned for the great majority of people—workers, the proletariat. They are not free; they are oppressed, exploited, alienated. They cannot be free under capitalism and bourgeois rule. Marx is also persuaded that real freedom for all—not only workers, but also peasants, and even capitalists and members of the middle class—cannot be achieved under capitalism and bourgeois rule.

Universal human emancipation, Marx maintains, is a problem that the conventional wisdom holds cannot be solved. Marx is savagely critical not only of feudalism, aristocracy, bourgeois conservatism, and liberalism—old and new status quo ideologies. He is also mordantly critical of traditional "radical" ideologies such as utopian socialism, or anarchism. Moreover, he is highly critical of those radicals who believe that a minority of insurrectionaries can make a successful revolution.

The status quo ideologies of his day affirmed that in this world there will always be rich and poor, exploited and exploiter. Conventional realists affirmed that there will always be illusions—religious, economic, political, social—to ensnare and enslave people.

Marx was aghast at the evils of his day, which—in his judgment—the conventional wisdom was unable to overcome. These evils were to be seen in the miserable, exploited lives of working people, in endemic class conflict, in the great chasm between rich and poor, in war, in the false lives led by all in bourgeois society. Status quo ideologies, reformist ideologies, even anarchist or insurrectionist ideologies Marx held to be incapable of understanding and changing the world—unable to rid the world of the evils he saw.

Let me turn next to Marx's alleged breakthrough, which will shed more light on his problem and his view that communism "is the riddle of history solved."[1]

MARX'S ALLEGED CREATIVE BREAKTHROUGH

There can be no question that Marx saw his communist theory as a creative breakthrough. Although Marx was loath to talk about values and ethics in any traditional sense, and although he had his own special view of the scientific enterprise, and although he was not tuned in to the use of the word "prudence," it is clear that he saw his communist theory as an ethical, empirical, and prudential breakthrough. Let me now present Marx's own understanding of his breakthrough, so that the reader may have a fuller basis for judging Marx's theory. I will reserve for a later section my critique of Marx's theory as a creative breakthrough in politics.

Marx's Ethical Vision

A number of interrelated values characterize Marx's ethical vision: (1) universal human freedom; (2) integration, harmony, and peace; (3) a truly human being and community; and (4) rich individual and social development.[2] Marx saw communism as the riddle of history solved because it would lead to the overcoming of all evils. The advent of communism would result in universal human emancipation, the "total redemption of humanity."[3] Communism would end class conflicts and international conflicts. Communism would overcome alienation and exploitation and enable workers to be in control of their work-product, to enjoy their work-activity, to recover their humanity, and to be reunited with other human beings. Communism would, moreover, usher in the free, harmonious, creative, prosperous society.

For Marx a democratic and prosperous communism was only the basis for the "true realm of freedom," not the ultimate objective for human beings.[4] In the "higher phase of communist society," the operative motto would be "From each according to his ability, to each according to his needs!"[5] Such a communist society would permit genuine diversity in human life. Marx held that in the

> communist society, where nobody has one exclusive sphere of activity but each can become accomplished in any branch he wishes, society regulates the general production and thus makes it possible for me to do one thing today and another tomorrow, to hunt in the morning, fish in the afternoon, rear cattle in the evening, criticise after dinner, just as I have a mind, without ever becoming hunter, fisherman, shepherd, or critic.[6]

The "true realm of freedom" was a creative realm beyond "the realm of necessity," or necessary labor. Such a true realm of freedom would be possible in the "higher phase of communist society" that would be characterized by a generous increase of the productive forces of society, by abundant cooperative wealth, and by "the all-round development of the individual." In such a society, individuals could be genuinely free and fully creative.

Marx's Social Science

Marx maintained that his social science constituted a breakthrough in scientific understanding that made possible the advent of universal human emancipation.[7] Marx's social science utilizes a bold concept of criticism to focus on what is crucial, a materialist conception of history to provide incisive orientation, and an ambitious social scientific exploration of the bourgeois capitalist order to lay bare the pervasiveness of capitalist exploitation of the worker, the secret of that exploitation, the weaknesses and final death of capitalism.

As Marx himself recognized, his criticism is a *"ruthless* criticism of everything existing." Marx held that criticism must be "ruthless in two senses: The criticism must not be afraid of its own conclusions, nor of conflict with the powers that be." Marx thus attempts through his social science to get at the fundamental truth of human beings and the real world they live in. He seeks not only to understand the world truthfully and fully, but also to point toward that change in the world that would bring it in accord with that truthful understanding.[8]

Marx's materialist conception of history led him to emphasize the primacy of life, the decisive importance of the material forces of production, and the significance of the economic and social relations of production. The forces and relations of production produced and conditioned civil society. Marx's perspective led him to stress the coercive and oppressive role of the state under capitalism, and the dependence of society's superstructure of religion, law, education, philosophy on its economic foundation. For Marx, the "sum total" of "the relations of production constitutes the economic structure of society, the real foundation, on which rises a legal and political superstructure and to which correspond definite forms of social consciousness." For Marx, the "mode of production of material life conditions the social, political and intellectual life process in general."[9]

Marx saw history moving from Asiatic to ancient to feudal to modern bourgeois modes of production. And so, as economic systems emerged, served a purpose, encountered difficulties, and inevitably evolved, in the modern world bourgeois capitalism too would be superseded by communism, first in Europe—the most advanced capitalist arena—and then throughout the world. This would happen not because communists desired it to occur, but because of the irresistible operation of economic forces.

Capitalism's very nature and functioning, Marx maintained, would bring about its demise and the advent of communism. Capitalism brought into existence, and depended upon, the proletariat for its operation, profits, and success. Exploitation and oppression were inherent in the very nature of capitalism. Marx believed that he had laid bare that oppression and claimed to have disovered the secret of that exploitation.

Marx's account of the oppression of workers in the nineteenth century is vivid and shocking. Workers lived lives of "misery, agony of toil, slavery, ignorance, brutality, mental degradation."[10] The workers' condition—one of alienation, dehumanization, estrangement, stunted development—was clear for all to see. This condition was attributable to the capitalist's hunger for surplus labor, and therefore profit and capital.

The secret of the exploitation of workers, Marx held, was deceptively simple. The capitalist obtains "surplus value," and thus increases profits and maximizes capital, by extracting from his workers hours of work beyond "necessary working time"—that is, hours put in to earn a subsistence wage. The capitalist, that is, extracts from his workers additional hours beyond what the workers put in to obtain their subsistence wage, additional hours that produce commodities (and therefore value) for the capitalist. As Marx put it:

> Suppose the working day consists of 6 hours of necessary labor, and 6 hours of surplus labor. Then the free labourer gives the capitalist every week 6 x 6 or 36 hours of surplus-labour. It is the same as if he worked 3 days in the week for himself, and 3 days in the week gratis for the capitalist.[11]

The surplus value created by labor power uncompensated beyond wages was the secret of capitalist accumulation. Under capitalism, Marx wrote, "the wage-worker has permission to work for his subsistence, that is, *to live*, only in so far as he works for a certain time gratis for the capitalist." According to Marx, "the whole capitalist system of production turns on the increase of this gratis labour by extending the working day or by developing the [worker's] productivity, that is, increasing the intensity of labour power, etc."[12] Wage slavery, then, was the inevitable lot of the worker under capitalism, an economic system that lives on, and profits from, stolen labor.

Capitalism's weaknesses would, however, Marx insisted, bring about its self-destruction. These weaknesses made it impossible for capitalism to produce rationally and abundantly and consistently to satisfy universal human freedom and needs. Despite the advances that capitalism made over previous economic systems, it could not endure. A number of factors would bring about its downfall. These factors included competition, which heightened the exploitation of workers, a cycle of boom-and-bust (characterized by overproduction, market glut, declining prices and profits, and unemployment) and thus destructive industrial crises; monopoly; the frantic quest for global markets. Ironically, centralization and monopoly prepare the way for the communist takeover; and the global spread of capitalism prepares the way for communist forces in the larger world beyond Europe.

The growing "revolt of the working-class"—intensified by the "misery, oppression, slavery, degradation, exploitation" of workers—provided the mass base for the communist revolution. "Centralization of the means of production and socialisation of labour at last reach a point where they become incompatible with their capitalistic integument. This integument is burst asunder. The knell of capitalist private property sounds. The expropriators are expropriated."[13]

So it is, then, that capitalism produces, socializes, educates, and exploits the proletariat. Capitalism centralizes and "socializes" the process of production. Capitalism weakens itself economically in industrial crises. Capitalism suffers from a diminishing rate of profit. Capitalism is unable to overcome the contradiction between developing (partly socialized but erratic) forces of production and the economic and social relations of bourgeois society. In these and other ways capitalism thus sets the stage for its own demise.

Marx's social scientific analysis is also directed at the bourgeois super-structure, and at noncommunist alternatives and reformers. Marx was severely critical of the ideas and institutions of the entire bourgeois super-structure. These political, legal, religious, educational, social, and cultural institutions were designed to sustain and perpetuate bourgeois capitalistic rule. The key ideas of bourgeois liberalism—especially private property, family, religion, order—sustain capitalism, the bourgeois state, bourgeois law, the exploitative bourgeois institutions of marriage and family, and a religion that dulls the radical, man-oriented consciousness of the worker by focusing on the false consciousness of another life.[14]

Marx was caustically critical of the bourgeois state as a coercive and oppressive instrument to perpetuate capitalist rule. He never deviated from the conclusion that real freedom for the proletariat is impossible in the bourgeois state.[15]

Marx is also harshly critical of a variety of reformers, and he bitterly attacks other socialists—those he calls reactionary, conservative, or utopian. These socialists and reformers either do not understand the march of modern history, are not genuinely revolutionary, or are naive about economics, politics, and society. They do not understand what is required to make the revolution that will usher in a genuinely communist society. Similarly, Marx is critical of anarchists who do not understand that force must be used by the majority, not only in the revolution to overthrow capitalism but after that to consolidate and complete the achievement of communism. Here Marx's social scientific analysis of revolution anticipates his strategy of revolution-ary action, which we will examine in the next section.

Communist Theory as a Revolutionary Guide to Action

Marx's social science pointed toward action on behalf of universal human emancipation. Social science understanding must lead to effective action—to changing the world: to strategy and tactics to overthrow capitalism and the bourgeois state and usher in the new communist society. Marx believed that his communist theory thus prepared the way for momentous change.

Marx developed a theory of revolutionary change, involving four defi-nite stages, that took into account the circumstances that would dictate exact strategy and tactics at each stage. Marx is relatively more explicit about stages 1 and 2, preparing for, and then making, the communist revolution. He provides rough, if incomplete, guide lines for stage 3, consolidating the revolution, with the help of the dictatorship of the prole-tariat. He is much more sketchy about stage 4, achieving a mature commu-nism. What is clear, nonetheless, is that Marx believed that his theory constituted a breakthrough in preparing for, making, consolidating, and fulfilling a real revolution—here the communist revolution. Let us examine his revolutionary judgments in each of these four stages.

Stage 1: Preparing for the Revolution

Preparing for revolution dictates, initially, a judgment that a fundamental, radical, and transforming democratic communist revolution is required. Such a revolution must be based on majority worker control; must abolish bourgeois capitalism and private ownership of the major means of production and exchange; must destroy the coercive and parasitic bourgeois state; must via communism overcome alienation, exploitation, and oppression in a free, harmonious, productive, creative communist society.

Moreover, communists and their allies must look to the development of those material, economic, and political conditions that ensure that the time for revolution is ripe. Preparation calls for avoiding the mistaken revolutionary judgments of insurrectionists and anarchists who would launch a revolution prematurely, or the mistaken judgments of liberal reformers who see no need for a radical communist revolution.

Workers in stage 1, then, get set by organizing; by unionizing; by propagandizing; by becoming politically active; by working with progressive democratic forces; by pushing aggressively within parliamentary bodies, if they are open to suasion, for key democratic reforms—for example, universal suffrage, the ten-hour day; by avoiding deception by utopian socialists, bourgeois reformers, or even wrong-headed socialist reformers; by acting to prepare the proletariat, at or shortly after the revolution (depending on circumstances), to become the ruling class; by never losing sight of the need for the fundamental communist revolution.[16] Communists, as leaders of the working class, must be organized, armed, and militant; and they must maintain a distinct communist identity.

Stage 2: Making the Revolution

Making the actual communist revolution—and whether it could be done peacefully or would require force and violence—would depend on circumstances and a judgment about ripeness. Generally, Marx recognized four possibilities: (1) proletarian majority revolution; (2) a revolutionary alliance of workers, peasants, and progressive bourgeoisie, (3) legal, constitutional, peaceful revolution; and, more remotely, (4) communism via an agrarian revolution.[17]

1. *Proletarian Majority Revolution.* In oligarchic or authoritarian countries where workers constituted the immense majority, but in which they lacked the suffrage or other basic freedoms, a violent, illegal, swift, spontaneous, popular, democratic revolution by the working masses was Marx's preferred model. Force is necessary in this strategy since the majority of

workers cannot use peaceful means, and since bourgeois capitalists will not voluntarily accept communism.

2. *Alliance of Workers, Peasants, and Progressive Bourgeoisie.* This strategy, for less economically and politically advanced countries, such as France and Germany, looked to a liberal bourgeois revolution (supported by workers, peasants, and petite bourgeoisie), to be followed in time by a majority communist regime. In this revolution, force would have to be used both during and immediately after the revolution to crush the resistance of the authoritarian, oligarchic bourgeoisie.

3. *Legal, Constitutional, Peaceful Revolution.* Later in his life Marx held that because of changing circumstances in certain advanced capitalist and more democratic countries (e.g., England)—where workers were (he thought) in a majority, enjoyed crucial freedoms, and could exercise the suffrage—peaceful, constitutional, and legal means might possibly be used by workers to achieve power. Marx's judgment here, we should note, is hedged with reservations and characterized by fears. He worries about the genuinely democratic commitment of the bourgeoisie in such countries. He worries about a bourgeois counterrevolution. He also worries about the militancy and resolve of the working class. Marx's general position, expressed in 1871, was frank: "We must declare to the governments: we know that you are the armed power directed against the proletariat; we will agitate against you in peaceful ways where that is possible for us, and with arms where it is necessary."[18] Marx opted for a policy of restraint for restraint, and force for force.

Engels outlived Marx (who died in 1883), and in the year of his own death in 1895 expressed hope about the possibilities of peaceful change in countries that enjoyed universal suffrage, hope even for Germany. We cannot be absolutely sure that Marx in 1895 would have shared Engels' views. We can only say that in his own lifetime Marx saw some possibility for legal and peaceful change in England and America; that he thought force would probably be needed on the Continent; but that he was responsive to changing circumstances that might lead him, pragmatically, to alter his views on the possibility of legal and peaceful change in such countries as Germany and France. The main emphasis in his writings, even in his later years, is still the emphasis on the need for a radical and fundamental revolution—probably necessitating force—to usher in proletarian rule and communism. Such force, he never forgets, might be required to forestall a nondemocratic and probourgeois counterrevolution or to defeat it after a proletarian legal victory.[19]

4. *Communism via an Agrarian Revolution.* Strategies 1 and 2 (proletarian majority revolution, alliance of the majority classes) are clearly the central ones in Marx's nineteenth-century lifetime. Strategy 3 (legal, peaceful, constitutional revolution) is, in some advanced countries, a possibility, but not a strong probability. Even less probable, although considered briefly but

not developed fully, is strategy 4 based on a possible agrarian revolution in Russia.[20] Here Marx stated that a communist revolution might emerge from the discontent of the peasant masses in a country like Russia and might be based on certain communal Russian agricultural arrangements. Marx had in mind the Russian *obshchina*, a form of primeval common ownership of land. Marx was "iffy" about the possibility. "If the Russian Revolution becomes the signal for a proletarian revolution in the West, so that both complement each other, the present Russian common ownership of land may serve as the starting-point for a communist development."[21] Given Marx's social science, which stressed the evolution of capitalism into communism, and the crucial role of the proletariat, it seems clear that Marx could not place fundamental reliance upon a peasant revolution in a relatively backward capitalist country, such as Russia. Indeed, the strategy of an agrarian revolution as the route to communism would probably not receive the attention it gets—given its minor treatment in the corpus of Marx's writing—were it not for the twentieth-century reality of the Russian and Chinese Revolutions. Although neither of these revolutions was crucially related to a tradition of the agricultural commune, the Russian Revolution did have a peasant component and, of course, the Chinese Revolution utilized peasant support to build a powerful communist base and, eventually, to overthrow the Nationalist government of China.

Stage 3: Consolidating the Revolution

Marx was adversely critical of the judgment of liberal or socialist reformers, who believed that they could significantly alter the oppression of the proletariat. He was also adversely critical of anarchists and other simple-minded revolutionaries who believed that the simple overthrow of the bourgeois state would miraculously usher in communism. Unlike the reformers, Marx insisted that the bourgeois state must not simply be taken over but destroyed. Peaceful, gradual, and piecemeal reform will not do the job. And unlike anarchists and other simple-minded revolutionaries, Marx recognized that it would take time, after the revolution, to usher in a full-fledged communist society. The new communist society would not miraculously appear after the revolution. The coercive and parasitic bourgeois state must not only be smashed but be replaced by proletarian rule and democratic economic, political, and social institutions. Workers and their revolutionary allies must unhesitatingly use their political powers, in the first stage of the consolidation of the revolution, to ensure the building of the communist society. Workers must be unafraid to use the dictatorship of the proletariat to advance the consolidation of the revolution. In 1875 Marx wrote: "Between capitalist and communist society lies the period of the revolutionary transformation of the one into the other. There corresponds to this also a political transition period in which the state can be nothing but the *revolutionary dictatorship of the proletariat.*"[22] Oddly, from the point of view of liberal democrats, this interim stage would be both democratic and dictatorial: democratic because it is based on majority and popular rule; dictatorial because it is illegal, in the interegnum between the majority revolution and a communist constitution, and because it requires revolutionary force.[23]

It is not perfectly clear how long, in the period of consolidating the revolution, the dictatorship of the proletariat would prevail. Long enough, presumably, to ensure the complete destruction of the old capitalist, bourgeois order and the creation of the new communist order. Richard Hunt sums up Marx's position on consolidating the revolution as follows: Marx

> expected the state as parasite to disappear immediately through deprofessionalization, the state as dictatorship, if required initially, to disappear by definition with the establishment of a new [communist] legality, and the state as coercive power to disappear substantially with the end of expropriation and bourgeois resistance, but only completely and absolutely after a new generation had so internalized the rules of social intercourse that no external coercion whatsoever would be required.[24]

Stage 4: Achieving Mature Communism

Marx argues that the advent of mature communism means the achievement of a classless, conflictless society. The state as a coercive organ will have ceased to exist. In the communist community the "free development of each" will be "the condition for the free development of all."[25] Abundant cooperative wealth will make possibile a free, rich, peaceful, and creative life according to the communist motto: "From each according to his ability, to each according to his needs."[26]

In the mature communist society, serious judgments about political, economic, and social problems will be nonexistent or minimal because, presumably, people will behave responsibly because they have been socialized properly.

Thus, the difficult judgments characteristic of the early stages of the communist revolution will no longer be necessary in the mature communist society.

Let me turn, next, to a critique of Marx's alleged revolutionary breakthrough to universal human emancipation in the communist society. This critique will highlight the strengths and weaknesses of Marx's argument, and will argue that Marx's theory cannot be considered a genuine creative breakthrough. In my conclusion I will extend this critique to argue that Marx's theory—unlike that of Williams and Madison—is not squarely in the tradition of prophetic politics.

WHY MARX'S COMMUNIST THEORY IS NOT A CREATIVE BREAKTHROUGH IN POLITICS

Despite the powerful and often illuminating character of Marx's communist theory, it fails to meet the test of a genuine creative breakthrough in politics because of its serious limitations and flaws. These weaknesses are to be found in the ethical, social scientific, and prudential aspects of Marx's theory. Let me examine each of these aspects in turn.

Marx's Values

Despite Marx's own adverse criticism of utopian socialists, we have to conclude that Marx's own vision is, alas, a naive and foolishly utopian vision. Marx's goals of universal emancipation, peace, community, prosperity, and creativity are laudable. So is his occasional acknowledgement of the need for a democratic communist constitution. Yet Marx is naive in believing that a completely conflictless harmonious society can ever come into existence. He is naive in believing that the state as a coercive organ will cease to exist, and that individuals in his mature communist society will behave rightly because of their socialization in a rightfully ordered communist society. He is naive in assuming the possibility of universal peace.

Marx's foolishly utopian vision leads him to neglect the ongoing, realistic need for a constitution and government able to monitor the never-ending struggle for power characteristic of people, interests, nations. He does not adequately stress the inevitability of a constitution required to help fallible political actors satisfy their vital needs, protect their fundamental interests, and advance their perceived desires. He neglects, in his ethical vision, the desirable and inevitable constitutional mechanisms required to harness the enduring struggle for power: mechanisms required to deal with persistent conflicts; to advance willing cooperation; to achieve necessary accommodation.

Marx's values are, unfortunately, not fully explicated or defended; they are asserted. With, perhaps, the important exception of alienation, Marx does not ably or fully argue on behalf of his values. And even his values of integration, harmony, and peace reflect a foolishly utopian conviction that alienation can be completely overcome in the communist society.

Marx is also ethically naive in believing that the achievement of a communist economy will miraculously usher in his preferred communist society of democratic abundance, human freedom, and creativity. This vision, we have to conclude, was an ethical vision unsupported by empirical understanding of the actual operation of a communist economy. Marx is largely oblivious of the actual operation of worker-control, of potential conflicts between economic directors and workers on the assembly line, of potential clashes between centralized decision-makers and decentralized operators on factory and farm.

Ethically speaking, Marx's key values, although superficially attractive, remain distressingly vague and undeveloped. Marx fails, moreover, in developing a full-fledged theory of constitutionalism to ensure that his values will be fulfilled. And, disturbingly, Marx misses other key values essential for the maintenance of a genuinely democratic, constitutional, and more fulfilling society: values such as love, compassion, tolerance, repentance; values such as realistic distrust even of people with good intentions.

We are thus led to the conclusion that Marx's superficially appealing values are too often foolishly utopian and not genuinely prophetic. Consequently, we cannot conclude that Marx's values constitute a genuine creative breakthrough in politics. What, next, can we say of Marx's social science?

Marx's Social Science

We must also raise serious questions about the social scientific accuracy of Marx's understanding of the historical process, of the operation of capitalism and liberal democratic states, of revolutionary violence, and of the functioning of communism. Marx thought he understood why and how capitalism had emerged, and why and how communism would replace capitalism. But how accurate is his social scientific diagnosis and prescription?

Marx's social science is, in many respects, powerfully illuminating, but nonetheless limited and seriously flawed. There can be no doubt that Marx revealed a horrendous gap between the proletariat's often dreadful condition *and* human freedom and development. He also presented us with a social scientific explanation for the existence of this gap. Much of his criticism of nineteenth-century capitalism, and of the operation of the bourgeois state and society, is on the mark. But we may have serious reservations about his social scientific conclusion about the inevitable collapse of capitalism and the inevitable triumph of communism.

If Marx, in important respects, is a powerful social scientist, his social science is nonetheless limited and flawed—limited because of what he excluded from his range of vision; and flawed because of his scientific astigmatism.[27]

Bourgeois, capitalistic society doesn't quite function in the way Marx said it did. It is by no means clear that the contradictions Marx saw operating in capitalism will lead to capitalism's destruction. It is by no means clear that the people in liberal democracies are unable to reform capitalism, to correct its worst abuses. It is by no means scientifically clear that communism is the inevitable alternative to capitalism as an economic system and to liberal democracy as a political system.

If Marx is accurate in describing the often-dreadful working conditions of the proletariat in the nineteenth century, and in noting how, for example, capitalists profit at the expense of workers, he fails to anticipate some late-nineteenth-century and some twentieth-century developments. He fails to appreciate in progressive liberal democracies the viability of a regulated capitalism, the power of workers to protect their economic, political, and social interests, and the ability of a liberal democracy to address (modestly if not radically) capitalistic abuses and the call for social justice. He does not grasp the resilience, vitality, or staying power of capitalism or of liberal democracy; nor does he anticipate (or, if he appreciates, approve) the emergence of democratic socialism functioning in a still largely capitalist society as a realistic alternative to communism.

Although he may have perceived important trends toward a concentration of capitalist enterprises in the nineteenth century, he mistakenly contends that declining profits, the growing misery/organization/militancy of workers, and severe economic crises (rooted in capitalism's contradictions) will inevitably pave the way for capitalism's demise.[28]

Moreover, because of his central preoccupation with capitalism, the proletariat, economics, and class struggle Marx also missed a number of forces that have proved to be hostile to his goals of freedom, peace, community, and development. He missed, for example, nationalism and nationalistic rivalries; he missed racism, sexism, anti-Semitism. In addition, on the important subject of alienation, Marx neglected other varieties of alienation that may be unrelated to an oppressive capitalist economy: varieties of alienation rooted in our human sense of our mortality, finiteness, fallibility; varieties of alienation rooted in large organizations, mass societies, the frustrations of a materialistic civilization.

The weaknesses of Marx's social science force us to conclude that his social science does not constitute a genuine creative breakthrough in politics. The Marxist social scientific understanding of how to achieve universal human emancipation is too seriously flawed to be considered such a genuine creative breakthrough in politics.

Marx's Prudential Judgments

The judgments in Marx's theory of revolutionary communist action emerge as powerful and illuminating, but also as limited and flawed. On one hand, his judgments are powerful and illuminating insofar as they highlight the importance of both economic conditions and political power in achieving a revolutionary breakthrough for workers and their allies. Marx sees clearly the importance of political struggle as a way, in conjunction with economic struggle, for oppressed workers to exert pressure on behalf of their own freedom. Marx makes a convincing case on behalf of violations of freedom, and other values, in the nineteenth century. Marx thoroughly appreciates the importance of universal suffrage and other basic democratic freedoms and institutions, when they were available, in the struggle for both political and economic power. He wisely rejects the minority *putsch* as a way to advance communism. He astutely perceives that the anarchist belief that the state could be immediately abolished is unrealistic. He persistently refuses to be taken in by bourgeois reformers not really interested in, or social democratic reformers deflected from, fundamental, radical changes that would get at the root of, and remedy, the oppression and exploitation of workers. There is evidence, then, supporting the proposition that Marx is a tough-minded, radical, democratic communist, and not a totalitarian democrat who believes in a minority revolution, a vanguard party, the systematic use of terror, and total control by the state of all aspects of life.

On the other hand, we also have reasons for seeing many of Marx's judgments as limited and flawed. Most important, his revolutionary theory does not fully satisfy the criteria of a prophetically just revolution. This standard is, I concede, an exacting one, and might seem to be offered in order to make impossible the justification of the communist revolution. Such, however, is not my intention. It is my intention to hold all revolutions—and all politics—to an exacting prophetic standard, and especially a revolutionary politics that would radically transform the world.

Although Marx's values of freedom, integration, humanity/community, and development are in the abstract quite compatible with the ends for which a just revolution can be fought, we must question Marx's judgment that communism would, in logic or experience, necessarily advance those values, and at a price we are willing to pay. Moreover, Marx assumes— again without convincing evidence—that workers will not only come to be the majority of the population in all countries, *but* that they will support communism as the way to freedom and that, consequently, there will be majority support for the communist revolution and society. Given our reservations mentioned above, we have all the more reason to probe carefully the rational, humane, effective means Marx would employ to achieve the communist revolution and society.

Marx is rightly impatient, but does he give up too quickly on the wisdom of legal, peaceful revolution? Does he correctly sense that communism would probably never be achievable in a legal, peaceful revolution, and therefore place his prime emphasis on violent revolution? Does he fail to calculate prudently the costs of a violent revolution, of the temporary dictatorship of the proletariat, of the continued use of coercion until the advent of mature communism as against the benefits of communism? Does he fail to articulate a communist constitution that would ensure the participatory democracy and worker economic control he favors; that would guard against the abuse of power; that would address the realities of the conflicts of interests and the struggles for power that characterize every society? Does Marx simply fail to face up to these issues because of his faith in the wisdom, humanity, and decency of the proletarian communist majority? Because of his unwillingness to appreciate the dangers of the abuse of power even by communists with good intentions?

Does Marx's recognition of the need for difficult judgments in the first two, or three, stages of the communist revolution tend to disappear in the fourth stage, the stage of mature communism, because with the advent of the conflictless, classless communist society there would no longer be any need for difficult judgments? Underlying the weaknesses in Marx's judgment here there is, it would seem, a romantic, indeed utopian, predilection, a belief that with the destruction of the old capitalist, coercive society a new harmonious communist society—a social, altruistic, caring, fulfilling society—will come into existence; a belief that egoism, selfishness, divisions, conflicts of interests, oppression, struggle, and evil will all disappear in the communist society.

Although Marx is justifiably critical of most governments in his day because they were not democratic and were often oppressive, he did not fully appreciate the reform potentialities of nascent liberal democratic regimes that were beginning to emerge at the end of his life, and that became more powerful in the twentieth century. He also fails to see the adaptive capabilities of capitalism as an economic system, adaptive capability that would function in both the economic and political domains, permitting capitalism to survive. He had good reason to be suspicious of most regimes in his lifetime; but although he presses hard for key reforms in his day, he still does not see that in time liberal democratic regimes might, in their own self-interest, move even more significantly to remedy some of the worst problems of an unregulated capitalism and of oligarchic political rule. Needless to say, Marx would not have been satisfied with such reforms; he would not have been satisfied with changes short of communism. Was he asking too much to press for the complete overthrow of capitalism and its replacement by communism.

We turn, next, to our conclusion about Marx's communism as a creative breakthough in the tradition of prophetic politics.

CONCLUSION

In some respects Marx emerges as a powerful political theorist because—in the tradition of prophetic politics—he links ethical concerns, social scientific analysis, a call for bold action, and a vision of the future. His values engage us. They appeal to our own strong ethical sense of universal liberation and fulfillment.

Moreover, Marx's social scientific analysis of nineteenth-century conditions under bourgeois capitalism and early liberal democracy illuminates vital matters and raises serious questions about human fulfillment. Most important, Marx illuminates the plight of working people and offers a provocative economic explanation of their exploitation. He seeks to break through beyond the illusions that prevent people from understanding their alienation. He endeavors to uncover the forces and conditions of social change, the key power of economics in shaping our lives, the crucial role of classes and class conflict in human history. Marx's social scientific thought stresses the connection between values that are coming to be in history, the shaping economic and social forces of human life, and revolutionary action to bring a brave new communist world into existence.

Marx's theory of revolutionary action demonstrates for many the fruitful tie between theory and practice. Action to achieve the communist society is guided by a philosophy of history that seemingly ensures success in making the revolution, in consolidating the revolution, and in achieving the higher phase of communist society.

For some the power of this theory is not seriously affected by its crucial limitations and flaws—limitations and flaws affecting its values, its social science, its theory of action, and its vision of the future. However, any fair appraisal of Marx calls upon us to appreciate both his strengths and weaknesses.

Marx is partially in the tradition of a secular prophetic politics. In some respects he has deepened our understanding of such prophetic values as freedom, peace, humanity/community, and rich individual and social development—and thus of the good political life. Yet his failure to do justice to the value of constitutionalism and to other important prophetic values—such as love, compassion, repentance—suggests serious trouble ahead for a theory unable to appreciate that key values can be sustained only in a genuinely constitutional society, one acutely aware of the dangers of the abuse of power, one keenly suspicious of those who claim a monopoly on truth, a vigilant society in which deep caring about human rights unites people in common respect for human integrity. We must search beyond Marx (although incorporating some of Marx's ethical insights) to arrive at a deeper, fuller, and more satisfactory understanding of the good political life.

Marx's theory is closest to prophetic politics in Marx's theoretical commitments to freedom, in his indictment of freedom's violations, in his call for action to end those violations, and in his advocacy of a democratic and fulfilling communism. His theory moves away from a secular prophetic politics when it is unable to establish the link between communism and freedom, when Marx fails to spell out more clearly a defensible calculus of costs and benefits, when he neglects to articulate a democratic communist constitution that would limit the abuse of power and preserve an open society.[29]

Marx is also partially in the prophetic tradition in his commitment to fearless criticism of the existing order in light of his ethical values. His social scientific criticism is clearly motivated, I believe, by his values and is dedicated to demonstrating both the gap between ethical aspirations and existential reality *and* the reasons for this gap. He is partly successful in highlighting the ways in which economic systems, especially capitalism, can alienate and enslave, divide and weaken, degrade and narrow, retard and stunt human beings in the workplace, in political life, and in society. He makes a valuable, if sometimes overemphasized, contribution to our empirical understanding of the role of classes and class conflict in human society. He certainly calls attention to the difficulties—contradictions—of capitalism as an economic system. He highlights the enormous influence of economic forces in history in shaping politics, law, education, and other aspects of society.

Yet Marx's social science—committed to fearless criticism—is badly flawed in key respects. His empirical analysis of the operation of capitalism is simply not correct in a number of instances. The fated self-destruction of capitalism as a result of contradictions and severe crisis, and as a result of the growing power of the proletariat in advanced capitalistic countries, has not occurred. In addition, Marx's social scientific logic does not persuade us that the destruction of capitalism is inevitable. The growing misery of workers as a result of the irrepressible urge of capitalists to enhance profits at the expense of workers is not to be found, at least not in the Western world. Capitalism, despite severe economic crises, and despite the continued exploitation and alienation of workers, has demonstrated a resilience and staying power, and a willingness to live with reforms (some radical, some quite modest), some of which have paradoxically reduced its power but probably enhanced its life. Liberal democracies have demonstrated that they are not simply and solely puppets of the dominant capitalist ruling class. They have modestly, if not adequately, responded to popular, and worker, cries for key economic and social reforms. Similarly, democratic socialist governments have been able, peacefully, to achieve governmental power and to enact modest socialist programs. Marx especially misses the importance and value of the democratic constitution as the safest vehicle for advancing the interests of workers and others oppressed in or left out of the economic, political, and social system.

Marx, moreover, misses a great deal in his analysis. Because of his concentration on the proletariat and capitalism, he misses the oppression of other groups and other oppressive forces. He misses—or, at least, does not adequately appreciate—racism, anti-Semitism, sexism, and the oppressive rule and role of whites, anti-Semites, and patriarchy. He misses the way in which nationalism (as an idolatrous secular religion) functions as a more powerful force than class in obtaining the allegiance of all peoples, including workers. He does not adequately stress the ways in which minorities within nations are often oppressed by dominant majorities, regardless of class. And he does not fully appreciate how conflicts between nations can destroy the brotherhood and sisterhood of workers and inflict dreadful damage on human freedom, peace, humanity/community, and rich human developments. Marx also fails to see other important causes of malaise—whether ecological imbalance or forms of human alienation unrelated to the workers' control over their primary work activity.

Marx's social science, in brief, leaves a great deal to be desired. We have to search more fully and deeply (again incorporating some parts of Marx's social science) for a social science that more universally explores the gap between prophetic values and existential reality.

It is difficult to reach the judgment that Marx's theory of revolutionary action is a wise theory. His extravagant early judgment (which I do not believe he ever abandons)—that communism is a solution to the riddle of history—cannot be easily sustained. It is by no means clear that a majority of the population in advanced capitalist countries, even a majority of workers in such countries, are or would become communists and endorse the desirability or wisdom of a communist revolution. Marx's theory of revolutionary action is seriously flawed by a failure to address the difficult but necessary problem of the calculus of costs. Marx does not satisfactorily address the question of how the costs of loss of life and freedom in making the revolution, the costs of despotic actions during the period of the dictatorship of the proletariat, or the continuing costs for workers and noncommunists under mature communism will be balanced by the presumed benefits of mature communism. Marx does not articulate a satisfactory theory of the just revolution, certainly not of the prophetically just revolution. And he fails to commit himself—clearly, explicitly, fully, generously—to a democratic constitution for his communist society. The absence of a democratic and constitutional framework for his theory of revolutionary and communist action puts his theory at grave risk. If we have doubts about key aspects of Marx's ethical and social scientific breakthroughs, we have even greater doubts about Marx's theory of revolutionary action.

Marx's short-range and long-range vision of the future of economics, politics, society, and culture in his mature communist community—its principles, practices, problems—is defective because he does not clearly establish the logical or empirical link between his inspiring goals of freedom, peace, humanity, community, and development—clearly in the prophetic tradition—and the actual fulfillment of those goals in a communist world by fallible humans. The vagueness of Marx's picture of the future mature communist community, the absence of a more fully developed democratic and constitutional framework within which communism can go forward, his failure to analyze and criticize the probability of a classless, conflictless, harmonious society—these considerations force us to conclude that Marx himself, despite his own adverse criticism of utopian socialists, is himself a utopian socialist. In some key respects Marx is not as creative or imaginative as some of the socialists he excoriates. Continuing prophetic scrutiny of the achievement of the necessary and sufficient conditions of freedom and development is apparently not required in Marx's communist society, or—if required—could be left to an intelligent and vigilant people. We pay dearly for Marx's noble faith in the people unsupported by a prophetically interpreted democratic constitution. Similarly, the need to project futuristic scenarios in order to identify future problems of that communist society is a task badly neglected by Marx. Marx's failure here leaves a dangerous vacuum that can be filled by those who are, unlike Marx, totalitarian. Marx's neglect also means that he would not do justice to other important problems—whether racism, anti-Semitism, sexism, war, nationalism, ecological malaise—and that he would not develop a more comprehensive theory of political health. Such a comprehensive and integrating political theory awaits a new generation of scholars able to build on Marx's work as a powerful but flawed prophet, scholars able to profit from both Marx's notable strengths and his serious weaknesses.[30]

Our examination of spurious and flawed breakthroughs—in Calhoun and Marx—helps us to better understand the achievements of both past genuine breakthroughs with Williams and Madison, trials of present breakthroughs, and the difficulties of future breakthroughs. To a present breakthrough in progress—European Union—we turn next in Chapter 6.

NOTES

1. See *Economic and Philosophical Manuscripts of 1844* in Robert C. Tucker, ed., *The Marx-Engels Reader*, 2nd ed. (New York: W. W. Norton, 1978), p. 85.

2. See Neal Riemer, *Karl Marx and Prophetic Politics* (New York: Praeger, 1987), Ch. 2, "Marx's Guiding Values and the Superior Universal Order," pp. 25–42. Throughout my treatment of Marx I draw generously from my book on Marx.

3. See *Contribution to the Critique of Hegel's Philosophy of Right: Introduction* (1844), in Tucker, *The Marx-Engels Reader*, p. 64.

4. *Capital*, Vol. III, in Tucker, p. 441.

5. *Critique of the Gotha Program* (written in 1875, published in 1891), in Tucker, p. 531.

6. *The German Ideology*: Part I, in Tucker, pp. 490–491.

7. I use social science to characterize Marx's scientific approach. Marx's science is, of course, more than narrowly empirical. It involves a broad theory of historical and social change. It also involves concepts that are philosophical in character.

8. See *Theses on Feuerbach* (1845), in Tucker, p. 145. Thesis 11 reads as follows: "The philosophers have only *interpreted* the world, in various ways; the point, however, is to change it."

9. *A Contribution to the Critique of Political Economy*, Preface, in Tucker, p. 4.

10. *Capital*, Vol. I, in Tucker, pp. 430–431; and see also pp. 371, 373–374, and 409–411.

11. *Capital*, Vol. I, in Tucker, p. 365.

12. *Critique of the Gotha Program*, in Tucker, p. 535.

13. *Capital*, Vol. I, in Tucker, p. 438.

14. Riemer, *Karl Marx and Prophetic Politics*, p. 64.

15. Only in his brilliant, if sometimes unpersuasive and sometimes inconsistent, analysis of the advent and rule of Louis Bonaparte in France, does Marx deviate from his general conviction that the bourgeoisie is fully in control of the state. See *The Eighteenth Brumaire of Louis Bonaparte* (1842), in Tucker (orig. 1972 edition), p. 474, where Marx argues that the bourgeois "to save its purse" "must abandon the crown"; that in the interest of saving "property, family, religion" the bourgeoisie will relinquish political power.

16. Riemer, *Karl Marx and Prophetic Politics*, p. 83.

17. Ibid., pp. 85–97.

18. Quoted in Richard N. Hunt, *The Political Ideas of Marx and Engels*, Vol. II, *Classical Marxism* (Pittsburgh, Pa.: University of Pittsburgh Press, 1984), p. 330.

19. Riemer, *Karl Marx and Prophetic Politics*, p. 94.

20. Ibid., p. 95.

21. From Marx's preface to the Russian edition of *The Communist Manifesto*, quoted in David McLellan, ed., *Karl Marx: Selected Writings* (Oxford: Oxford University Press, 1977), p. 584.

22. *Critique of the Gotha Program*, in Tucker, p. 538.

23. See Riemer, *Karl Marx and Prophetic Politics*, pp. 98–99. In this interpretation I follow Richard N. Hunt, *The Political Ideas of Marx and Engels, Vol. I: Marxism and Totalitarian Democracy, 1818–1850* (Pittsburgh, Pa.: University of Pittsburgh Press, 1974), especially pp. 293, 215, 296–297, 319, 334, and 341.

24. Hunt, *The Political Ideas of Marx and Engels*, Vol. II, p. 246.

25. The Communist Manifesto, in Tucker, p. 491.

26. *Critique of Gotha Program*, in Tucker, p. 531.

27. Riemer, *Karl Marx and Prophetic Politics*, p. 71.

28. Ibid., pp. 71–72.

29. Ibid., pp. 118–120. For a fuller critique of the tough questions about the future of mature communism that Marx failed to address, see, ibid., pp. 133–143.

30. Ibid., pp. 147–151.

CHAPTER 6

European Union: Beyond War, Economic Malaise, and Political Turmoil via Transnational Integration

INTRODUCTION

In this chapter we turn from Marx's Promethean, utopian effort to achieve universal human emancipation to the ambitious, yet more modest, attempt by West European countries to achieve European Union. The Union they seek is not a U.S. federal-style Union designed to reconcile liberty and large size; but it is an effort to reconcile peace, economic prosperity, democracy *and* the historic sovereign powers of a large number of West European states. The Union they seek has a more ambitious agenda than Roger Williams' attempt to achieve religious liberty and peace, respect for religious pluralism, and democratic governance; but it does reflect the need to reconcile political pluralism (in the historic military and economic competition of sovereign states) *and* some supranational integrating features. Moreover, the problem of protection of vital state interests, via voting procedures (including at times a veto) to protect a minority of states—or a single state—against a majority, continues to bedevil the politics of European Union, and to remind us of Calhoun's dilemma. As we examine progress toward European Union, it will be helpful to keep in mind insights gained from our examination in previous chapters of the creative and spurious creative breakthroughs we have examined. As we do so, however, we must leave room for the sometimes unique, creative exercise that is characteristic of genuine breakthroughs in politics.

How can West European nations move beyond war and destructive political and economic rivalry toward permanent peace, enduring prosperity, and solid constitutional democracy? This is the difficult problem to be explored in this chapter. I will be focusing primarily on West European nations and their post–World War II struggle to achieve an integrated community. My central concern will be the European Community, which is now known as the European Union.[1]

The problem facing Europeans took on a momentous urgency after two catastrophic world wars. World War II had followed a devastating World War I that severely weakened Europe and opened up the door to communism in Russia and Fascism in Italy and Germany. World War II also followed the worldwide Great Depression that began in 1928. That great economic catastrophe was fed by protectionist policies, further weakened European nations, and facilitated the advent of Nazism in Germany.

The consequences of war, economic malaise, and political authoritarianism in the twentieth century in Europe have been frightful. Considering war alone we see revealed the dreadful human costs of a seriously flawed nation-state system, a foolish militarism, and fanatical authoritarianism. The figures make the mind reel!

The total number of people who were killed or died in World War I is 9,972,000. This includes 8,418,000 soldiers who were killed or died of wounds and 1,374,000 civilians who were killed or died from injuries.[2] Key West European nations were devastated. In Germany 1,774,000 soldiers were killed or died of wounds, 225,000 German civilians were killed or died from injuries, for a German grand total of 1,999,000. In France comparable figures were 1,363,000 and 150,000, for a French grand total of 1,513,000. The British lost 908,000 soldiers and 9,000 civilians, a total of 917,000. Italian losses totaled 760,000—460,000 soliders, 300,000 civilians. And, of course, a major East European power, Russia, also suffered grievous losses, as did soldiers of the Austro-Hungarian Empire in Central Europe. Thus, 1,700,000 Russian soldiers alone were killed or died of wounds, and soldiers from Austria-Hungry suffered 1,200,000 casualties.[3]

Moreover, the deaths in World War II are even more horrendous than those in World War I. Excluding soldier and civilian deaths from non-European countries (Australia, Canada, China, India, Japan, the United States), total European deaths amounted to 26,452,000. This included, for example, 557,000 British soldiers and 61,000 British civilians; 202,000 French soldiers and 108,000 French civilians; 3,250,000 German soldiers and 500,000 German civilians; 149,000 Italian soldiers and 783,000 Italian civilians; 64,000 Polish soliders and 2,000,000 Polish civilians; 7,500,000 Soviet soldiers and 7,500,000 Soviet civilians; 410,000 Yugoslavian soldiers and 1,275,000 Yugoslavian civilians.[4]

These casualties of European wars are twentieth-century figures only. They do not take into account European wars in earlier centuries, wars that also brought death, destruction, and misery to millions of people.

To the grim statistics on soldier and civilian deaths in war in Europe must be added information about other painful consequences attributable to war: (1) nonlethal wartime injuries; (2) suffering from starvation or malnutrition; (3) the dreadful ravages of disease; (4) horrible violations of liberty and justice and humane governance; (5) the agonizing plight of refugees; (6) the painful misdirection of resources—human labor and material—to the end of destruction rather than construction; (7) the anguish of widows, orphans, and others caused by the loss of loved ones; (8) ecological damage caused by war; and, of course, (9) the staggering total monetary cost of war, estimated at some $1,348,000,000,000 for all of World War II, much of which cost was borne by Europeans.

The violations of life and liberty in Europe during World War II are mind-boggling. The Holocaust—the destruction of 6 million Jews in Europe by the Nazis—could not have been accomplished without World War II. The creation of millions of "slave laborers"—people forced to work for the Nazi war machine—would not have been possible in peacetime.

Disturbingly, after World War II, the "realistic"[5] conventional wisdom continued to affirm that war will always be with us; that war among the great powers is inevitable. The "realistic" conventional wisdom affirmed that the best that sovereign nation-states can achieve in international relations is a tolerable balance of power. The "realistic" conventional wisdom affirmed that political, ideological, geographical, and economic rivalry leads invariably to military clashes.

More pointedly, according to the "realistic" conventional wisdom, traditional nationalism—with its worship of the sovereign nation-state—is too powerful to allow any significant movement toward European Union to occur. Nations will simply not give up their sovereignty. A transnational or supranational authority is impossible. Economic rivalry and economic autarchy (self-sufficiency) cannot be avoided.

The "realistic" conventional wisdom—reflecting the undeniable history of war between nations; of political rivalries; of economic competition; of ideological differences; of the persistence of jealous, sovereign nation-states; of national states composed of people who speak different languages, use different currencies, adhere to different cultural standards—thus affirms that the present and future will reproduce the past. It is simply impossible, in Western Europe, to avoid nationalistic rivalry, economic conflict, and war. More pessimistic purveyors of the conventional wisdom also declare that devastating economic depressions, ineffective democratic governments, and authoritarian regimes are also inevitable.

This chapter focuses on those in Western Europe who denied the "realistic" conventional wisdom and not only sought, but achieved, a creative breakthrough in relations between West European states. This break-through—to what is now called European Union—is, however, still in process. The achievement of complete economic integration in Western Europe has not yet occurred. Moreover, complete political union in Western Europe remains an illusive goal. And the fuller economic and political integration of *all* of Europe is an even more distant goal. Nonetheless—despite the fact that neither the fuller deepening of West European Union nor the widening of European integration (to include, for example, Central and Eastern Europe) has yet happened—few will deny that a highly significant breakthrough did occur in Western Europe in the post-World War II years. It is clear, then, that a breakthrough in Western Europe occurred, and is still occurring.

The breakthrough occurred in stages: with initial progress in the 1950s and mid-1960s; with stagnation (with some exceptions) in the period of the mid-1960s through the 1980s; and with regeneration in the late 1980s and into the 1990s. Thus the breakthrough has been characterized by advance and relapse and advance, and by the complicated pulls and pushes of national and community politics. Often one is led to believe that the miracle of European Union does not lie in its initial founding in the 1950s, but that it has survived the difficulties, internal and external, of nearly five decades since then.

EUROPEAN INTEGRATION AND UNION: A SIGNIFICANT BREAKTHROUGH STILL IN PROCESS

The major breakthrough occurred first with the Coal and Steel Community (Schuman Plan, May 9, 1950; Treaty of Paris, April 18, 1951). This momentous breakthrough was then followed by another: the European Common Market (Treaty of Rome, March 25, 1957, which came into effect January 1, 1958). Signficant steps to consolidate the breakthroughs achieved by these treaties were then taken, first, by the Single European Act (December 1985, coming into effect in July 1987); and then by the Maastricht Treaty on European Union (agreed to December 1991, signed February 1992).

The central objective in these efforts was to so integrate the economies of key participants—particularly France and Germany—as to make war impossible, to enhance trade and economic prosperity, and to advance their political (that is, their democratic and constitutional) health. The Paris Treaty started with the integration of coal and steel. The Rome Treaty aimed at a customs union. The Single European Act sought to advance the achievement of a single market. Maastricht aimed at a monetary and economic union and at a common foreign and security policy.

A key initiative for the movement toward the closer integration of Europe came from Jean Monnet, who had urged French Foreign Minister Robert Schuman to act. Schuman had responded as follows:

... the French Government proposes to take action immediately on one limited but decisive point ... to place Franco-German production of coal and steel under a common High Authority, within the framework of an organisation open to the participation of the other countries of Europe.... The solidarity of production thus established will make it plain that any war between France and Germany becomes not merely unthinkable, but materially impossible. . . . [T]his proposal will build the first concrete foundation of a European federation which is indispensable to the preservation of peace.[6]

The ideas of Monnet and Schuman—and the motivation behind the Coal and Steel Community—were articulated in the preface to the Paris Treaty (1951) that established the Coal and Steel Community. The Treaty thus resolved to substitute for dangerous age-old rivalries the merging of their essential coal and steel interests; "to create, by establishing [such] an economic community, the basis for a broader and deeper community among peoples long divided by bloody conflicts; and [thus] to lay the foundation for institutions which will give direction to a destiny henceforward shared." The Paris Treaty affirmed that "world peace" could only be "safeguarded" by such "creative efforts." The Paris Treaty insisted "that Europe can be built only through practical achievements which will . . . create real solidarity" via "common bases for economic development."[7]

The European Coal and Steel Community (ECSC) originally included six countries: the Federal Republic of Germany, France, Italy, Belgium, Netherlands, Luxembourg.

After failing to establish a European Defense Community in 1954, which also crippled the immediate possibility of a treaty for a European Political Community, advocates of fuller economic integration nevertheless pressed on, benefiting from the leadership of Paul-Henri Spaak of Belgium. The Treaty of Rome (1957) established the European Economic Community. The heart of the Rome Treaty was the effort to achieve a common internal market—a customs union—among France, Germany, Italy, Belgium, the Netherlands, and Luxembourg (and other nations that would join the Community) by eliminating barriers to intra-European trade. The Rome Treaty also looked forward to a common external tariff and "the progressive abolition of restrictions on international trade." The Rome Treaty emphasized, again, the vital importance "of an ever closer union among the peoples of Europe," and stressed the objective of constantly improving "the living and working conditions of their peoples." The Rome Treaty stressed the importance of "concerted action in order to guarantee steady expansion, balanced trade and fair competition." The Treaty explicitly recognized the need to reduce "the differences existing between the various regions and the backwardness of the less favoured regions." The Treaty emphatically underscored the linkage between the pooling of resources and the preservation and strengthening of peace and liberty.[8]

The European Community started with the ECSC six. Subsequently, and after hesitations and temporary defeats, they were joined by nine others: the United Kingdom, Ireland, Denmark (1973); Greece (1981); Spain, Portugal (1986); Sweden, Austria, and Finland (1995).

Steps toward European Union have not been easy, effortless, or swift. But movement toward a common internal market did move along. The first steps to bring the national customs tariffs of the original six together did not occur until January 1, 1961. It was not until July 1, 1968, that the Customs Union came into effect, along with the total elimination of internal tariffs among the six and the establishment of a common customs tariff.

Enlargement occurred slowly. British entry into the Common Market was held up for years, first by British opposition and hesitations, and then by French vetoes by Charles de Gaulle.

Movement on a common agricultural policy took time, and—although successful in one respect in enhancing the prosperity of most farmers—created budgetary and other problems when in effect.

Efforts to establish a European Monetary System and greater political cooperation have been slow, difficult, and incomplete. Rhetorical pronouncements in favor of completion of European Union have been easier than concrete steps toward fuller union.

Nonetheless, Western Europe has continued to try to achieve closer integration and a version of European Union. Thus, in 1985 the Single European Act was signed, and came into effect in 1987, with its provisions to come into full force on January 1, 1993. This act was designed to speed up decision-making on the achievement of the internal market by eliminating 300 nontariff barriers—physical, technical, and fiscal—to the internal market.

Similarly, at Maastricht the nations of the European Community agreed to a Treaty on European Union in December 1991 and signed it in February 1992. This Treaty finally called for an economic and monetary union (EMU) that would "go far to complete the economic competences [powers] that a federal Union requires."[9] Maastricht also sought to move toward greater political union by opting for a common foreign and security policy and greater cooperation on "justice and home affairs." By giving increased power to the European Parliament, Maastricht also sought to enhance the democratic character of the European Community, and to respond to criticism that the institutions of the Community were too elitist. Other institutional reforms in the Maastricht Treaty included enhancing majority decisions, widening the scope of the Court of Justice, and establishing a common citizenship.[10] The Maastricht Treaty thus endeavored to move more forcefully toward economic and monetary union, a common foreign and security policy, and cooperation on justice and home affairs.

Even in 1996 it still is not clear whether all of the ambitious goals of the Maastricht Treaty will be fulfilled. The road to more complete (a deeper)

European Union will still be long and bumpy. A broader European Union remains an even more distant goal. It is doubtful that a federal European Union on the U.S. model will ever appear. Nonetheless, a European Community has evolved. Its exact character is unique. It may perhaps best be characterized as a neofunctional, neofederal union.[11] It is certainly not a sovereign state. Yet it is more than an old-fashioned intergovernmental organization. It is characterized by certain supranational features; yet it is not identical to any current federal or confederal political community. Whether, and how, it will evolve into a very loose federal or confederal political community still remains to be seen.

In this newly created European Union it would be foolhardy to affirm that its constituent sovereign states have disappeared, or that national self-interest played no part in facilitating the significant, if still modest, achievements of the European Community, and that complete European Union is around the corner. Nevertheless, it would also be a serious mistake to lose sight of the most significant breakthrough that has taken place in Western Europe.

Four major propositions are undeniable:

1. War between Germany and France, or between other nations in Western Europe in the European Union, is now clearly impossible.

2. Despite difficult economic times through which the Community has passed or will pass, it is the case that the economic strength of Community members has been significantly enhanced, and that the members of the Community are now better positioned economically to compete and prosper in Europe and in the larger world.

3. Constitutional democracy has been significantly strengthened in all members of the Community.

4. The European Union is generally better positioned to aid the cause of peace, economic advance, and constitutional democracy in other parts of Europe, and in other parts of the world.[12]

Let me now turn to reemphasize that the breakthrough has been ethical, empirical, and prudential. These aspects of the breakthrough are, of course, closely related, and sometimes overlap. If I separate them out for analysis, it is because I want to emphasize that a breakthrough occurs on three fronts. Initially, a creative breakthrough embodies an ethical vision (of what ought to be) that goes beyond the status quo and the conventional wisdom. Second, it is based on a new or fresh grasp of empirical realities—past, present, or future (a perceptive grasp of what has been, is now, or will be). Third, a creative breakthrough is characterized by bold but wise judgments (of what can be done) that facilitate sensible advance toward that bold ethical vision in light of realities that have not been fully perceived or adequately appreciated.

The Ethical Vision

European Union is inspired by an ethical vision of a peaceful, prosperous, democratic united Western Europe. This ethical vision rejects the conventional wisdom of inevitable and harmful nationalistic rivalry and divisions, balance of power policies, catastrophic war between European nations, periodic devastating economic depressions, selfish national economic self-sufficency (autarchy). This ethical vision also rejects either democratic weakness or political authoritarianism. Particularly important as part of this ethical vision is the recognition of the need to endorse some supranational features and to reject the proposition that national sovereignty can never be divided.

Jean Monnet, a key founding father of European Union, was one of those who articulated this vision and attempted to move toward its fulfillment in Western Europe. An ardent proponent of the need for allied unity in World War I and World War II, he early perceived that Europeans must "choose unity or gradual decline."[13] His wartime experiences underscored for him the importance of economic union—in peace as well as in war.[14] He candidly confessed that at the time of his post–World War I work with the League of Nations (as deputy to the League's secretary-general) he did not recognize the pooling of sovereignty as a way to solve international problems.[15] It was, it seems clear, the crisis of World War II and the travail of West European nations after that war that led him to see the necessity of radical change.[16] His lifelong concern with uniting people and nations in order to solve troublesome problems that divide them led him to propound the idea of a Coal and Steel Community—the idea of joint sovereignty over part of their joint resources[17]—as the initial way to integrate key aspects of the economies of historic rivals—France and Germany—so as to avert war. This would be a concrete step on the road to a more complete economic union, which would further diminish the fear of nationalistic rivalry, sovereign state jealousies, armaments, protectionism, and war. It would ensure not only peace, but also prosperity and democracy. It would be the "practical" and "ambitious" "start" that would "tackle" the evils of national sovereignty "boldly," if on a "narrower front."[18] Coal and steel, Monnet clearly recognized, were the keys to economic power and the raw materials for forging weapons of war. To pool these essential resources across frontiers would reduce their malign influence and transform them into a guarantee of peace."[19]

Hence, Monnet sought to get the French government to act. He wanted the French government to propose placing *"the whole of Franco-German coal and steel production under an international Authority open to the participation of the other countries of Europe."*[20] Monnet wisely recognized that such a proposal has a vital political objective: "to make a breach in the ramparts of national sovereignty which will be narrow enough to secure consent, but deep enough to open the way towards the unity that is essential to peace."[21]

Monnet and his colleagues clearly envisaged the Coal and Steel Community as laying the foundation of a European Federation and permanent peace: *"By the pooling of basic production and the establishment of a new High Authority whose decisions will be binding on France, Germany, and the countries that join them, this proposal will lay the first concrete foundations of the European Federation which is indispensable to the maintenance of peace."*[22]

As we have noted earlier, French Foreign Minister Robert Schuman shared the vision of Monnet and Monnet's colleagues, and succeeded in getting the French government's support for the project.

West German Chancellor Konrad Adenauer also shared the Monnet/Schuman vision. Strikingly, both French and German national interests would be served by the Coal and Steel Community. French fears of a future militant and aggressive Germany would be stilled; West Germany would gain political recognition and security.

Adenauer wrote in his *Memoirs* that the aim of the Schuman plan was not economic but highly political. France was still fearful that when Germany recovered it would attack France. Germany, on the other hand, sought greater security. Rearmament, Adenauer recognized, depended upon increasing coal, iron, and steel production. The Schuman plan would enable both countries to detect the first sights of any such rearmament, and this would ease France's fears.[23]

This particular bold ethical vision of a united Europe ensuring peace, prosperity, and democracy was an enduring vision with Monnet, and one shared by Schuman, Adenauer, Alcide De Gasperi, Spaak, and other (but not all) West European leaders. Monnet emphasized, as did Schuman, the revolutionary, unique character of the new Coal and Steel Community.

In responding to Harold Macmillan, Monnet wrote that the Schuman proposals were revolutionary. Monnet insisted that cooperation between nations, although essential, was not enough. Monnet stated that Europeans must seek a fusion of their interests, and not simply another diplomatic effort to maintain a balance of those interests.

Monnet held that the Schuman proposals provided an opportunity to build a new Europe through "the concrete achievements of a supranational regime within a limited but controlling area of economic effort." Monnet insisted that the indispensable first principle of these proposals is the "abnegation of sovereignty in a limited but decisive field." Such action, he maintained, was crucial to the solution of Western Europe's grave problems.[24]

Schuman agreed on the uniqueness of the new Community: "never before have States undertaken or even envisaged the joint delegation of part of their national sovereignty to an independent supranational body."[25]

The conventional wisdom, it must be reemphasized, did not share the bold ethical vision of Monnet and Schuman and Adenauer.

The British Labour Party, for example, was worried about a supra-national authority, and was leery of jeopardizing its own socialist experiment, Britain's special relationship to its Commonwealth, or to the United States.[26] The British generally, including many Conservatives, were also leery of going beyond international cooperation, They, too, were particularly worried about jeopardizing their role as banker to the Sterling Area, about jeopardizing Commonwealth links, and their special relationship with the United States.

On the continent, de Gaulle and his followers in France were insistent on maintaining French national sovereignty. De Gaulle could only endorse a Europe of the States. Michel Debré's opposition to the ECSC dredged up historical fears of Germany: "You must realize that nation's lust for power, its lack of respect for freedom, its political instability and, I would add, its total failure to learn the lessons of the past."[27]

Debré did not appreciate that Adenauer, and other German leaders, might have learned some lessons from the past. At the inaugural meeting of the Council of Europe in 1952, Adenauer emphasized that the Council stood at the crossroads of two kinds of sovereignty, national and supranational. He held that although the Council must protect the national interests of its member states, it must not make such protection its paramount task. Rather, its key task was the promotion of the interests of the European Community. Hence, Adenauer argued, the Council must leave the Community's supranational institution—the High Authority—a great deal of freedom to develop.[28]

Monnet's vision—as we have indicated—saw the Coal and Steel Community as a first step on the way to a more completely unified Europe. When on November 9, 1954, he resigned as president of the High Authority of the ECSC in order to head up the Action Committee for the United States of Europe, he emphasized this point. He saw the Coal and Steel Community culminating in a United States of Europe. Monnet underscored the importance of the broader economic base that a larger European community would make possible. The union of European peoples in the United States of Europe will help to raise Europe's standard of living and to preserve peace.[29]

Monnet endorsed the Treaty of Rome, which established a Common Market for the six, and looked forward to more complete economic, monetary, and political union. There is little doubt that his vision—and those who shared his vision—inspired the Single European Act and the Maastricht Treaty on European Union.

That vision may seem unrealistic and impossible to fulfill for many. It cannot, however, be denied that even if the vision of a completely united Europe remains unfulfilled, it has in fact contributed to a significant breakthrough to peace, prosperity, and democracy in Western Europe.

The New Empirical Understanding

Let us now examine more fully the empirical character of the break-through. What did Monnet and other proponents of European Community and Union discover about the political, economic, and social behavior of nations, peoples, and interests—past, present, and future? What empirical evidence of a resolution of a troubling problem can we identify in the movement for European Union?

First let me address the most troubling problem: war and peace. The empirical evidence of fifty years of peace in Western Europe is here incontestable, even though scholars will argue as to the exact causes of such peace. Certainly, the integration of coal and steel has played a part in overcoming tensions, fears, and troubles between France and Germany. And closer economic and political ties within the Community have served to dissipate traditional national rivalries that once made war easier. Now it is impossible to argue persuasively, empirically, that France, the United Kingdom, Germany, Italy—for example—will be involved in another major European war, or even in smaller wars on the European continent that plagued European powers in earlier centuries.

To highlight fifty years of peace in Western Europe is not to deny the role that fear of Soviet military aggression and the role that the North Atlantic Treaty Organization (NATO) have played in maintaining peace. But, clearly, West European economic strength and political stability—much of it attributable to the Paris and Rome Treaties—played an important part in ensuring peace in those fifty years.

Apropos economic and political strength: Economically and politically, the European Community has helped to rescue the nations of Western Europe from internal weaknesses and dangerous isolation and made them more effective in satisfying the economic and democratic needs of their citizens.[30] Economic prosperity and constitutional democracy have been signficantly enhanced. The economies of the Community's nations have been strengthened. Ailing industries and agriculture have been assisted.

As barriers to trade within the Community have come down, as a Customs Union came into play, trade within the European Community has increased significantly. So has trade beyond the Community. Per capita income of citizens in the European Community has increased. And even though recession and unemployment may plague the Community from time to time, there can be little doubt that nations in the Community are better positioned to deal with such economic woes than they have ever been in their respective histories. Although the more complete free movement of capital, people, goods, services still has to be achieved, enough progress has been made to sustain the argument that the Community may well become the most powerful economic power in the twenty-first century.

Lester Thurow writes:

> If it [Europe] makes the right moves, it can become the dominant economic
> power in the twenty-first century, regardless of what Japan and the United
> States do. . . . If Europe can truly integrate the EEC (337 million people)
> into one economy and gradually move to absorb the rest of Europe (more
> than 500 million people) into the House of Europe, it can put together an
> economy that no one else can match.[31]

The social achievements of the Community in helping to improve industrial and social standards, hours and conditions of work, and the equitable
treatment of women should also be noted. They point toward strengthening
the fabric of constitutional democracy.

Finally, we must take note of the role of the European Court of Justice in
enhancing the rule of law in the Community; and of the role the European
Parliament plays in enhancing democracy, modestly, in the Community.
However modest these legal and democratic breakthroughs are, they contribute to the fashioning of that complex economic, political, legal, and
social web that ties the nations and peoples of the Community together, and
thus advances peace, prosperity, and democracy.

The Wise Decisions

Prudentially, and with some minor exceptions, the decisions of Monnet,
Schuman, Adenauer, De Gasperi, Spaak, Jacques Delors, and others have
proved wise. In moving beyond traditional notions of national sovereignty—particularly the idea that sovereignty could never, ever be divided
within or abandoned by a nation-state—they have convincingly demonstrated that functional, economic agreements among nations that transcend
traditional notions of sovereignty could be achieved. The nation-state has
by no means been abolished; and national interests have played, and will
unquestionably continue to play, a major part in the European Union.

Although it is clear, as Alan S. Milward has argued, that the European
Community rescued the nation-state,[32] it is equally true that nations have
seen the wisdom of moving beyond traditionally selfish views of national
interest to a more enlightened view of national interest that affirms that
some surrender of sovereignty—via the Coal and Steel Community or, more
modestly, via the Common Market—may in fact protect the vital interests
of the nation-state better than a narrow view. To say this is not to contend
that nations gave up all battles to protect national interests. It is to say that
these nations recognized that they could best protect vital, and sometimes
not so vital, national interests by operating politically within the framework
of a European Community, with some supranational features. Some national decisions may not have been as generously prudent as those advocated by more idealistic proponents of European Union; but they do

demonstrate a capacity for prudent—if hard-headed—decisions that often carried political actors beyond timid, fruitless, unwise national decisions.

Some of the prudential judgments of leading figures in the movement toward European Community and Union can here be highlighted.

Initially, we can underscore—again—Monnet's prudential recognition that Europe must unite or decline, and his subsequent efforts to strike for union at the right time with the right idea, and with the right method. This recognition led Monnet and other architects of European Community and Union to affirm that some transcendence of traditional notions of sovereignty was required. Crisis would lead leaders and people to recognize the vital importance of necessary change. Such change must go beyond "mere cooperation."[33] National sovereignty would have to be relinquished on a narrow front by pooling and integrating the coal and steel resources of fearful neighbors—France and Germany; by placing these resources under a sovereign authority. This—to repeat—would be the "breach in the ramparts of national sovereignty which will be narrow enough to secure consent, but deep enough to open the way towards the unity that is essential to peace."[34] Thus the Schuman proposals provided the basis for building a new Europe through "the concrete achievement of a supranational regime within a limited but controlling area of economic effort."[35] Later, with the Common Market, the breakthrough to peace, prosperity, and democracy could be broadened.

Monnet's judgment about progress in the breakthrough needs to be underscored. Monnet was determined, yet patient. Again and again, he insisted that Europe will not be built all at once, or as a single whole; rather, Europe will be "built by concrete achievements which first create *de facto* solidarity."[36]

Although Monnet was a firm believer in European Union, and often talked about a confederated or federal Europe as a goal, he was wisely realistic, or prudent, at the end of his service in 1975 with the Action Committee for the United States of Europe about naming the final form of such a Europe or describing its political authority.

Monnet did not doubt that the process he had initiated would lead to a United States of Europe. However, he saw no point in imagining what precise political form such a union would take, whether—for example— European Union would be a federation or confederation. He recognized that the new Europe was without precedent.[37]

The prudential judgments of other key leaders also deserve attention. German Chancellor Konrad Adenauer, for example, quickly recognized the merit of Schuman's plan. His actions, which—we should not forget—were to benefit Germany politically and economically, even at a price, indicate that he and Germany had learned a valuable lesson. As Adenauer said to Monnet "I have waited twenty-five years for a move like this." Adenauer emphasized that Germany had no secret plan to dominate. Historical events since 1933 had taught Germany the folly of efforts to dominate Europe. "Germany knows that its fate is bound up with that of Western Europe as a whole."[38]

Similarly, one of Adenauer's successors as chancellor of West Germany, Ludwig Erhard, also indicated, in 1965, the prudential lesson that had been learned. Erhard stated that the German people had learned that a policy of hegemony is bound to fail because it arouses other European nations against it.[39]

CRITIQUE

In this critique I should like to focus on three key questions: (1) How sound, really, is the ethical vision that has guided European Union? (2) How accurate has been the Community leaders' grasp of empirical realities— past, present, and future? (3) How do we assess the prudential problems that have faced the proponents of European Union in the past, face them currently, and will face them in the future?

Initially, there can be little doubt that the ethical vision of peace, prosperity, and constitutional democracy is fundamentally sound. Similarly, the vision of a democratic and constitutional European Community, resting in part on at least some institutions with supranational characteristics, is equally attractive. That such a European Community can in time be deepened and enlarged is also appealing so long as it is clear that this can be done successfully without altering the ability of the Community to maintain peace, enhance prosperity, and strengthen constitutional democracy. The potential ability of the Community to enhance peace, prosperity, and constitutional democracy beyond Europe is also an aspect of the vision that must be applauded.

What is not clear, however, is the ultimate political character of European Union. Will it be a federal union on the model of the United States? (Highly unlikely.) Or a unique neofederal, neofunctional hybrid? (Perhaps.) Or what? The fuzziness of this ultimate vision—and differing answers on these questions by supporters of the Union—need not detract from the central accomplishments, however incomplete, achieved by European Union to date. Similarly, the historical difficulties in modestly accomplishing some of its aims should not detract from these accomplishments—accomplishments impossible, we argue, without a bold ethical vision. The dreadful consequences allegedly attendant upon the modest surrender of national sovereignty to some European Union institutions have simply not materialized.

Second, is the Community's grasp of empirical realities accurate? The recognition of the empirical linkage between (1) the integration of coal and steel and (2) peace has proved to be accurate. Of course, other factors—for example, NATO—also played a role in ensuring peace in Western Europe;

but it would be a serious mistake to underestimate the role that the Coal and Steel Community has played in advancing Franco-German reconciliation and making war between these historic enemies now impossible. Similarly, the Common Market has also assisted in linking the economic interests of West European nations in such a way that, again, war between or among them is now impossible.

It is now undeniable that the economic and political linkages of the European Community via the Coal and Steel Community and then the Common Market have also enhanced the prosperity and constitutional democracy of West European nations and peoples. Again, other factors (for example, U.S. economic, political, and military support) undoubtedly played a role in these developments. Yet the contribution of the Community to these ends is also clear. One careful student of European Union, Alan S. Milward, has argued that the Community actually functioned to rescue the nation-states of Western Europe: strengthening their economies, enabling them to deal with sick industries, supporting agriculture, providing for other helpful economic adjustments.[40] It is certainly the case that the Community saw a significant increase in trade among Community nations, a significant increase in their export trade beyond the Community, and a general increase in per capita income among citizens of the Community.

European Union has, moreover, emerged as a powerful actor in the economic world, able—for example—to negotiate as an entity in General Agreement on Tariffs and Trade (GATT) deliberations; and possessed of an economic potential that may enable it to become the dominant economic community in the world.

There are, of course, realistic observers of Europe who are less sanguine than the federalists about either the economic or political prospects for European Union. Paul Kennedy, for example, concludes his assessment of "Europe and the Future" as follows:

> In sum, the burden is upon European federalists to outline how they can create a thriving unified body which will assume a responsible world role *without* hiding behind walls, adopting selfish policies, and running against the trends toward globalization; how they can further EC's internal development at the same time as they seek to cope—and help poorer nations to cope—with global changes. Should it actually manage to reconcile these aims, Europe might find that the next century will be kinder to it than the present century has been. As things now stand, however, resolving such a cluster of major challenges seems unlikely—in which case, both Europe and the rest of the world will suffer the consequences.[41]

It is certainly true that a number of European Union objectives have not yet been fulfilled, objectives related to the deepening of European Union: an economic and monetary union (involving a common currency, a central European Union bank); a common foreign and security policy. Moreover, the European Parliament, although strengthened considerably by Maastricht, has not yet acquired really significant powers. Not all barriers to intra-Community trade have yet been eliminated. Majority voting in *all* decisions by the Community's High Commission has not yet been achieved. In brief, the European Union still has a long and difficult road ahead in the accomplishment of the vision of more complete union.

As the deepening of European Union has not been fully achieved, so problems of enlargement remain on the unfinished agenda. Although East Germany is now in the Union, along with such European Free Trade Association (EFTA) nations as Sweden, Finland, and Austria, questions remain about the inclusion of the nations of Central and Eastern Europe. Particularly important, and especially troubling, is the question of the future inclusion of Russia. Some critics fear that the European Union will get a severe case of economic and political indigestion if it tries to absorb Central and East European countries—let alone Russia as well—that have such a long way to go before they are credible pluralist democracies and healthy market economies.

These undeniable problems of deepening and enlarging highlight the incomplete character of the breakthrough, or—put differently—the undeniable fact that the breakthrough is still in process. Nonetheless, these problems should not detract from the important scientific judgment that a breakthrough did occur, even though the fuller consolidation of the breakthrough remains.

We do not have to share the reasonably optimistic assessment of John Pinder, an extremely well-informed neofederalist, that a "federal Union is not unlikely to become a reality in the 1990s," to believe further consolidation of the breakthrough to European Union will continue—slowly and carefully—in the years ahead.[42]

Third, how, indeed, do we assess the prudential problems that faced proponents of European Union in the past, face them now in the present, and will face them still in the future?

It seems reasonably clear that the functional, economic approach to integration, community, and union—embodying a conscious decision to go beyond mere international cooperation to secure some supranational institutions—was a wise decision. Although functional and economic, we must remember that this approach clearly rested on a wise political assessment of how to advance Franco-German reconciliation. Monnet was wise to opt for a Coal and Steel Community under a supranational authority—thus creating an institution that would indeed breach the "ramparts of national sovereignty" by being "narrow enough to secure consent, but deep enough to open the way towards the unity that is essential to peace."[43] In this fashion he avoided a massive direct assault on national sovereignty; his action was a prudent finesse of the still troubling problem of national sovereignty.

It does not take away from the wisdom of Monnet and Schuman, on the French side, and Adenauer, on the German side, to recognize that both French interests in security and economic benefits and German interests in political recognition and economic benefits would be served by a supranational Coal and Steel Community.

Similarly, it does not take away from the wisdom of the six who went on to form the Common Market to recognize that national self-interests were served in the process, and that the institutions of the Coal and Steel Community and the Common Market did indeed help to "rescue" the nation-states of Europe that had been so devastated by the World War II.

Questions remain about the wisdom of the British and other EFTA nations—those seeking a free trade association, but unwilling to join the European Economic Community, with its Common Market—in not promptly joining the European Union at the beginning. The British may have suffered from their refusal to join early on, and from France's several vetoes of British membership subsequently.

Serious questions remain, too, about the wisdom of a number of Community policies, particularly in regard to support of agriculture. Certainly, French and community farmers, for example, benefitted from Community policy; but Community agricultural subsidies were highly expensive, "ate" up a disproportionate share of the Community's budget, and led to higher food prices in France and throughout the Community. *The Economist*, a harsh critic of EC agricultural policy, but not alone in such criticism, described EC support for agriculture as "the single most idiotic system of economic mismanagement that the rich western countries have ever devised."[44] Only belatedly, and still incompletely, has the Community moved to reform agricultural policy.

Most pressing now are problems involving the deepening and enlarging of European Union. If the key to European peace is Franco-German reconciliation, and this has been achieved by the initial efforts of the Community, is there a need for deepening or enlarging? Or will the fuller guarantee of European peace—not only in Western Europe, but in Central and Eastern Europe—require both deepening and enlarging? Moreover, will Europe not be fully secure, for example, until Russia is brought within the framework of European Union?

At this stage past history and present leadership suggest that we can look forward both to prudent, modest deepening and prudent, modest enlarging in the interest of consolidating a most sigificant, if still not completed, creative breakthrough in politics.

CONCLUSION

The history of this breakthrough reveals, then, highly significant, if still limited, successes; some failures; a political process of bargaining and compromises; the continued influence of national and special interests; difficulties in dealing with tough problems; setbacks and relaunches; ambitious goals for union often difficult to fulfill.

Yet despite the limited successes, setbacks, and overly ambitious goals, no one can deny certain propositions:

1. That war between the nations of Western Europe is now impossible.
2. That the integrated economy of Western Europe has enhanced prosperity.
3. That constitutional democracy in the nations of Western Europe has been greatly strengthened.

These are momentous achievements and need to be constantly kept in mind as we assess the continuing difficulties of consolidating the breakthrough.

The nations of Western Europe have come to recognize that it is in their self-interest to consolidate the breakthrough, and modestly advance it in some areas—both by deepening and enlarging. The movement toward fuller economic and monetary union, and toward a common foreign and security policy, will undoubtedly take time, patience, and bargaining. So will the admission of Central and East European nations.

It is still too early to ascertain if the end of the Cold War, the breakup of the Soviet Union, and the demise of communism in Russia and the nations of Central and Eastern Europe will lead to a slowdown of the consolidation of the breakthrough.

It is reasonably certain that the United States, whose security concerns after World War II led it to strongly support the movement toward integration and Union, will still favor a strong and more united Europe.

Thus, this remains a highly significant breakthrough in history and politics. Although by no means complete and certainly not perfect, it does demonstrate the possibility of moving beyond narrow, selfish, unwise, fruitless conceptions of national interest toward a more enlightened national interest that concedes the value of some supranational institutions. This breakthrough also demonstrates the strengths of a modest supranational approach in a key region of the world, an approach that has enabled nations to work together to deal with common economic, and some political, problems, and that may in the future enable them to deal effectively with key security and larger political and security questions.

What is particularly heartening about this breakthrough to enduring peace, enhanced prosperity, and more secure constitutional democracy in Western Europe is that it highlights a creative process that rival countries in other parts of the world may employ to deal with their bitter and protracted national enmities.

Monnet, for example, wondered about the applicability of the European model to the Arab-Israeli conflict. He wrote that the hostility between Israel and the Arabs did not seem to him "more insuperable than that between

France and Germany had been for more than seventy years." He maintained that what had ended Franco-German enmity was neither warfare nor diplomacy, but a new approach to economic and political relationships. This new approach might one day persuade Arabs and Israelis that they had great economic and political tasks to perform together. Monnet argued that what Europeans had achieved against great odds could also be achieved elsewhere in the world.[45]

Of course, there are important differences between Franco-German rivalries and Israeli-Arab rivalries. Yet the prospect of integrating economies and thus creating economic incentives for peaceful relations, prosperous economies, and democratic development makes as good sense in the Middle East—or in other trouble spots around the world—as in Western Europe.

We turn, next, in Chapter 7, to examine a case not for a signficant breakthrough in process, but for a future breakthrough.

NOTES

1. In this chapter I will be using the words "Community" and "Union" interchangeably. For a comprehensive account that explores the history, institutions, policies, and programs of the Union, see Desmond Dinan, *Ever Closer Union? An Introduction to the European Community* (Boulder, Colo.: Lynne Rienner, 1994). For a rich, comprehensive, and revealing biography of a key architect of the Community, see François Duchene, *Jean Monnet: The First Statesman of Interdependence* (New York: W. W. Norton, 1994). For selections on sometimes competing visions of a united Europe, and diverse explanatory theories of actual developments, see Brent F. Nelsen and Alexander C. G. Stubb, ed., *The European Union: Readings on the Theory and Practice of European Integration* (Boulder, Colo.: Lynne Rienner, 1994). For some current perspectives, largely economic, on the prospects for the deepening and widening of integration after the Maastricht Treaty, see C. Randall Henning, Eduard Hockreiter, and Gary Clyde Hufbauer, eds., *Reviving the European Union* (Washington, D.C.: Institute for International Economics, 1994).

2. See David Wood, *Conflict in the Twentieth Century* (London: International Institute for Strategic Studies, 1968), p. 24. These figures exclude non-European belligerents and certain smaller European belligerents that played a minor role in the war. Reprinted in Neal Riemer and Douglas W. Simon, *The New World of Politics: An Introduction to Political Science*, 3rd ed. (San Diego: Collegiate Press, 1994), p. 332.

3. Estimates vary; the figures in Ruth Leger Sivard's *World Military and Social Expenditures 1985* (Washington, D.C.: World Priorities, 1985), p. 11, are higher than those in Wood. Thus Sivard's totals for France were 1,630,000; for Germany, 2,400,000; for the United Kingdom 1,016,000. Sivard also calculates that the Russians lost 2,950,000 soliders; and Austria-Hungry 2,300,000.

4. See the table in Riemer and Simon, *The New World of Politics*, p. 333. This table draws upon data in Wood, *Conflict in the Twentieth Century*, p. 26, and Quincy

Wright, *A Study of War* (Chicago: University of Chicago Press, 1942, 1965), p. 1542. Again Sivard's figures in *World Military and Social Expenditures* tend to be larger. She estimates, for example, total World War II casualties for Germany at 4,000,000; for the USSR at 20,950,000; and for France at 675,000.

5. I put "realistic" in quotes to emphasize a narrow-minded, unimaginative, selfish variety of political realism. My quarrel is not with broad-minded, imaginative, generous political realists.

6. Quoted in John Pinder, *European Community: The Building of a Union, Updated following the Maastricht Treaty* (Oxford: Oxford University Press, 1992), p. 1.

7. See Richard Vaughan, *Post-War Integration in Europe* (London: Edward Arnold, 1976), pp. 60–61.

8. Ibid. The Community also attempted to do for atomic energy what it had done for coal and steel by way of a European Atomic Energy Community. This effort, largely because of de Gaulle's insistence on a separate French atomic military force, has not been a success.

9. Pinder, *European Community*, p. 222.

10. Ibid., pp. 224–228.

11. Ibid., especially pp. 213–222.

12. The inability of the European Union to help bring peace to Bosnia in the early 1990s indicates, however, how difficult it can be to achieve peace in a complex and tangled part of Europe.

13. Jean Monnet, *Memoirs* (London: Collins, 1978), p. 75.

14. Ibid., pp. 78–79.

15. Ibid., p. 80.

16. Ibid., p. 109. Monnet wrote: "people only accept change when they are faced with necessity, and only recognize necessity when a crisis is upon them."

17. Ibid., p. 293.

18. Ibid., p. 274.

19. Ibid., p. 293.

20. Ibid., p. 295.

21. Ibid., p. 296.

22. Ibid., p. 298.

23. See ibid., p. 303.

24. Ibid., p. 315.

25. Ibid., p. 322.

26. See *European Unity: A Statement by the National Executive Committee of the British Labour Party* (London: Transport House, 1950), p. 6 and p. 4; cited in Monnet, *Memoirs*, pp. 314–315.

27. Debré, quoted in Monnet, *Memoirs*, p. 366.

28. See ibid., p. 381.

29. Ibid., pp. 339–400.

30. See Alan S. Milward, *The European Rescue of the Nation-State* (Berkeley: University of California Press, 1992).

31. See Lester Thurow, *Head to Head: The Coming Economic Battle Among Japan, Europe, and America* (New York: Warner, 1993), p. 252. Thurow's assessment is predicated on the solution of two major problems:

> This does not mean, however, that Europe will win. It just means that it can win if it can make exactly the right moves—no matter how well either the United States

or the Japanese play the economic game. The right moves involve two major problems. The economies of Western Europe really have to integrate, and that integration has to be quickly extended to Middle and Eastern Europe. The ex-communist economies of Middle and Eastern Europe have to become successful market economies. Neither is an easy task (p. 253).

Nonetheless, in the competition with the United States and Japan, Thurow maintains that Europe has the edge:

A case can be made for each of the three contenders. Momentum is on the side of the Japanese. It is difficult to bet against them. The Americans have flexibility and an unmatched ability to organize if directly challenged. They start out with more wealth and more power than anyone else. But strategic position is on the side of the Europeans. They are the most likely to have the honor of having the twenty-first century named for them. (p. 257).

For what some consider to be a more realistic assessment, see the balanced, thoughtful, sober account of Paul Kennedy in his *Preparing For The Twenty-First Century* (New York: Vintage, 1994), Chapter 12, "Europe and the Future," pp. 255–289.

32. Milward, *The European Rescue.*
33. See Monnet, *Memoirs*, pp. 271–272.
34. Ibid., p. 296.
35. Ibid., p. 135.
36. Ibid., p. 300.
37. Ibid., p. 523. Monnet added significantly: "The Community itself is founded on institutions, and they need strengthening; but the true political authority which the democracies of Europe will one day establish still has to be conceived and built." For the perspective of a later president of the European Commission, another Frenchman who greatly helped to move the Community toward fuller Union, see Jacques Delors, *Our Europe: The Community and National Development* (London: Verso, 1992). This book, first published in French in 1988, notes in the Preface to the English edition (p. vii) that the "European Community . . . is . . . passing through further stages on the way to integration: monetary union and a nascent political union," but that this "is not happening without some difficulty." Delors looks toward fuller integration, but cautions:

Europe is not a panacea. It would be foolish to wait for Christmas 1992, in order then to hang up one's stocking by the chimney in the hope of finding in it, at the beginning of 1993, the wrapped present of a Europe miraculously unified, with a prosperous economy, declining unemployment, and uncontested authority in the world (p. 152).

38. See Monnet, *Memoirs*, p. 310.
39. Quoted in ibid., p. 480. Other German and French leaders—Willy Brandt, Helmut Schmidt, Valery Giscard d'Estaing, Georges Pompidou, François Mitterrand—also played important roles in advancing the development of European Union.
40. Milward, *The European Rescue.*
41. Kennedy, *Preparing for the Twenty-First Century*, p. 289.
42. See Pinder, *European Community*, p. 222. For Pinder's presentation of the forces against and favoring federal union, see pp. 207–213.
43. Monnet, *Memoirs*, p. 296.
44. Quoted in Kennedy, *Preparing for the Twenty-First Century*, p. 280.
45. Monnet, *Memoirs*, pp. 510–511.

CHAPTER 7

Protection Against Genocide:
Toward a Global Human Rights Regime

INTRODUCTION

Can an effective Global Human Rights Regime be put into place to both prevent and stop genocide?[1] This is the terribly neglected, and excruciatingly difficult, problem that calls for a creative breakthrough in the future of international politics. In my affirmative answer, outlined in the thought experiment that follows, I shall argue that the creative breakthrough supporting such an affirmative answer calls for (1) strengthened institutions in a Global Human Rights Regime, guided by (2) a cogent theory of prudent prevention, (3) an operative theory of effective staged implementation, and (4) a wise theory of just humanitarian intercession.

The problem to be explored in this chapter is underscored by the tragic failure of the international community to develop an effective response to the evil of genocide in a post–World War II world traumatized by the Holocaust, a world that saw the passage of the UN convention against genocide, but a world still characterized by persistent, systemic, and egregious violations of human rights. In this chapter I will focus primarily on the imperative of developing a Global Human Rights Regime capable of dealing with genocide. My assumption is that if we can break through in dealing effectively with genocide, we can then consolidate that breakthrough in dealing with other flagrant violations of human rights.

The UN Convention on the Prevention and Punishment of the Crime of Genocide (adopted 1948; in force 1951) defines genocide as "any of the following acts committed with the intent to destroy, in whole or in part, a national, ethnic, racial, or religious group" by—for example—"Killing members of the group; . . . Causing either bodily or mental harm to members of the group; . . . Deliberately inflicting on the group conditions of life calculated to bring about its physical extermination in whole or in part."[2] Moreover, by interpretation or amendment, the antigenocide convention should also clearly protect political groups or economic classes from genocidal killing.[3]

I take for granted that the problem of genocide is a real problem. First, genocide persists. Despite the global revulsion against the Nazi extermination of 6 million Jews and other target groups in the Holocaust—a revulsion that contributed to the UN's Genocide Convention—genocide has continued in the post–World War II world. It continued in Cambodia (now Kampuchea), in East Pakistan (now Bangladesh), in Bosnia, in Iraq, in Rwanda, and in other areas of the world.[4]

Second, genocide remains a problem because of the continuing dominance of a short-sighted conventional wisdom, which too often "realistically" notes the seeming inevitability of egregious violations of human rights, the principle of noninterference in the internal affairs of nation-states, the absence of a national self-interest in humanitarian intercession, and the costs and dangers of intervention.

THE OUTLINE OF A CREATIVE BREAKTHROUGH
IN POLITICS ON GENOCIDE

The persistence of the problem of genocide prompts us to address four neglected needs and thus to outline the key features of a creative breakthrough required to attend to these needs. The fuller defense of this breakthrough also requires us to take serious note of, and to respond to, the adverse criticism of this possibility.

Strengthened Institutions

The first need is to strengthen the institutions of a Global Human Rights Regime. By a Global Human Rights Regime I understand all those actors—the United Nations, key nations, certain regional organizations, committed nongovernmental organizations—dedicated to the protection of human rights. These actors in a Global Human Rights Regime are committed to those norms, principles, institutions, policies, and practices concerned with the protection of human rights. The norms, for example, are articulated in the UN Declaration of Human Rights, in the UN Convention Against Genocide, and in other key UN documents. Here I will concentrate on institutions and the will to make them work. Key principles, policies, and practices will become clearer as I subsequently address theories of prudent prevention, staged implementation, and just humanitarian intercession.[5]

Currently, we have a number of diverse political actors who respect and try to abide by these norms—certain nation-states committed to the protection of human rights; certain regional actors (e.g., West European Union) equally respectful of human rights; most organs of the United Nations; a number of nongovernmental organizations (e.g., Amnesty International)—highly dedicated to human rights. Focusing only on the most promising of global human rights organizations—the United Nations—we find, however, that some of its key institutions are weak and often untested. Thus the UN Security Council is potentially strong but actually weak in its ability either to prevent or intercede against genocide. The UN Commission on Human Rights lacks stronger powers to be effective.[6] The recently created UN High Commissioner on Human Rights is untested. UN policies and practices are theoretically promising, but weak. Clearly, there is a need—especially in such a promising global organization—to develop stronger institutions, policies, and practices that could make prudent prevention, effective staged implementation, and just humanitarian intercession genuinely meaningful.

The breakthrough I envisage requires a UN Security Council with the will to act; and this, in turn, means a will to act on the part of the permanent members of the Security Council. If the Security Council has power but often lacks will, other key UN institutions lack both power and will. The creative breakthrough proposed here envisages a strengthening of the UN High Commissioner for Human Rights and the UN Commission on Human Rights. The UN High Commissioner, in particular, working closely with an empowered UN Commission on Human Rights, has a particularly important role to play in monitoring the status of human rights and in utilizing the power of publicity. Strategy here would be to increase the powers of these organs to investigate and publicize genocidal threats or acts. The UN High Commissioner for Human Rights, working with the UN Commission on Human Rights, would then be required to recommend to the UN Security Council more stringent actions to prevent or stop genocide.

Several new UN institutions also need to be put into place. For example, to make monitoring more effective, a UN Human Rights Monitor needs to be established for every region of the world in order to cover every country. A UN Human Rights Protection Force should be ready to move in the event that protection against genocide requires its use. Similarly, a UN Protectorate Agency could ensure temporary guardianship of a country after a genocidal regime is removed and until a human-rights-respecting regime is put into place in such a country.[7]

As key institutions of a Global Human Rights Regime are strengthened or developed, it will be helpful to address more clearly the broader operative political theory—the guiding principles, policies, and practices—that

will guide those institutions. Again, neglected needs highlight the imperative of appropriate responses.

Prudent Prevention

The second neglected need is to articulate a cogent theory of prudent
prevention of persistent, systemic, egregious violations of basic human
rights. In this chapter I focus on the prevention of genocide.[8] My argument
here is simple and compelling: It is far better to prevent genocide than to
have to cope with it after it has occurred.

A theory of prudent prevention rests on three cardinal principles. *First,
it will be important to encourage the development of mature constitutional democracies.* This is the best preventive principle because mature constitutional
democracies do not practice genocide against their own citizens. Thus with
the growth of mature constitutional democracies the danger of genocide
would decline. Moreover, a world of mature constitutional democracies
would contribute to a peaceful world because such democracies do not
wage war on each other; and war is unquestionably the condition that
makes possible the worst violations of human rights, including genocide.[9]

The world's existent mature constitutional democracies, regional organizations sensitive to the protection of human rights, the United Nations, and
committed human rights nongovernmental organizations (NGOs)—key
members of a Global Human Rights Regime—have an ethical and prudential reason to foster constitutional democracies in a host of ways. The
protection of human life is an ethical imperative. Prudentially, such actors
recognize that such protection makes a global climate safer for each nation's
vital interests, and safer too for the vital interests of regional organizations
and the United Nations. These vital interests are clearly served when
humanitarian intercession is not needed, and when the costs and dangers
of legitimate intercession are either eliminated or minimized.

The Global Human Rights Regime would have the important, yet deli-
cate, task of monitoring the evolution of constitutional democracies around
the globe, and of supporting national, regional, and UN policies to assist in
the maturation of constitutional democracies. The monitoring would look
to the existential status of nations around the globe, with particular emphasis on genocide. Monitoring would also look to the empirical investigation
of the necessary and sufficient conditions—social, cultural, political, economic—for the development and maturation of constitutional democracies. National, regional, and global policies to achieve these conditions
would then logically flow from such monitoring. At a minimum such
policies would stress the development of democratic civil societies, healthy
economic and social systems, and functioning democratic constitutions and
political institutions.

Second, it will be essential to develop the philosophy and practice of deterrence of genocide. Deterrence is the next best preventive medicine. Deterrence is based on the premise that mature constitutional democracies will not come into existence immediately, or all over the globe. Authoritarian and despotic regimes will continue to operate for many years ahead. Consequently, a strategy of prevention must also contemplate additional ways of stopping egregious human rights violations—specifically acts of genocide—before they occur. A policy of deterrence is one such way. A policy of deterrence would warn potential egregious violators of human rights that they will pay a high price for such violations. Deterrence would be premised on reliable monitoring to identify potentially egregious violations. Publicity, in turn, would serve to signal violators, as well as the global community, that the global human rights regime is aware of dangerous conditions, and that egregious violations are unacceptable. The high price of egregious violations would include an escalating series of actions—political, economic, judicial, military. The credible threat of such actions would be designed to forestall egregious violations.

Third, it will be crucial to develop the philosophy and practice of preemptive action in the event that deterrence doesn't work. Preemptive action is a fallback preventive strategy. All three principles of a theory of prudent prevention rest on the irrefutable proposition that it is unquestionably better to prevent genocide than to stop it once it has occurred.

Preemptive action could include political, economic, or judicial sanctions, with military intercession being the ultimate sanction. Military intercession would be based on overwhelmingly credible evidence of a clear and present danger of genocide. The fuller conditions under which deterrence and preemptive action can occur, and policies and practices of implementation, will be spelled out as I speak to the following needs and thus speak to the issue of effective staged implementation and the issue of just humanitarian intercession.

Effectively Staged Implementation

The third need is to work out an operative theory of wisely staged implementation. Such an operative theory of implementation would guide a Global Human Rights Regime, and particularly the relevant UN organs of that regime. Four key points in such a theory can be indentified.

First, it is vitally important to develop effective and respected machinery for monitoring/investigating/reporting. Ideally, the UN High Commissioner on Human Rights, working with an empowered UN Commission on Human Rights, would coordinate the diverse national, nongovernmental, and United Nations monitoring that is currently going on in the arena of human rights. Reliable information about potential or actual genocide is the primary basis for a sensible response.

Second, the power of publicity must be employed to deter potential egregious violations—where there is a clear and present danger of the eruption of genocide—and to solidify global support for just humanitarian intercession to stop genocide in progress. Such publicity would also be employed in cases of actual egregious violations—actual acts of genocide. Key UN organs (the UN High Commissioner on Human Rights, the UN Commission on Human Rights, the UN Security Council), effective regional organizations, key nations, and NGOs would function to publicize egregious violations.

Third, effective remedies—political, judicial, economic, military—must be on hand, to be prudently chosen and employed to prevent or stop genocide. Such remedies to have any chance of success, must have the support of UN members willing and able to implement decisions of the UN Security Council. These decisions, for example, may involve such political actions as withdrawal of diplomatic recognition; such judicial remedies as trial and punishment of those guilty of genocide; such economic sanctions as a trade embargo, freezing of a country's assets; and such military sanctions as the use of force to stop genocidal actions.

Fourth, it will be essential to work out the problem of what might be called "human rights consolidation," namely, what it takes to ensure that human rights will continue to be respected after initial efforts of prevention or intercession have been successful. Consolidation might involve (1) temporary maintenance of a UN Human Rights Protection Force in the country involved; (2) placing the country involved temporarily in the status of a UN Protectorate; or (3) other prudent measures.

Just Humanitarian Intercession

The fourth tragically neglected need is to articulate a cogent theory of just humanitarian intercession.[10] Such a theory would include the following eight principles.

1. An appropriate authority is required to bring the doctrine of just humanitarian intercession into action. The UN Security Council, for example, would be such an appropriate authority.
2. Just humanitarian intercession could be invoked only in support of a just cause—for example, intercession to prevent or stop genocide.
3. Military intercession would function as a last resort, after other pacific means—political, economic, judicial—have been tried and found wanting.
4. Normally the consent of parties at risk—for example, targeted victims and their supporters—would be required for just humanitarian intercession.
5. The appropriate authority interceding would be required to make a prudent appraisal of the benefits and costs of intercession.

6. Just humanitarian intercession must be based upon the expectation of a reasonable chance of success—immediate success in preventing or stopping egregious violations.
7. The interceding authority must employ humane and proportionate means to prevent or stop egregious violations, in the interest of minimizing harm, especially to the innocents involved in the conflict.
8. Just humanitarian intercession must also calculate the long-run reasonable chance of success, success—for example—in putting into place a human-rights-respecting regime to ensure the ongoing protection of human rights.

These eight principles of just humanitarian intercession are, of course, easier to state than to implement. Yet it is important to set forth the larger philosophy that guides both the deterrent and preemptive aspects of prudent prevention, and the conditions for actual intercession when preventive measures fail.

These four interrelated needs urgently call for the development of a responsible and effective Human Rights Regime. But can such a regime be put into place, especially in light of the difficulties attendant upon the very endeavor to fulfill these four needs?

THE ADVERSE CRITIQUE: FOUR DIFFICULTIES

Let me here attempt to present in summary fashion some of the adverse criticisms that might be made of my outlined creative breakthrough to a Global Human Rights Regime capable of coping with genocide. Any breakthrough must come to grips with four interrelated difficulties.

Difficulty I: Strengthening the Institutions of a Global Human Rights Regime

Adverse critics contend that a Global Human Rights Regime can develop neither the institutions nor the will to curtail genocide. They note that a Global Human Rights Regime is currently very loosely structured and lacks the power to do the very ambitious job sketched for it. They underscore the point that there is no convincing evidence that the United Nations, for example, is able to go beyond its own attractive rhetoric in protecting against such admitted evils as genocide. Its preventive power is nil; and its actual power to stop genocide negligible. The evidence in support of this contention is found, for example, in a number of UN failures—in Bosnia, in Rwanda, as well as in earlier failures to take any action against Pol Pot and the Khmer Rouge in Cambodia or against other genocidal attacks.

Strengthening the powers of the UN High Commissioner for Human Rights or the UN Commission on Human Rights is politically unrealistic. So is the proposal to put into place UN Human Rights Monitors and a UN Human Rights Protection Force.

Adverse critics also note that a Global Human Rights Regime lacks clearly authorized, agreed-upon principles, policies, and practices; and there is no compelling evidence that these will come into existence in the near or even distant future.

Finally, in their argument against the reality and sense of strengthening UN institutions, adverse critics point to the dominance in international law, at the United Nations and in custom and practice, of the view of sovereignty that precludes outside interference in a nation's domestic affairs, and that is hostile to outside meddling.[11] This view of national sovereignty, critics argue, militates against strengthening of institutions of a Global Human Rights Regime with power to intervene against genocide.

Difficulty 2: Prudent Prevention

Three troubling questions must be addressed here. Is it utopian to think it is possible to move the world toward mature constitutional democracy? Can a policy of deterrence be put into place and will it work? Is premptive action realistic? Realistic critics answer in the negative on all three questions.

Difficulty 3: Articulating a Theory of Wisely Staged Implementation

Here adverse critics note that monitoring of egregious violations has not been strong and effective. Efforts to make it stronger and more effective—such as a proposal to place a UN Human Rights Monitor in every world region for surveillance of suspect countries—will not be accepted by the nations most in need of watching. Such critics also contend that publicity is an impotent weapon against a determined and callous offending nation, particularly if it is a big and powerful nation, or a nation allergic to "illegitimate interference" in its domestic affairs. Political actions will simply not prevail against a determined violator. Judicial remedies are laughable: offending nations or offending leaders, particularly if they are powerful, will not be deterred by the threat of trials for crimes against humanity. Economic sanctions will not work. Military intercession is always risky, difficult, costly, perilous. Moreover, these adverse critics conclude, there is little confidence that after successful intercession, a human-rights-respecting regime can come into play.

Difficulty 4: Just Humanitarian Intercession

Here adverse critics raise a number of troubling questions, which parallel the doctrine of just humanitarian intercession.

1. Is it possible to get agreement on the appropriate authority to take action? Will there be a will to take action? And will the appropriate authority have adequate forces to do the job? Will nations be willing to contribute to

a regional or UN Human Rights Protection Force? Is it realistic to rely upon a volunteer Human Rights Protection Force? Is unilateral national action acceptable?

2. Is it possible to get agreement on the meaning of just cause—on the basic human rights that are to be protected? How many slaughtered victims constitute genocide?

3. How easy or difficult will it be to ascertain what is a last resort, so that military intercession can be invoked because all pacific means have been tried and found wanting?

4. How easy or difficult will it be to obtain the consent of distressed parties, targeted victims, particularly in complex situations—as in Bosnia and Rwanda—where atrocities have been attributed to both sides?

5. What conclusions will a "reasonable" person arrive at after calculating costs and benefits—particularly if that "reasonable person" is a political realist dedicated conscientiously to the prudent protection of the nation's vital interests, and not to a regional or global vital interest; and particularly if intercession threatens a Vietnam-style "quagmire" or is directed at a powerful nation-state (such as China)?

6. How easy or difficult will it be to determine whether the intercession, especially if military, has a reasonable chance of stopping the immediate egregious violations?

7. What, indeed, are humane and proportionate means?

8. Assuming that military intercession momentarily stops the egregious violations, what confidence can the interceding force have that a human-rights-respecting regime will be put into place to ensure ongoing protection of human rights?

All of these questions—all of which imply skepticism about the doctrine of just humanitarian intercession—emphasize that it may be easier to articulate a theory of just humanitarian intercession than to employ it in real international situations.

These four difficulties, adverse critics charge, add up to a disturbing conclusion: The endeavor to establish a strengthened Global Human Rights Regime incorporating the ideas of prudent prevention, wisely staged implementation, and just humanitarian intercession is unrealistic, foolish, utopian. This endeavor betrays an ignorance of the realities of international politics, of the meaning of prudent protection of vital national interests, and of international law.

What, then, can be said in response to this adverse criticism?

THE FULLER DEFENSE OF A BREAKTHROUGH TO A GLOBAL HUMAN RIGHTS REGIME

Although it would be foolish to ignore the difficulties posed by the critics in the previous section, it would be equally foolish to ignore the four badly neglected needs outlined earlier in the chapter and the possibility of a creative breakthrough. A creative breakthrough along the lines outlined earlier is, I maintain, a theoretical possibility; consequently, the real question is the actual probability of that possibility. I shall argue that a fuller defense suggests a more convincing case for the probability of that possibility than the adverse critics are willing to concede.

The fuller defense starts with the strong ethical appeal of a global regime able to to prevent and stop genocide. Narrow-minded realists may scoff about the significance of this appeal in international politics; but broad-minded realists will affirm its importance. Most certainly this ethical factor operates to keep open the commitment to a Global Human Rights Regime along the lines I have suggested, even if there are doubts about its full functioning in today's world.

The ethical promise of global protection against egregious violations of human rights does not, therefore, need extended defense. What may need defense, however, is the ethical priority to be given to the prevention of and protection against genocide. However, a strong case can be made for this priority once two things become clear: first, that the priority given to the battle against genocide does not necessarily prejudice action in protection of a wide range of human rights less severe than genocide; second, that the battle against genocide necessarily involves protecting a range of human rights violations that are often premonitory (or early warning) signals of a coming genocide. Such human rights violations, for example, are exemplified by torture of political opponents, religious persecution, racial discrimination, and violations of other basic human rights, including freedom of speech, press, association. Moreover, the priority to be given to the battle against genocide is premised on the argument that a breakthrough against genocide prepares the way for breakthroughs in the protection of human rights less severe than genocide. Thus, the breakthrough against genocide—itself a highly defensible ethical goal—should make possible the development of those institutions, principles, policies, and practices that can subsequently be used in the protection of less egregious violations of human rights than genocide.

Candidly, those who seek a breakthrough to a strengthened Global Human Rights Regime incorporating a guiding theory of prudent prevention, effectively staged implementation, and just humanitarian intercession confront a past and present seemingly hostile to such a breakthrough. Yet a closer look at past and present may offer some encouraging empirical evidence that a brighter future than the skeptics envision may lie ahead. It is, I suggest, foolish to remain stuck in the conventional wisdom when there is good reason to believe that it may be possible to break through beyond the "realities" of the conventional wisdom and, sensibly, to create new "realities" more in tune with the more adequate protection against genocide. Let us, then, in this thought experiment, take another look at the probability of the possibility of strengthening the institutions of our Global Human Rights Regime, and of pursuing policies of prevention, of effective staged implementation, and of just humanitarian intercession in the battle against genocide.

Most significant in the effort to strengthen the institutions of a Global Human Rights Regime is the end of the Cold War and the relative empowerment of the UN Security Council. This relative empowerment was dramatically illustrated by the UN's action (with, of course, U.S. leadership, will, and commitment) in defeating Iraq's effort to gobble up Kuwait. UN action, however incomplete, at least signalled that the UN Security Council—a key actor in a Global Human Rights Regime—could act decisively under certain conditions free of the restraints of the Cold War.

Despite undeniable difficulties in Somalia, Bosnia, Cambodia, Rwanda, and Haiti, there is evidence that the end of the Cold War makes possible stronger institutions at the United Nations and elsewhere. Of course, it remains to be seen whether the newly established UN High Commissioner for Human Rights can develop along the lines I have suggested in my thought experiment. Similarly, the empowerment of the UN Commission on Human Rights still has to be accomplished. But the probability of the possibility of the development of strengthened institutions—including UN Human Rights Monitors and a UN Human Rights Protection Force—is not a distant and foolish utopian dream but a distinct prospect.

Existing institutions for monitoring (many of them highly effective)—at the United Nations, within such nations as the United States, and including a number of very effective NGOs—suggest that an even more effective monitoring establishment can be put into place. It is not naive to see in place in the very near future a most effective program of global monitoring of human rights.

Similarly, a UN Human Rights Protection Force (already modelled to some extent on present UN Peacekeeping Forces) is not a fantastic idea. Whether such a Force should combine the functions of both military intercession to stop genocide and consolidation of a human-rights-respecting regime in the offending country is a question that can profitably be debated. But the possibility—indeed, the probability—of such a Force is not foolishly utopian.

Next, the case for prudent prevention is not as unrealistic as adverse critics maintain. Take the problem of encouraging the development of mature constitutional democracies. There is now considerable evidence to suggest that steps can be realistically taken to enhance the growth and development of democratic and constitutional countries, and thus to create the firm future foundation for the prevention of genocide. This task is not foolishly utopian. We have in fact seen the growth and development of democratic and constitutional countries in post–World War II Germany, Italy, and Japan—remarkable constitutional developments in major, powerful offending nations in history. Of course, important circumstances (unconditional surrender, military occupation) may have encouraged such democratic and constitutional development in the defeated foes of the allies in World War II. Yet we cannot deny that fascist and militarist regimes were in fact replaced by democratic and constitutional countries. The fuller story of this replacement may not always be apt for other authoritarian and despotic regimes; but certainly some relevant lessons can be learned from that experience. Importantly, the current democratic and constitutional status of Germany and Japan indicate that significant democratic and constitutional transformation can occur even in great powers once given over to persistent, systemic, egregious violations of human rights.

Today, of course, circumstances in other countries—China, Iran, Iraq, Vietnam, North Korea, Russia, for example—may make the path of transformation different and more difficult than in the cases of a defeated Germany, Italy, or Japan. (And we should not forget the tragic fact that it took a dreadful war to bring about the transformation in Germany, Italy, and Japan.) Yet it would be defeatist and unrealistic to deny the possibility of change in authoritarian countries, even in such powerful states as China and Russia.

Moreover, we must not forget the remarkable transformations of other authoritarian regimes. For example, Greece, Spain, and Portugal moved away from right-wing regimes (Greece), or fascist regimes (Spain and Portugal) and are now functioning as constitutional democracies—all within the framework of European Union. These changes occurred without military defeat in war and military occupation.

Similarly, right-wing authoritarian regimes in Latin America have been replaced by governments committed to constitutional democracy—for example, in Brazil, Argentina, and Chile. The path to constitutional democracy in these countries has often been rocky, and the advent of really mature constitutional democracy still has to be achieved. But it is unrealistic to deny the partial progress that has been made in Latin America.

Most significantly a powerful communist state, the Soviet Union, has been peacefully replaced by the Commonwealth of Independent States, and the guiding ideology of the Soviet Union, communism—an ideology hostile to the protection of human rights—has been repudiated. This transformation has also included the emergence of Russia as a great power that has significantly, if not fully, repudiated its oppressive human rights heritage, and is seeking amid great difficulty to develop into a constitutional democracy. Again it would be foolish to assert that mature constitutional democracy has emerged in Russia. Yet it would be even more foolish to close one's eyes to the remarkable change in Russia that has occurred, and may—painfully, and with some setbacks—still occur.

Other transformations in a democratic and constitutional direction have occurred in other formerly communist nations in Eastern Europe, once dominated by the Soviet Union. These transformations include the reunification of formerly communist East Germany with democratic and constitutional West Germany, and the slow, halting painful progress of other former Soviet-dominated countries of Eastern Europe toward constitutional democracies. Some of these countries—for example, the Czech Republic and Poland—have made greater progress than others. But the change from old-style repressive communist regimes is undeniable.

These developments—with great portent for the protection of human rights—occurred despite the conventional wisdom that affirmed that it was utopian to think of the breakup of the Soviet Union, of the demise of communism, and of a day when all countries of Eastern and Central Europe would be moving, however painfully and however slowly, toward constitutional democracy.

Most recently we have seen another seemingly unbelievable event: a free general election and a black man's presidential election (Nelson Mandela) in a South Africa once dedicated to apartheid and white rule forever. This transformation, too, unquestionably also deemed utopian by the conventional wisdom, is another piece of evidence supporting the proposition that movement toward constitutional democracy can occur even in regimes that were once stuck in the most authoritarian systems. Genocide, per se, may not have characterized all such authoritarian systems, but a wide range of other human rights were clearly violated in persistent, systemic, and egregious ways.

These developments, then—especially in Germany, Japan, Italy, Spain, Greece, Portugal, Brazil, Argentina, Russia, South Africa—provide a genuinely realistic hope for movement toward democracy and constitutionalism in other countries and in other parts of the world. Clearly, then, a Global Human Rights Regime can profit from a study of these remarkable transformations and developments. A Global Human Rights Regime can encourage constructive policies derived from that study as well as from other policies derived from a general knowledge of the necessary and sufficient conditions of constitutional democracy.

The case for deterrence as an instrument of prevention is not easy to make, but the ethical sense of stopping egregious violations before they occur is so overwhelming that the study of the policy and machinery of deterrence must not be undermined by short-sighted realists and other advocates of a timid conventional wisdom who affirm that little or nothing can be done to deter such offenders. Theoretically, it should not be difficult to identify all those national regimes that should be subjects of scrutiny as case studies for possible deterrence of genocide. They are authoritarian regimes of the Left or Right that currently maltreat political opponents, or people of certain races and religions. To argue on behalf of a theory of deterrence to prevent egregious violations before they occur is not to argue that prudence will easily dictate the application of deterrence in connection with each and every authoritarian regime. I argue only that we must *begin* to develop a theory of deterrence, so that we shall be clearheaded about its application in the first few test cases in which we employ the theory. Clearly, protection against genocide will be enormously advanced if this second aspect of a theory of protection via prevention can become an operational reality in the global community. It will take time to develop the policy and machinery of deterrence. It probably would be wise to employ deterrence, at the start, in cases where success is guaranteed, or almost guaranteed. Then, gradually and prudently, the range of cases in which the doctrine of deterrence would come into play can be extended.

Much of the argument and strategy articulated above about deterrence is relevant to the argument on behalf of preemptive action. Here, however, the case for a preemptive strike to forestall genocide is even more difficult to make because the stakes are higher insofar as they could involve military intercession. Such preemptive military intercession should in my judgment be rarely used. But, again, given the ethical sense of saving lives before egregious violations occur—in other words, given the logic of prevention over "cure"—the weapon of the preemptive strike should be included in the arsenal of weapons to be employed—rarely, prudently, carefully—as occasion demands. Very careful consideration should be required to demonstrate that a just preemptive intercession is in order. The threat of preemptive humanitarian intercession may often serve as a deterrent and make actual military intercession necessary. But in those normally rare cases where there is a clear and present danger of genocide, the policy and machinery of preemption should be ready for use. The UN High Commissioner for Human Rights, who would normally be in charge of recommending a preemptive strike to the UN Security Council, would have to have an overwhelmingly compelling case before making such a recommendation, and the Security Council would have to concur only on being convinced that such an overwhelming case exists. Clearly, these precautions against easy and loose preemptive strikes may deny the interceding force of the element of suprise in its action against a potential offender. Yet this loss may well be justified if it ensures that the most careful and thorough justification for action is established prior to any preemptive strike. Other difficulties facing this option will be addressed when I consider the doctrine of just humanitarian military intercession *after* genocidal violations have occurred.

Next, we come to the difficult and crucial task of effective staged implementation, the task of enforcing an escalating strategy for protecting human rights. Fortunately, as we have noted, there is already a good deal of policy and machinery in place. Monitoring, investigating, and reporting are already modest realities and can be significantly enhanced. Acting on behalf of the Global Human Rights Regime, a committed and resourceful High Commissioner for Human Rights can coordinate much of the work now being done by NGOs, individual nations, regions, and the United Nations itself. Power to acquire more information can be obtained, especially if a

Human Rights Monitor can be established in every region of the world. There will, of course, be resistance to such monitoring, in general, and to a Human Rights Monitor in every world region; but the long-term prospects for effective monitoring are, nonetheless, promising.

Similarly, publicity with regard to the results of findings on human rights can be enhanced and can increasingly serve as a powerful weapon in the creation of a supportive public opinion on human rights. The use of modern means of communication to get the word out on protection against genocidal violations will be increasingly effective.

Our creative political imaginations should not be limited to some of the usual political or diplomatic pressures that can be brought to bear against offending parties. Here too the test of success will be a pragmatic one. Withdrawal of diplomatic recognition, ending of foreign aid, other political and economic pressures (including freezing or seizure of assets, limitations on travel) can be brought to bear on offending countries and their leaders. And, it should be clear, nations (generally acting pursuant to UN Security Council decisions) will normally be the political actors to make enforcement decisions effective. Nations will normally implement decisions to assess fines, seize or freeze assets, limit the travel of egregious violators of human rights.

One often hears that economic sanctions do not work to protect human rights. The story here may be a mixed one, but limited successes in South Africa and Zimbabwe (formerly Rhodesia) suggest that sometimes economic sanctions may play a more important role than is often held. Bosnia certainly suggests that, alone, economic sanctions against the former Yugoslavia did not bring an end to "ethnic cleansing" and other violations of human rights. Yet we do not know for sure what limited effect sanctions may have had in curtailing somewhat the brutal activities in that country. Clearly, more research is in order on the effectiveness of economic sanctions (what kind, how administered, etc.) in protecting against genocidal violations. It is especially important to keep in mind the effect of sanctions on innocent children, women, and men.

The effectiveness of judicial trials in enhancing protection againt genocidal violations needs to be more fully tested. It is important to develop such trials as a plausible tool in the human rights arsenal. Their effectiveness will, in turn, depend upon the development of a constitutional global culture strongly supportive of human rights and willing to act on information of genocidal violations. The effectiveness of judicial trials will be further strengthened by the penalties meted out to violators. Here the door is open to pragmatic experimentation to see which penalties can be most effective. Experience will also demonstrate whether, for example, a Global Human Rights Court needs to be established to try genocidal offenders, and how such a Court can be effective in apprehending, trying, and punishing genocidal offenders.

Finally, we come to the ultimate sanction: the use of military force in humanitarian intercession. This is a concededly difficult and dangerous weapon in the battle to protect human rights. It should normally be employed as a last resort and used very sparingly. However, used prudently it can be an effective weapon of last resort. I repeat: it is a difficult and dangerous weapon and must be used accordingly. Its use will always involve an agonizingly tough prudential decision on balancing costs and benefits. The task of those concerned with a creative breakthough in this domain is to minimize the perils, and maximize the promise, of humanitarian intervention. Since just humanitarian military intercession is such an important part of a Global Human Rights Regime, let me in the following paragraphs recapitulate the compelling argument on wise guidelines to be followed in such intercession, and emphasize how such guidelines may serve to distinguish between just humanitarian intercession and illegitimate intervention.

The doctrine of just intercession would thus require (1) that the decision to intercede be made an appropriate authority (preferably the UN Security Council), normally on the recommendation of the UN High Commissioner on Human Rights; (2) that a just cause for intervention be clearly established (based on reliable, authentic information of genocidal violations—or, in the case of preemptive intercession, on reliable, authentic information of a clear and present danger of such violations); (3) that military intercession normally be a last resort (after pacific means of intercession have been tried and found wanting); (4) that the intercession be welcomed by the people or victims (actual or potential) in the offending country; (5) and (6) that the military intercession, (5) based on a careful calculation of costs and benefits, have (6) a strongly reasonable chance of success; (7) that the means of intervention be humane and proportionate to the end sought (protection against genocide); (8) that the end (protection against genocide) be not temporary or transient but durable, that—in brief—just results be accomplished and be as permanent as human affairs can permit.[12]

Next, let me address the argument that just humanitarian intercession is a cover for illegitimate intervention. Historically, we must concede that so-called humanitarian intercession has often, in fact, been a cover for illegitimate intervention in the internal affairs of other states. Consequently, great care is required to avert illegitimate intervention and to protect nation-states from unwarranted meddling. Such great care can be advanced if a strong case must be made—as I have argued—for following the principles of just humanitarian intercession outlined above. The making of such a strong case can provide the safeguards against illegitimate intervention.

Nations have a crucial role to play in the protection against genocide. And they should be encouraged to play that valuable role. However, protecting against illegitimate intervention and securing the development of global constitutionalism call for primary use of regional and global (UN) organizations. Action by the United Nations can serve to some extent to counter the argument that just humanitarian intercession is simply a cover for illegitimate intervention by big, bullying states acting in their own selfish interests. Intervention can be ill- or well-advised depending on fulfillment of the principles of just humanitarian intercession. Buttressed by a convincing doctrine of just humanitarian intercession, and by a standby volunteer Human Rights Protection Force, intercession—in the very rare cases in which it will be invoked—can prudently go forward. Intercession almost always, but not necessarily, will be a costly enterprise, a powerful reason for considering it carefully and employing it only on very limited and very special occasions. Nonetheless, carefully conceived and executed, it can be effective.

The idea of protection of basic human rights against genocidal violations is not a diabolic Western invention. I affirm the universality of basic human rights, reject the arguments of radical cultural relativists on human rights, yet recognize the historical particularity of some aspects of human rights.[13] Basic human rights (at least at the rhetorical level) are recognized globally. Their protection makes great sense. Even if human rights are not always adequately protected, especially by authoritarian or despotic regimes, or are not always respected by political, religious, and tribal fanatics around the globe, there is considerable global support for the protection of life against genocidal attacks. Moreover, the evidence revealed by the collapse of the Soviet Union and Soviet communism, and by the replacement of other authoritarian regimes of the Left or Right, strongly suggests that large numbers of people in those countries understand the meaning of human rights, want them respected and want to be adequately protected. There is also considerable evidence to support the proposition that human rights, even though they clearly owe a great debt to the Western constitutional tradition, are deeply rooted in human needs and find support in all the world's great religions.

It is most important that individual nations act to protect basic human rights in their own polities. Clearly, they must avoid giving aid and comfort to nations that engage in persistent, systemic, egregious violations of human rights. Moreover, it is important for them to take other prudent actions against violators of human rights. Having said this it is important, nonetheless, also to declare that sometimes—in a modest and careful and constitutional way—nations may also have an ethical obligation, related to their constitutional obligation, to support regional and global policies and measures to protect against genocidal violations beyond national borders. Indeed, the effectiveness of a Global Human Rights Regime will depend upon the support that individual nations in the United Nations can bring to that Global Human Rights Regime. Individual nations must appreciate the important role they have to play in building on national, regional, and UN precedents, and thus furthering the protection against genocide.

Regional declarations and practices deserve special attention. Here developments in Western Europe can serve as a model for other regions of the world that have been less effective in protecting human rights. The irony here is that Western Europe has the most effective regional human rights regime in place; yet in the post–World War II world, there has been less need for a Western European regime to act because of the absence in Western Europe of egregious violations. Nonetheless, the experience of these regional human rights regimes in dealing with lesser human rights violations provide valuable empirical lessons for the development of constitutional machinery to protect against egregious violations elsewhere in the world.

We must also take note of other significant developments, apropos the protection of human rights, that have occurred or are occurring in international law. Fernando Tesson's work represents the most radical effort to enhance the protection of human rights under international law. Tesson makes a strong legal and moral argument on behalf of just humanitarian intercession. International law, and the theory and practice of the United Nations, Tesson contends, are compatible with such intercession. Fundamentally, those who argue on behalf of just humanitarian intercession maintain that persistent, systemic, egregious violations of human rights—such as genocide—trump the principle of Article 2, Paragraph 7 of the UN Charter (no interference in the internal affairs of a sovereign state). Tesson concludes his work on *Humanitarian Intervention: An Inquiry into Law and Morality* as follows:

> I have attepted in this book to defend three interrelated propositions: I argued, first, for a *jurisprudence* of international law—that international law and moral philosophy are essentially linked. Second, I defended a *substantive* moral philosophy of international relations—that the rights of states derive from human rights and consequently wars in defense of human rights are just. And third, I argued for a specific *legal* proposition— that the right of humanitarian intervention is consistent with the United Nations Charter and positively supported by state practice, when both are examined in the light of the normative theory mentioned above.[14]

Clearly, the effectiveness of a Global Human Rights Regime will be immensely enhanced if a clear basis in international law is established for prudent prevention and just humanitarian intercession.

The foregoing arguments underscore the prudential judgments that have to be made by an effective Global Human Rights Regime. Bold and successful prudential judgments have to made on a number of key issues: strengthening global institutions, prudent prevention, staged implementation, and just humanitarian intercession. Such prudential judgments must be capable of grappling with the dangers of illegitimate intervention, on one hand, and cowardly failure, on the other. Such prudential judgments must also be capable of dealing wisely with the real tensions involved in the undoubtable costs and benefits of policies designed to make prudent prevention a reality, to effectuate a policy of effective staged implementation, and to ensure that just humanitarian intercession will be followed. Only careful assessment of actual practice will inform us of the success of the difficult prudential judgments required to make a Global Human Rights regime an operational reality.

CONCLUSION

This thought experiment can only point the general way toward a prophetic breakthrough to a global human rights regime capable of preventing and stopping genocide. Only time will tell if this future breakthrough occurs and is then consolidated. The breakthrough, however, depends significantly upon imaginative and creative leaders and imaginative and creative followers. Thought experiments—and a creative breakthrough is always, early on, such a thought experiment—can be transformed into reality only when they are taken seriously by creative leaders and when they make sense to thoughtful followers. It is easy in a political world that does not lend itself readily to change of the right kind, in a world in which it is so easy to be overwhelmed by external forces—powerful forces beyond our control—to be pessimistic or skeptical about the possibilities of creative breakthroughs in politics. I hope, however, that the argument I have made leads one to be skeptical about the skeptics: skeptical about the overwhelming cogency of the arguments of the adverse critics.

We conclude, then, that a creative breakthrough to a Global Human Rights Regime capable of protecting against genocide is a theoretical possibility. What will be tested in the future is the probability of that possibility. As we explore the probability of that possibility, it may be helpful to be reminded of what other penetrating students of politics have said about the human factor in politics.

Although Niccolo Machiavelli warned "that there is nothing more difficult to carry out, nor more doubtful of success, nor more dangerous to handle, than to initiate a new order of things,"[15] he also held that "fortune is the ruler of half our actions, but that she allows the other half or thereabouts to be governed by us."[16] Machiavelli's emphasis, of course, is on what human will can do in the 50 percent zone of freedom.

Next, I turn from the political realist Machiavelli to James Madison, who prudently but boldly helped shape a new Constitution and federal republic, and to Alexis de Tocqueville, who analyzed the new America that Madison had helped to create. Wrote Madison in *Federalist* No. 14:

> Hearken not to the voice which petulantly tells you that the form of government recommended for your adoption is a novelty in the political world; that it has never yet had a place in the theories of the wildest

projectors; that it rashly attempts what it is impossible to accomplish. . . . But . . . is the experiment of an extended republic to be rejected, merely because it may comprise what is new? Is it not to the glory of the people of America, that whilst they have paid a decent regard to the opinions of former times and other nations, they have not suffered a blind veneration for antiquity, for custom, or for names, to overrule the suggestion of their own good sense, the knowledge of their own situation, and the lessons of their own experience. To this manly spirit, posterity will be indebted for the possession, and the world for the example, of the numerous innovations displayed on the American theatre, in favor of private rights and public happiness. Had no important step been taken by the leaders of the Revolution for which a precedent could not be discovered, no government established of which an exact model did not present itself, the people of the United States might, at this moment, have been numbered among the melancholy victims of misguided councils, must at best have been laboring under the weight of some of those forms which have crushed the liberties of the rest of mankind.[17]

Madison saw the need to move beyond the conventional wisdom, beyond precedent, and to experiment, to innovate, in order to advance human liberties.

Tocqueville, too, urged people in politics to exercise their power to advance equality, freedom, knowledge, prosperity: "Providence has not created mankind entirely independent or entirely free. It is true that around every man a fatal circle is traced beyond which he cannot pass; but within the wide verge of that circle he is powerful and free; as it is with man, so with communities."[18]

So Tocqueville joins Madison and Machiavelli and other thinkers who emphasize the importance of human creativity, purposeful will, bold action. This emphasis can reinforce those who believe that creative breakthroughs are as possible in the future as in the present and the past.

NOTES

1. My initial intent in this inquiry was to include all human rights. I then concluded that the most urgent need was to focus on genocide. Initially, I also limited myself to the doctrine of just humanitarian, military intercession. I then concluded that there was an urgent need to focus on prevention as well as military intercession and to broaden the meaning of intercession to include political, economic, and judicial sanctions as well as military intercession. In probing these matters it also became clear that separate attention was required to the related problem of strengthening the global institutions that would carry out the tasks of prevention and intercession; and that, additionally, the related problem of effective staged implementation (involving monitoring, publicity, sanctions, and consolidation) deserved separate treatment.

2. The full text of the Convention on the Prevention and Punishment of the Crime of Genocide may be found in Leo Kuper, *The Prevention of Genocide* (New Haven: Yale University Press, 1985), Appendix 1, pp. 241–246.

3. On this point I follow Leo Kuper, *Genocide: Its Political Use in the Twentieth Century* (New Haven, Conn.: Yale University Press, 1981), especially pp. 9–10, and Chapter 8, "Related Atrocities," pp. 138–160.

4. It is estimated that 1 million out of 7 million people in Cambodia were killed or died during the infamous reign of Pol Pot and the Khmer Rouge in Cambodia between 1975 and 1979. Although out of power, Pol Pot and the Khmer Rouge continue to operate in Cambodia. A million Bengalese in East Pakistan (now Bangladesh) were killed and 10 million displaced by Pakistan in 1971, the year Bangladesh achieved independence from Pakistan. On ethnic cleansing in Bosnia, see U.S. Department of State, *Country Reports on Human Rights Practices for 1993* (Washington, D.C.: U.S. Government Printing Office, 1994), p. 806: "Ethnic cleansing" and warfare in Bosnia have resulted in the deaths of some 200,000 Bosnians; over 800,000 have become refugees outside Bosnia; another 1.2 million have been displaced within the nation.

> Techniques employed by the BSA [Bosnian Serb Army], which the Serbs themselves referred to as "ethnic cleansing," included: laying siege to cities and indiscriminately shelling civilian inhabitants; "strangling" cities (i.e., withholding food deliveries and utilities so as to starve and freeze residents); executing noncombatants; establishing concentration camps where thousands of prisoners were summarily executed and tens of thousands subjected to torture and inhumane treatment; using prisoners as human shields; employing rape as a tool of war to terrorize and uproot populations; forcing large numbers of civilians to flee to other regions; razing villages to prevent the return of displaced persons; and interfering with international relief efforts, including attacks on relief personnel.

And so on: for Saddam Hussein's brutal actions against Kurds in Northern Iraq and against Shia Muslims in Southern Iraq; for the insane slaughter in Rwanda; for the continuing atrocities in the civil war in the Sudan; and so on.

5. For other views on the concept of an international regime, see Stephen Krasner, ed., *International Regimes* (Ithaca, N.Y.: Cornell University Press, 1983, p. 186: "Regimes can be defined as sets of implicit or explicit principles, norms, rules, and decision-making procedures around which actors' expectations converge in a given area of international relations." Jack Donnelly, *International Human Rights* (Boulder, Colo.: Westview Press, 1993), p. 57, follows Krasner's definition: "An *international regime* is typically defined as a set of principles, norms, rules, and other decision-making procedures that are accepted by states (and other international actors) as binding within a particular issue area." Donnelly notes, p. 57, that the "principles and norms that govern human rights regimes" are outlined in such documents as the Universal Declaration of Human Rights and the International Human Rights Covenants. Some rules, and decision-making and implementation procedures for some actors in the human rights regime, are to be found, for example, in the activities of the UN Commission on Human Rights, the UN Human Rights Committee, and other human rights organizations.

6. For the weaknesses of the UN Commission on Human Rights, see Donnelly, *International Human Rights*, pp. 57–63. Donnelly notes that the Commission's investigative procedure is strictly confidential; this means that during the process

of investigation the United Nations "renounces the use of publicity, its most powerful weapon in the struggle for human rights" (p. 59). Donnelly also highlights "the slow pace of the 1503 procedure," (p. 59); notes (p. 60) that the "1503 procedure has little or no value as a preventive or early warning device," and is "simply weak" on enforcement. However, Donnelly notes (p. 60) that the Commission can, after investigation, "make the evidence that has been acquired, along with the commission's view on it, publicly available," but adds that "in practice, the commission has never fully exercised even these weak procedures."

7. Although in my outline of a creative breakthrough I concentrate on the United Nations, I do not exclude attention to protection against genocide at the level of effective regional organizations. The strengthening of comparable institutions at the regional level is quite in harmony with my argument.

8. Although my focus is on genocide, as the most egregious violation of a basic human right—the right to life—the ethical vision that animates a Global Human Rights Regime is also captured in such other UN documents as the International Covenant on the Elimination of All Forms of Racial Discrimination (adopted 1965, in force 1969); the International Covenant on Civil and Political Rights (1976); the International Covenant on Economic, Social, and Cultural Rights (in force 1976); the UN Convention against Torture and Other Cruel, Inhuman or Degrading Treatment or Punishment (signed 1984, in force 1987).

9. See David Forsythe, *Human Rights and Peace: International and National Dimensions* (Lincoln: University of Nebraska Press, 1993). To anticipate one criticism, let me note that mature constitutional democracies do engage in war, not with other mature constitutional democracies, but with other countries. Moreover, the track record of *maturing* constitutional democracies—such as the United States—in dealing with American Indians, blacks, or women has by no means been exemplary! And, of course, a similar point could be made of other *maturing* constitutional democracies—the United Kingdom, France, Belgium, Holland.

10. See Fernando R. Teson, *Humanitarian Intervention: An Inquiry into Law and Morality* (Dobbs Ferry, N.Y.: Transnational Publishers, 1988); Nancy D. Arnison, "International Law and NonIntervention: When Humanitarian Concerns Supersede Sovereignty," in U.S. Government, Hearing . . . 1992, *Humanitarian Intervention: A Review of Theory and Practice* (Washington, D.C.: U.S. Government Printing Office, 1993), pp. 107–124; David P. Forsythe and Kelly Kate Pease, "Human Rights, Humanitarian Intervention, and World Politics," in *Human Rights Quarterly*, Vol. 15, No. 2 (May 1993), pp. 290–314; Thomas R. Gillespie, "Unwanted Responsibility: Humanitarian Military Intervention to Advance Human Rights," in *Peace and Change*, Vol. 18, No. 3 (July 1993), pp. 219–246; Richard B. Lillich, ed., *Humanitarian Intervention and the United Nations* (Charlottesville: University Press of Virginia, 1973); Jerome Slater and Terry Nardin, "Nonintervention and Human Rights," *The Journal of Politics*, Vol. 48 (1986), pp. 86–96; R. J. Vincent, *Nonintervention and International Order* (Princeton, N.J.: Princeton University Press, 1974; R. J. Vincent, *Human Rights and International Relations* (Cambridge: Cambridge University Press, 1986); Hedley Bull, ed., *Intervention in World Politics* (Oxford: Clarendon Press, 1984); Jack Donnelly, "Human Rights, Humanitarian Intervention, and American Foreign Policy: Law, Morality and Politics," *Journal of International Affairs*, Vol. 37 (Winter 1984), pp. 311–328.

Clearly, the principles of just humanitarian intercession owe a great deal to just war theory. For a sample of the literature on just war theory, see Bernard T. Adeney, *Just War, Political Realism, and Faith* (Metuchen, N.J.: Scarecrow, 1988); Jean Bethke Elshtain, ed., *Just War Theory* (Oxford: Basil Blackwell, 1992); Robert L. Holmes, *On War and Morality* (Princeton, N.J.: Princeton University Press, 1989); John Kelsay and James Turner Johnson, eds., *Just War and Jihad: Historical and Theoretical Perspectives on War and Peace in Western and Islamic Traditions* (Westport, Conn.: Greenwood Press, 1991); William V. O'Brien, *The Conduct of Just and Limited War* (New York: Praeger, 1981); Paul Ramsay, *The Just War: Force and Political Responsibility* (New York: Scribners, 1968); Michael Walzer, *Just and Unjust Wars: A Moral Argument with Historical Illustrations*, 2nd ed. (New York: Basic Books, 1992); John Howard Yoder, *When War Is Unjust: Being Honest in Just-War Thinking* (Minneapolis: Augsburg, 1984).

See also the principles of the just revolution in Locke and Jefferson and Mazzini. For a modern exploration and application of the principles of the just revolution, see Neal Riemer, *Karl Marx and Prophetic Politics* (New York: Praeger, 1987), pp. 109–118.

11. "Nothing contained in the Charter shall authorize the United Nations to intervene in matters that are essentially within the domestic jurisdiction of any state." Article 2, Par. 7 of the United Nations Charter.

12. It is crucial that the fate of despotic leaders or despotic states be candidly addressed. There must be a strong likelihood that a constitutional government will replace despotic leaders in the offending despotic states and that human rights will be protected over time.

13. Here I share the general outlook of Jack Donnelly, *Universal Human Rights in Theory and Practice* (Ithaca, N.Y.: Cornell University Press, 1989).

14. Tesson, *Humanitarian Intervention*.

15. Niccolo Machiavelli, *The Prince*, Ch. VI (New York: Modern Library, 1940), p. 21.

16. Ibid., Ch. XXV, p. 91.

17. Quoted in Neal Riemer, *The Democratic Experiment* (Princeton, N.J.: Van Nostrand, 1967), pp. 14–15. Original source: *The Federalist* No. 14 (New York: Modern Library, 1937), pp. 84–85.

18. Quoted in Riemer, *The Democratic Experiment*, pp. 9–10. Original source: Alexis de Tocqueville, *Democracy in America* (1835), Phillips Bradley, ed., 2 Vols. (New York: Knopf, 1946), II, p. 334.

CHAPTER 8

Conclusion: The Unfinished Prophetic Agenda

INTRODUCTION

The fiftieth anniversary of the end of World War II has now come and gone; but the memory of war and destruction—and of bravery and sacrifice—lingers on. This memory prompts us to ask whether we can intensify our efforts to achieve creative breakthroughs in politics that might eliminate or significantly reduce throughout the entire world the horrors of war, of massive violations of human rights, of despotic governments, of insane nationalism, of religious fanaticism, of economic malaise. Can we demonstrate a bravery in achieving creative breakthroughs on our contemporary troublesome problems comparable, if not identical, to that of the Allied soldiers who stormed the beaches of Normandy and fought so valiantly on other key fronts of the war against Nazism and imperialism? Are we willing to make the relatively minor sacrifices to prevent war, egregious violations of human rights, and debilitating poverty? And to combat racism, sexism, ecological malaise, and cultural disorder? Can we break forth from our limited democratic and constitutional beachheads and win the larger global battle for constitutional democracy?

These questions take on a new urgency as we move through the first decade since the end of the Cold War and approach the twenty-first century. It is my hope that we can learn from the genuine creative breakthroughs, as well as the spurious ones, examined in the preceding chapters. It is my hope that we can also take heart from the great breakthrough still in process in Western Europe. And it is my hope, too, that we will not shy away from exploring such future breakthroughs as global protection against genocide and other egregious violations of human rights, however difficult such breakthroughs may seem.

I have argued in this book that we can learn from our study of creative breakthroughs in politics that such breakthroughs, although rare, have occurred in history, are still occurring, and can also be planned for the future. Such breakthroughs, I have maintained, involve significantly fruitful resolutions of real problems. These are major problems of war and peace: eliminating warfare based on religious controversies; overcoming the mutually destructive national and economic rivalries of the great Western European powers. These are major problems of liberty and authority: reconciling religious liberty and religious and secular order; reconciling liberty and large size; reconciling national sovereignty with transnational economic integration and European political community. These breakthroughs are, significantly, in the democratic and constitutional tradition.

Even the flawed and spurious breakthroughs attempted to deal with real problems: the protection of minority interests in a majority rule system (Calhoun); how to achieve universal human emancipation (Marx). These spurious breakthroughs, nonetheless, like the genuine ones we have considered (in Williams, Madison, European Union), reveal the importance of focusing sharply on the ethical, empirical, and prudential components of the breakthrough. To do so is to recognize, as in our Calhoun case study, that the protection of the economic and social interests of a slaveholding minority in the nation is ethically unacceptable, empirically unrealistic, and prudentially foolish. Similarly, although Marx's ethical vision of universal human emancipation is laudable, Marx's empirical diagnosis and revolutionary prudential recommendations are seriously flawed.

Genuine creative breakthroughs do not suffer from these ethical, empirical, and prudential weaknesses. Not only is their ethical vision sound; but so is their understanding of past, present, and future; and so is their prudential judgment. That ethical vision can, of course, indeed often must, go beyond the conventional wisdom; can and must involve an empirical understanding of emerging and future realities; and can and must involve bold, cogent prudential judgments about moving from where we are now to where we ought to be.

Roger Williams struck hard at the conventional wisdom which held that it is the obligation of secular rulers to maintain the one true religious faith, if necessary, by persecution and force. He demonstrated the crucial importance of religious liberty, and the compatibility of religious liberty and diversity with religious truth and secular order. He took a major step in harmonizing religious truth, religious diversity, and democratic order.

Madison struck hard at the conventional wisdom that insisted that it was impossible to reconcile liberty and large size, democratic liberty and national authority. A constitutionally organized extensive republic—a democratic federal republic—could indeed achieve such a reconciliation. Properly organized and led, reliant upon the protection of basic rights and a strong two-party system, such a republic could guard against a tyrannical majority faction either at the periphery or center of political power. Given the safeguards of a representative and constitutional system, majority rule would normally operate safely to protect both individual rights and the common good.

European Union—our creative breakthrough still in process—demonstrates the international possibilities of creative breakthroughs in politics. This breakthrough illustrates, even now, even before its deepening and enlarging, that bitter enemies over hundreds of years can by way of transnational integration move beyond war, narrow national economic self-interest, and political turmoil. The nations of Western Europe have demonstrated that they can transcend devastating national and economic rivalries by integrating their economies in such ways as to enhance their mutual prosperity and their political cooperation and cohesion. The breakthrough here has not been easy or flawless. But it has occurred. And its continuing consolidation—via deepening and enlarging—although slow and agonizing and painful, promises to extend the zone of peace and prosperity and constitutional democracy throughout Europe.

Our proposed future breakthrough on global protection against genocide was designed as a thought experiment. It was intended to stimulate attention to a pressing problem and invite constructive criticism. It is important to challenge the conventional wisdom that affirms that little or nothing can be done to protect basic human rights against genocidal violations around the world. It is important especially to challenge the conventional view of national sovereignty that affirms that the subject of genocide and human rights is an internal matter within the jurisdiction of the sovereign state, and that there is to be no meddling in the domestic affairs of a sovereign state.

It is important, too, to challenge those concerned with human rights to articulate a theory of a Global Human Rights Regime that will protect against genocide. Such a theory would focus on (1) strengthening key institutions, and the will to make them work; (2) attending to the important but badly neglected task of prevention of genocide (via the development of constitutional democracies, deterrence, and preemptive action); (3) working out the wise theory of effective staged implementation (via monitoring, publicity, and sanctions); and (4) articulating a cogent guiding theory of just humanitarian intercession when preventive measures have not been successful in protecting against genocide. Such a Global Human Rights Regime, we have argued, would normally make use of United Nations organizations (especially an envigorated Security Council) to implement protection; and would sagaciously employ the preferred policy of staged implementation: via monitoring, publicity, and political, economic, judicial, and military remedies. Key new features of such a strengthened Global Human Rights Regime would include (1) a UN Human Rights Monitor in every region of the world (with responsibility to be on the lookout for genocide in member states of the United Nations in that region) reporting to the newly appointed UN High Commissioner for Human Rights and to an empowered UN Commission on Human Rights; (2) a volunteer UN Human Rights Protection Force to give effect to UN Security Council decisions on political, economic, and military intercession; and (3) a UN Human Rights Court to deal with genocidal criminals.

There are many difficulties facing the development of an effective Global Human Rights Regime able to implement a policy of prudent prevention, staged implementation, and just humanitarian intercession. Yet a start must be made in improving current machinery in significant ways. The thought experiment of Chapter 7 was not intended to be the final word on a Global Human Rights Regime but a bold beachhead on the fortified frontier of indefensible national sovereignty, narrow-minded political realism, and other barriers erected by the "but it can't be done" mentality.

The final actual breakthrough on behalf of the global protection of basic human rights may not, of course, resemble the thought experiment I have sketched in every detail. But it will most certainly have to address the crucial problems of prudent prevention, staged implementation, and just humanitarian intercession—within the framework of a strengthened and effective Global Human Rights Regime. This proposed future breakthrough also calls our attention to other aspects of the unfinished agenda.

THE UNFINISHED AGENDA

Creative breakthroughs in politics, we have argued, are in the soundly prophetic—not the falsely utopian—tradition. They are in the tradition of a genuinely prophetic politics. They nourish the hope of those who seek to enhance the prospects for peace, freedom, and prosperity in a challenging world. This hope is not deflated by the prudent recognition that not even genuinely creative breakthroughs solve all difficulties in the major problem area. And this hope is not deflated by the prudent recognition that we cannot easily solve all problems everywhere in the world. Nonetheless, despite ongong difficulties even with acknowledged creative break-throughs, and despite the candid recognition of the immensity of our unsolved global problems, we can be encouraged to focus our attention on significant problems of the unfinished agenda.

Thus, much remains to be done to extend the arena of peace beyond the North American continent, beyond Western and Northern Europe, and now beyond most of South America. A World War III fought with nuclear weapons may now not be a live possibility; but nuclear proliferation remains a nagging problem. And little wars are a present ugly reality and a clear and present danger in too many areas of the world. What effective global policy and machinery can be put into place to stop the proliferation of nuclear weapons, and to curtail and minimize the harm of these—seemingly inevitable—little wars?

Assuming that we can be successful in preventing or stopping genocide, can we then move on to prevent or stop persistent, systemic, egregious violations of other human rights, including racist, sexist, and religious violations?

Can we really win the battle against poverty—not only in rich developed countries such as the United States, but throughout so many poverty-stricken developing nations of the southern hemisphere? And here I include not only poverty of income, but poverty of mind attributable to inadequate education, and poverty of resources to deal with problems of global health.

Can we take action now to address the multiple problems of ecological malaise? Breakthroughs are in order here to bring population and resources into balance, to protect against pollution, and to guard against other ecological disasters.

Finally, to round out this rough unfinished agenda, we need to address the problem of cultural disorder, or, positively, cultural creativity. We need, in brief, to take steps to enhance the quality of human life.

Each of these major problem areas demands fresh thinking. That fresh thinking, in turn, requires creative minds unafraid to question the conventional wisdom that would perpetuate the problem. Such fresh thinking also demands that we challenge the narrow-minded realists who insistently tell us "it can't be done." In particular, we need to reflect on the necessary and sufficient conditions of creative breakthroughs in politics.

Such reflections will be advanced, initially, if we identify the problem that calls for a creative breakthrough. Second, we need to appreciate that each problem has an ethical, empirical, and prudential dimension. The ethical dimension calls upon us to ask whether the guiding vision of the conventional wisdom is adequate or in need of modification or replacement. The empirical dimension calls upon us to challenge narrow-minded realists and to look to the discovery of potential realities, emergent realities, future realities in tune with a bolder ethical vision. The prudential dimension calls upon us to exercise bold wise judgment in shaping new but cogent public policies, in devising new and effective machinery, in implementing new rules and procedures. Bold but prudent experimentation must be the motto to be followed. Breakthroughs may be wisely sought first on a narrow front, with consolidation on a broader front to follow initial success.

Inspired by a genuinely prophetic vision, committed to a social scientific understanding of emergent realities, and guided by a bold prudential judgment, we can undertake the challenging task of achieving creative breakthroughs in the on-rushing twenty-first century.

CONCLUSION

Those who would address the unfinished agenda of creative break-throughs in politics can take heart from those who have demonstrated that creative breakthroughs in politics are possible. Roger Williams and James Madison and Jean Monnet are all in the tradition of a prophetic politics unashamed of its commitment to prophetic values, to vigorous criticism of the existing order (often the conventional wisdom), to bold but prudent constitutional action to break through beyond the conventional wisdom, and to imaginative scenarios to explore the emerging future. It is that prophetic tradition that will continue to nourish creative breakthroughs in politics.

Select Bibliography

Adeney, Bernard T. *Just War, Political Realism, and Faith*. Metuchen, N.J.: Scarecrow, 1988.

Arnison, Nancy D. "International Law and NonIntervention: When Humanitarian Concerns Supersede Sovereignty." In U.S. Government, Hearing . . . 1992, *Humanitarian Intervention: A Review of Theory and Practice*. Washington, D.C.: U.S. Government Printing Office, 1993.

Bainton, Roland H. *Studies of the Reformation*. Boston: Beacon Press, 1966.

Bull, Hedley, ed. *Intervention in World Politics*. Oxford: Clarendon Press, 1984.

Calhoun, John C. *A Discourse on the Constitution and Government of the United States*. In *The Works of John C. Calhoun*, Vol. 1. Columbia: General Assembly of the State of South Carolina, 1852.

———. *A Disquisition on Government* (1851). In John C. Anderson, ed., *Calhoun: Basic Documents*. State College, Pa.: Bald Eagle Press, 1952.

Coker, Francis W. *Readings in Political Philosophy*. New York: Macmillan, 1938.

Delors, Jacques. *Our Europe: The Community and National Development*. London: Verso, 1992.

Dinan, Desmond. *Ever Closer Union? An Introduction to the European Community*. Boulder, Colo.: Lynne Rienner, 1994.

Donnelly, Jack. "Human Rights, Humanitarian Intervention, and American Foreign Policy: Law, Morality and Politics." In *Journal of International Affairs*. Vol. 37 (Winter 1984).

———. *International Human Rights*. Boulder, Colo.: Westview Press, 1993.

———. *Universal Human Rights in Theory and Practice*. Ithaca, N.Y.: Cornell University Press, 1989.

Duchene, François. *Jean Monnet: The First Statesman of Interdependence*. New York: W. W. Norton, 1994.

Elshtain, Jean Bethke, ed. *Just War Theory*. Oxford: Basil Blackwell, 1992.

Everson v. Board of Education, 330 U.S. 1 (1947).

Forsythe, David. *Human Rights and Peace: International and National Dimensions*. Lincoln: University of Nebraska Press, 1993.

Forsythe, David, and Pease, Kelly Kate. "Human Rights, Humanitarian Intervention, and World Politics." In *Human Rights Quarterly*, Vol. 15, No. 2 (May 1993).

Gillespie, Thomas R. "Unwanted Responsibility: Humanitarian Military Intervention to Advance Human Rights." In *Peace and Change*. Vol. 18, No. 3 (July 1993).

Henning, C. Randall, Hockreiter, Eduard, and Hufbauer, Gary Clyde, eds. *Reviving the European Union*. Washington, D.C.: Institute for International Economics, 1994.

Herz, John H. *Political Realism and Political Idealism*. Chicago: University of Chicago Press, 1951.

Hofstadter, Richard. *The American Political Tradition and the Men Who Made It*. New York: Knopf, 1948.

Holmes, Robert L. *On War and Morality*. Princeton, N.J.: Princeton University Press, 1989.

Hunt, Richard N. *The Political Ideas of Marx and Engels, Vol. I: Marxism and Totalitarian Democracy, 1818–1850*. Pittsburgh, Pa.: University of Pittsburgh Press, 1984.

———. *The Political Ideas of Marx and Engels, Vol. II: Classical Marxism*. Pittsburgh, Pa.: University of Pittsburgh Press, 1984.

Kariel, Henry. *The Desperate Politics of Postmodernism*. Amherst: University of Massachusetts Press, 1989.

Kelsay, John, and Johnson, James Turner, eds. *Just War and Jihad: Historical and Theoretical Perspectives on War and Peace in Western and Islamic Traditions*. Westport, Conn.: Greenwood Press, 1991.

Kennedy, Paul. *Preparing for the Twenty-First Century*. New York: Vintage, 1994.

Krasner, Stephen, ed. *International Regimes*. Ithaca, N.Y.: Cornell University Press, 1983.

Kuper, Leo. *Genocide: Its Political Use in the Twentieth Century*. New Haven, Conn.: Yale University Press, 1981.

———. *The Prevention of Genocide*. New Haven, Conn.: Yale University Press, 1985.

Lillich, Richard B., ed. *Humanitarian Intervention and the United Nations*. Charlottesville: University Press of Virginia, 1973.

Lugo, Luis E., ed. *Religion, Public Life, and the American Polity*. Knoxville: University of Tennessee Press, 1994.

Machiavelli, Niccolo. *The Prince*. New York: Modern Library, 1940.

Madison, James. *The Papers of James Madison*, 17 vols. William T. Hutchinson & William M. E. Rachal and Robert A. Rutland & Charles F. Hobson, eds. Charlottesville: University Press of Virginia, 1977–.

Marx, Karl. *Capital*. In Robert C. Tucker, ed., *The Marx-Engels Reader*, 2nd ed. New York: W. W. Norton, 1978.

———. *The Communist Manifesto*. (1848). In David McClellan, ed., *Karl Marx: Selected Writings*. Oxford: Oxford University Press, 1977.

_____ . *Contribution to the Critique of Hegel's Philosophy of Right: Introduction* (1844). In Tucker.

_____ . *A Contribution to the Critique of Political Economy*, Preface. In Tucker.

_____ . *Critique of the Gotha Program* (1875, 1891). In Tucker.

_____ . *Economic and Philosophical Manuscripts of 1844*. In Tucker.

_____ . *The Eighteenth Brumaire of Louis Napoleon.* (1842). In Tucker.

_____ . *The German Ideology: Part I.* In Tucker.

_____ . *Theses on Feuerbach.* (1845). In Tucker.

Mill, John Stuart. *On Liberty* (1859). Indianapolis: Hacket, 1978.

Miller, Perry, ed. *Roger Williams: His Contribution to the American Tradition.* Indianapolis: Bobbs-Merrill, 1953.

Miller, Perry and Johnson, Thomas H., eds. *The Puritans: A Sourcebook of Their Writings.* 2 vols. New York: Harper and Row, 1963. [originally published in 1938].

Milton, John. *Areopagitica* (1644). New York: Payson & Clarke, 1927.

_____ . *Complete Poems and Major Prose.* New York: Odyssey Press, 1957.

Milward, Alan S. *The European Rescue of the Nation-State.* Berkeley, Calif.: University of California Press, 1992.

Monnet, Jean. *Memoirs.* London: Collins, 1978.

Nelsen, Brent F. and Stubb, Alexander C. G., eds. *The European Union: Readings on the Theory and Practice of European Integration.* Boulder, Colo.: Lynne Rienner, 1994.

O'Brien, William V. *The Conduct of Just and Limited War.* New York: Praeger, 1981.

Pfeffer, Leo. *Church, State and Freedom.* Boston: Beacon Press, 1953.

Pinder, John. *European Community: The Building of a Union, Updated following the Maastricht Treaty.* Oxford: Oxford University Press, 1992.

Polishook, Irwin H. *Roger Williams, John Cotton and Religious Freedom: A Controversy in Old and New England.* Englewood Cliffs, N.J.: Prentice-Hall, 1967.

Ramsay, Paul. *The Just War: Force and Political Responsibility.* New York: Scribners, 1968.

Ricci, David. *The Tragedy of Political Science: Politics, Scholarship, and Democracy.* New Haven, Conn.: Yale University Press, 1984.

Riemer, Neal. "The Case for Bare Majority Rule." *Ethics*, Vol. 62 (October 1951).

_____ . *The Democratic Experiment.* Princeton, N.J.: Van Nostrand, 1967.

_____ . *The Future of the Democratic Revolution: Toward a More Prophetic Politics.* New York: Praeger, 1984.

_____ . *James Madison: Creating the American Constitution.* Washington, D.C.: Congressional Quarterly Press, 1986.

_____ . *Karl Marx and Prophetic Politics.* New York: Praeger, 1987.

_____ , ed. *Let Justice Roll: Prophetic Challenges in Religion, Politics, and Society.* Lanham, Md.: Rowman and Littlefield, 1996.

_____ . "Madison: A Founder's Vision of Religious Liberty and Public Life." In Luis E. Lugo, ed., *Religion, Public Life, and the American Polity.* Knoxville: University of Tennessee Press, 1994.

_____ , ed. *New Thinking and Developments in International Politics: Opportunities and Dangers.* Lanham, Md.: University Press of America, 1991.

_____ . "Reinhold Niebuhr, Political Realism, and Prophetic Politics." Paper, Annual Meeting of American Political Science Association, September 3–6, 1992.

_____. *The Revival of Democratic Theory*. New York: Appleton-Century-Crofts, 1962.

Riemer, Neal, and Simon, Douglas W. *The New World of Politics: An Introduction to Political Science*, 3rd ed. San Diego: Collegiate Press, 1994.

Rosenau, Pauline Marie. *Post-Modernism and the Social Sciences: Insights, Inroads, and Intrusions*. Princeton, N.J.: Princeton University Press, 1984.

Rosenthal, Joel H. *Righteous Realists: Political Realism, Responsible Power, and American Culture in the Nuclear Age*. Baton Rouge: Louisiana State University Press, 1991.

Sivard, Ruth Leger. *World Military and Social Expenditures 1985*. Washington, D.C.: World Priorities, 1985.

Slater, Jerome, and Nardin, Terry. "Nonintervention and Human Rights." *The Journal of Politics*, Vol. 48 (1986).

Smith, Michael Joseph. *Realist Thought from Weber to Kissinger*. Baton Rouge: Louisiana State University Press, 1986.

Tesson, Fernando R. *Humanitarian Intervention: An Inquiry Into Law and Morality*. Dobbs Ferry, N.Y.: Transnational Publishers, 1988.

Thurow, Lester. *Head to Head: The Coming Economic Battle Among Japan, Europe, and America*. New York: Warner, 1993.

Tocqueville, Alexis de. *Democracy in America*. (1835). Phillips Bradley, ed. 2 vols. New York: Knopf, 1946.

U.S. Department of State, *Country Reports on Human Rights Practices for 1993*. Washington, D.C.: U.S. Government Printing Office, 1994.

Vaughan, Richard. *Post-War Integration in Europe*. London: Edward Arnold, 1976.

Vincent, R. J. *Human Rights and International Relations*. Cambridge: Cambridge University Press, 1986.

_____. *Nonintervention and International Order*. Princeton, N.J.: Princeton University Press, 1974.

Walzer, Michael. *Just and Unjust Wars: A Moral Argument with Historical Illustrations*, 2nd ed. New York: Basic Books, 1992.

Wood, David. *Conflict in the Twentieth Century*. London: International Institute for Strategic Studies, 1968.

Wright, Quincy. *A Study of War*. Chicago: University of Chicago Press, 1942, 1965.

Yoder, John Howard. *When War Is Unjust: Being Honest in Just-War Thinking*. Minneapolis: Augsburg, 1984.

Index

About the Author

NEAL RIEMER is Andrew V. Stout Professor of Political Philosophy, Emeritus, Department of Political Science, Drew University. His most recent books are *Let Justice Roll: Prophetic Challenges in Religion, Politics and Society* (1996) (editor & coauthor); *The New World of Politics* (1994) (coauthor); and *New Thinking and Developments in International Politics: Opportunities and Dangers* (1991) (editor & coauthor). In spring 1996 he was the Distinguished Visiting Honors Professor at the University of Central Florida.

ISBN 0-275-95595-8

90000>

EAN

9 780275 955953

HARDCOVER BAR CODE